Civilizing Sex

p. 11
children born out of wedlock
"The unchaste act that produces
him is a sin against society."

p. 137 ff
Homosexuality

Civilizing Sex

On Chastity and the Common Good

PATRICK G. D. RILEY

T&T CLARK INTERNATIONAL
A Continuum imprint
NEW YORK • LONDON

2005

T & T Clark International
The Tower Building, 11 York Road, London SE1 7NX

T & T Clark International
Madison Square Park, 15 East 26 Street, New York, NY 10010

T & T Clark is a Continuum imprint.

First published 2000

ISBN 0 567 08708 5 (HB)
ISBN 0 567 08766 2 (PB)

British Library Cataloguing-in-Publication Data
A catalogue record for this book is available from the British Library

Typeset by Waverley Typesetters, Galashiels

To

la gentile signora AnnaMaria Paltrinieri in Riley,

who made me write this book

and

the Rev. Alfred Wilder, OP,

who made me rewrite it.

CONTENTS

Part II
THE STRUCTURE

ACKNOWLEDGMENTS

Anyone who has tried to put together a work of philosophy will understand his debt to others, and will look with a more tolerant eye on the tedious list of persons that often finds itself at the beginning of such a book. He will also gain fresh insight into the willingness and even eagerness of men to contribute to the common good, in this case by helping ensure the truth – that is the wholesomeness – of a book. Of the many who have shown such good will during the writing of this work, I single out some whose help was decisive: the Rev. Stanley Jaki, OSB, the first to suggest the historical approach adopted in the body of this book: the Revs John E. Lynch, CSP, and Neil J. McEleney, CSP, friends from youth, and here guides in matters of history and Scripture respectively; the Rev. Lawrence Boadt, Paulist of a younger generation and expert on the Old Testament; Dr German Grisez, Dr William E. May, and Msgr William B. Smith, superb ethicists all; Rabbi Samuel Dresner, who showed me the relevance of the prophets to our own tragic times; and Dr Edward Macierowski, who helped with the Greek and Latin texts, and wrestled over many a metaphysical problem with me.

A special debt must be acknowledged to the Josephite Society, in the persons of the Very Revs John Filippelli, SSJ, Eugene McManus, SSJ, and Charles McMahon, SSJ, for the hospitality that made the writing of this book possible.

My chief debt is to a man who lived seven centuries ago, yet who is a father to me and many of my generation. Like any father, St Thomas can never be fully repaid, so this work of thanks falls under that part of justice known as *pietas* (see *Summa Theologiae,* II-II. 80).

PREFACE

I have been told this book is useless. Those who think sexual freedom is destructive don't need it, while those who think sexual freedom is a good thing, especially those who so to speak are profiting from it, won't read it. Or if they do, they won't be persuaded by it.

So ran the objection.

It is true that the sexually indulgent are unlikely to be moved by argument. My purpose however in writing this book was not to convert, but rather to offer historical and philosophical support for the conviction that marriage and marital fidelity are necessary preservatives of every society, and an indispensable means of rescuing our own.

But marriage does far more for a society than preserve or rescue it. Marriage actually builds it. In creating a family and giving it stability, marriage provides civil society with its primary cell.

The family given us by marriage is the first school of culture: it is the native environment in which the accumulated discipline, wisdom, knowledge, and arts of the larger society are first handed from one generation to the next. That virtue which preserves this environment by confining genital activity to marriage we call chastity. Because chastity preserves the first school of civilization, we deem it a *civilizing* force in

In references to the *Summa Theologiae* of Thomas Aquinas, only the *locus* is given. Translations from St Thomas are by the present writer.

society. Chastity is also civilizing in the sense that it tames the sexual drive, described by Plato in the opening pages of the *Republic* as 'a mad and savage master.'

This brings us to the twofold use of the word *civilizing* as employed in the title of this book, *Civilizing Sex.* The sexual drive is civilized by containing it within marriage, while sexual activity, so channeled, becomes a civilizing force by undergirding the stable family and providing children educated for participation in the larger society and for the formation of new and functional families.

Broadly speaking, then, this book is a philosophical and historical enquiry into the impact of sexual behavior on civic life. More specifically, it investigates the relation of a particular virtue, chastity, to the common good; this is reflected in the subtitle, *On Chastity and the Common Good.*

Since virtue, every virtue of every citizen without exception, is a constituent of the common good of civil society, we can correctly conclude that chastity itself is a constituent of the common good. We might, then, resolve the question *a priori.* But philosophy is not that simple, nor is life. Hence the need, if one is to examine the question in its practical and even in its theoretical dimensions, to survey history: the history of the observance and violation of this virtue, and their effect on civic life, and the history of thought on these phenomena and on their underlying aetiology.

There is another reason counselling us to move beyond *a priori* argument on the role of chastity in the common good: the currency of bogus notions about the common good and about chastity. Until the mid-eighties, when history began catching up with the prevailing wisdom, these widespread errors made it difficult for men and women to conceive of chastity, or any virtue at all, as an integral part of the common good.

Not so with liberty. For the past two centuries it has been widely accepted in the West as the chief good of civic life. Liberty long ago replaced virtue as the key word in political discourse. The very sound of the word stirs hearts. It is a staple of political oratory.

Philosophy, of course, cannot dismiss liberty as mere rhetoric. Philosophy must agree that liberty is a constituent of the common good. Yet distinctions must be drawn: the distinctions that are ignored in so much talk of liberty, distinctions without which liberty long ago became a justification for crimes without number.

Once the work of distinction begins, liberty reveals a wealth of metaphysical, psychological and political meanings, the most relevant to our immediate purpose being *perfection of the power to choose freely*. This perfection enables the person to grow in virtue; in fact the perfection of free will, achieved through making the right choices habitually, is itself virtue.[1] Thus liberty in this special sense, because it is virtue, becomes a part of the common good.

The dynamic of this argument returns us, via liberty, to chastity. Chastity is so signally a part of virtue, whose elements are interwoven into a unity,[2] that the word *chastity* is sometimes used as a synecdoche for the whole of virtue: a will unpolluted by self-interest or deceit, and directed firmly to good. But chastity remains, in the primary sense, a particular virtue, and is linked to the inner liberty cited above (the perfection of the power to choose freely), as is any virtue, though in its own particular way. Indeed the tyranny exercised by

[1] St Thomas holds: 'Virtue, according to its name, displays the perfection of a power' (*Disputationes de Virtutibus in communi*, I).

[2] Aristotle makes the point in *Nicomachean Ethics*, VI. 13 (especially 1144^{b}30–1145^{a}4). St Thomas expands on Aristotle's treatment in I-II. 65. 1.

Aquinas is fully aware that every day we meet men who manifest some virtues yet are in thrall to some base vice. The example he cites suits our present purposes perfectly: men who are generous but not chaste. But the virtues found in such men, he holds, are 'merely some inborn or habitual inclination in us toward doing good,' and are not interconnected, nor are they to be confused with 'perfect moral virtue,' which is 'a habit inclining us toward a good deed well done.'

St Thomas also confronts the objection that because some men are not called upon to perform the acts of certain virtues, they cannot have the habit of performing them. His response is that a man who is virtuous in matters that all men must deal with has been made ready to practice other virtues, such as the 'magnificence and magnanimity' required of statesmen (I-II. 65. 1, ad 1).

lust over its thralls is a byword. Shakespeare well describes that vice as perjured and even murderous.[3]

To be sure, the tyranny and the liberty spoken of in most political discourse, and appealed to even by demagogues, are quite distinct from virtue and vice. Yet this outward liberty, the liberty of common political parlance, must itself be accepted as an element of the common good. Precisely how such liberty relates to chastity and how such tyranny relates to lechery are not apparent, or at any rate may not dawn upon the thinker until he descries those relations in history.

On the nexus between liberty and chastity the ancients held strong notions, born of experience. Because slavery was a universal institution, they had ample opportunity to witness the sexual exploitation of slaves, attested in Aristophanes, Demosthenes, Livy, Pliny, Plutarch, and Strabo, to mention only some.[4] Aristotle, on the grounds that family life made a man prize liberty, advised that slaves not be allowed a family of their own, 'for if they have wives and children in common, they will be bound to one another with weaker ties, as a subject class should be, and they will remain obedient and not rebel.'[5]

When in this work we speak of *the ancients* we mean writers and public figures not only of the Greece and Rome of classical antiquity but of another and quite different ancient civilization: the Israel of biblical times. Because these cultures are direct ancestors of our own, because they exalted and fought for the survival of the personal and public ethos that is our precious and unique heritage, because they live in us to this day, this survey singles them out for study among all the cultures of ancient times.

Into the half-millennium following the breakup of the Western Empire this work does not attempt to delve. With the collapse of centralized authority, with the arrival – never

[3] Sonnet CXXIX.

[4] For citations from such authors, see William L. Westermann, *The Slave Systems of Greek and Roman Antiquity* (Philadelphia: American Philosophical Society, 1955), *passim.*

[5] *Politics*, II. 4 (1262[b]). Here he uses the term 'husbandmen,' but he later specifies: 'husbandmen should be slaves' (II. 10 [1330[a]]).

wholly welcome – of new and less cultured peoples, and with the retreat of letters into monasteries, history in Europe followed a turbulent and turbid course. Much of the essential history is unrecorded, warranting the name given those centuries: the Dark Ages.[6]

Yet at the opening of the millennium which has just ended, a highly organized civilization presents itself. Its ample records reveal institutions, structures of society, a cast of mind, and habits of life representing a triumph, necessarily limited, of Christian ideas. The Middle Ages, while far from perfect, offer history's best example of a society whose institutions hold up marriage for esteem and protect it. Indeed that society rose up in a mighty military and intellectual effort to defend marriage and marital chastity from a revival of Manichaean dualism known most widely as Albigensianism, and more correctly as Catharism, the religion of the Pure. With the history of that struggle our study ends.

Why halt there? Because the onslaught of the Pure was the last principled, concentrated attack on chastity to be repulsed, the last great crisis of chastity to be resolved.

We will not, then, follow the fortunes of chastity in later times. Beyond the scope of this study are vast historical changes that, we might well think, have impinged on chastity, such as the Great Schism in Christendom or the social, economic, and political upheavals consequent upon the Protestant Reformation. Beyond the scope of this study is the philosophical revolution begun by Niccolo Machiavelli

[6] Ecclesiastical documentation, such as penitentials and the records of local councils, is relatively plentiful however. Availing himself of those sources, George Hayward Joyce writes of these centuries: 'When in the West the Roman Empire went down before the Barbarians, and civilization seemed threatened with complete and permanent dissolution, it is not disputed that the rebuilding of the social order was in chief measure the work of the Catholic Church. . . . When the Northern tribes accepted the faith of Christ, she strove alike by exhortation and by a rigid ecclesiastical discipline to make them conform their lives to the code of the Gospel. But her efforts for that end were directed in large measure to enforcing the law of Christian Marriage. The Penitentials and the decrees of local councils afford abundant evidence of this; and many examples will occur in the pages of this book' (*Christian Marriage: An Historical and Doctrinal Study*, 2nd edn. [London: Sheed & Ward, 1948], pp. v–vi).

when, citing chastity among others, he denied the virtues their classic role in public life.[7] Finally, and most significantly, beyond the scope of this study is the secularization that ensued under the name of Enlightenment, a secularization we are all still undergoing even if the rationalism that served as its pretext has petered out.

In fact the eighteenth-century Enlightenment mounted the first direct attack on chastity since the Cathar attack half a millennium and more before. We must of course beware of thinking that the Enlightenment sprang fully armed from the forehead of eighteenth-century philosophy: the principles of Enlightenment, sown by Machiavelli, were cultivated by seventeenth-century thinkers to whom the philosophers of the Enlightenment appealed. These early heirs of Machiavelli, notably Thomas Hobbes and John Locke, fomented that revolution in the notion of virtue which along with secularization and the abolition of mystery is the essence of Enlightenment.[8]

Thus enlightened men of the eighteenth century dismissed chastity as a relic having no role to play in civil society. Yet as the Enlightenment passed a climax in the ferocities, carnal as well as sanguinary, of the French Revolution, its campaign against chastity and the family lost momentum, and eventually retreated before a widespread counter-attack carried out in literature and laws on the Continent, in England, and in the United States.

Enlightenment then pursued the campaign against tradition through politics and, more effectively, through the struggle to dominate higher education. Before the nineteenth century had ended, control of education on the European continent was in the hands of secularizers. American universities, with hardly a struggle, followed.[9] (The

[7] *The Prince*, ch. 18.

[8] *Pace* Immanuel Kant, who defined Enlightenment as 'man's emergence from his self-imposed immaturity,' and ascribed that immaturity to 'laziness and cowardice' (*What is Enlightenment?*, from *Kants gesammelte Schriften* [Berlin and Leipzig: Walter de Gruyter & Co., 1904–], vol. 8, p. 35).

[9] See Henry C. Johnson, Jr., '"Down from the Mountain": Secularization and the Higher Learning in America,' *Review of Politics*, 54 (1992), p. 551.

resulting change of curricula and focus means that much of the history recounted in the pages that follow, history that was once the common patrimony of cultured men, may come as a surprise to all but specialists.)

Then, in the sixties, American universities were rocked by a series of student revolts that all but razed even the detritus of classical culture, provoked serious questions about the meaning of culture itself, of education itself, and unmasked the inability of American academics to explain their very reason for being.[10] Simultaneously, the American political scene, where statesman and demagogue alike had routinely invoked the name of God, became a secular preserve. The stage was set for a renewed attack on marriage and chastity, the first concentrated attack since the glory days of the Enlightenment.

That is what we find ourselves facing. Since the sixties, our society has been reeling beneath an attack on chastity from a secularist, hedonist philosophy that is Enlightenment redivivus. The few decades since have sufficed to demonstrate the destructive effects of that hedonism, and have provided its opponents with lethal arguments, lethal precisely to the degree to which those effects are lethal. Still the battle hangs in the balance, largely because the major media are manned preponderantly by proponents of advanced ideas.[11] It is too

[10] The most familiar account of the student rebellion is Allan Bloom's, in *The Closing of the American Mind* (New York: Simon & Schuster, 1987), pp. 313–35. The subsequent, and final, chapter is a brilliant survey of the decomposition of the contemporary university.

[11] 'A predominant characteristic of the media elite is its secular outlook,' wrote S. Robert Lichter and Stanley Rothman in *Public Opinion* (Oct.–Nov. 1981).

They continued: 'Exactly 50 percent eschew any religious affiliation. . . . Very few are regular churchgoers. Only 8 percent go to church or synagogue weekly, and 86 percent seldom or never attend religious services' (p. 43).

Drs Lichter and Rothman said their survey of journalists working at ten major print and electronic media of the New York–Washington power axis showed that half of the journalists held that adultery was not wrong, while three-quarters approved of homosexual acts.

A study by John Dart and Jimmy R. Allen contradicted the Lichter–Rothman report: 'The nation's journalists are not largely irreligious, contrary to the much-quoted (and misquoted) Lichter-Rothman study' (*Bridging the Gap:*

early to predict the outcome, whether the retreat of those ideas or the decline of the West into, first, the anarchy and then the tyranny inevitable with the collapse of that indispensable cell of civil society which is the family.

Political societies can falter and fail, chiefly through a failure of culture. But where the family stands firm, even a society in ruins bears within itself the germ of its regeneration. And the family can stand firm, with husband and wife bound by the strongest friendship known to man,[12] only if husband and wife understand the reason for their friendship, and do their best to preserve it, and all that depends on it, through the virtue of chastity.

Religion and the News Media [Nashville, Tenn.: The Freedom Forum First Amendment Center at Vanderbilt University, 1993], p. 6).

In delivering this judgment, Dr Allen and Dart themselves misquote the Lichter–Rothman report, which never claimed to speak for 'the nation's journalists' but only for those employed by elite media such as the *New York Times*, *Time*, and TV network news – the media widely thought to be the most influential both with a TV-watching public and with the classes more likely to read.

[12] Thus St Thomas, *Summa contra Gentiles*, III. 123.

INTRODUCTION: A PRIMER OF POLITICAL PHILOSOPHY

I ask your pardon, Sir, for entering theology instead of sticking to philosophy, which was my only subject. But I was led there without realizing it, and it is hard not to get into it whatever truth one is treating, because it is the center of all truths.

Blaise Pascal to M. Le Maistre de Saci (attributed)[1]

The Scope of this Book

In common parlance, any discussion of God is theological. There is no compelling reason, in this work of political philosophy, to avoid that broad use of the term.[2] Nor for that matter is there any substantial reason to keep God himself

[1] From N. Fontaine's account of a meeting between Pascal and several gentlemen of Port-Royal in 1655, taken from his memoirs and reproduced as *Entretien avec M. de Saci* in *Pascal: œvres complètes*, ed. Jacques Chevalier, Bibliothèque de la Pléiade, vol. 34 (Paris: Librairie Gallimard, 1954), pp. 572–3.

John Henry Newman makes the point in *The Idea of a University*: 'Admit a God, and you introduce among the subjects of your knowledge, a fact encompassing, closing in upon, absorbing, every other fact conceivable. How can we investigate any part of any order of Knowledge, and stop short of that which enters into every order? All true principles run over with it, all phenomena converge to it; it is truly the First and the Last' (Discourse II. 3).

[2] St Thomas too uses the term this way, to include what among modern scholastics came to be called theodicy, the study of God through natural reason. But he also uses the term in the sense of the application of reason to revelation. See Brian Davies, OP, 'Is Sacra Doctrina Theology?', *New Blackfriars*, Mar. 1990, 141–7.

out of it. Yet for decades a rigorous secularism so dominated American politics, jurisprudence, and media that any association between God and politics was anathema.[3]

That may be why mention of virtue, and certainly the virtue of chastity, long ago vanished from politics. For despite centuries of effort to prescind from God in moral speculation, God seems inseparable from virtue in life itself.[4] And the absence of virtue from political discourse until very recently is one measure of how far we had ventured from the classic political tradition, given voice by thinkers and politicians from Plato to Robespierre and beyond who made *virtue* the key word in their political lexicon. For not only was the virtue of the citizenry seen to play a leading role in civic life, but law itself was conceived to be based on a virtue, the paradigmatic virtue of justice.

It is from this political tradition that the present essay on chastity and the common good takes its bearings. But we depart from the mainstream. Perhaps it would be more accurate to say, at the risk of appearing immodest, that with the help of modern archaeology we move ahead of the mainstream. With new evidence before us, but with classical notions of the nature of law as our leading principles, we find the Decalogue to be the foundational document of Western civilization, including its political structure.

The full argument for this is found in Chapter 1. Suffice it to say here that we do not halt at arguing that morality, symbolized by the Decalogue, is basic to politics, though of course we hold that. We move far beyond it to argue that these Ten Commandments and the Covenant of which they

[3] This still has its champions in high places. The Democratic Party's refusal to put the name of God in its 1992 platform despite the recommendation of Sen. Joseph Lieberman of Connecticut is one of many straws in a wind that still blows strong even if it is no longer prevailing (see Larry Witham's report in the *Washington Times*, 4 July 1992).

[4] See for example the claim of Socrates, when on trial for his life, that had he shirked his philosophical vocation 'I might justly have been brought here for not believing that there are gods' (Plato, *Apology*, 29[a]); also, his final argument that if he persuaded the jury to violate its oath of office, 'I would be teaching you not to believe that there are gods' (ibid., 35[d]).

are the stipulations, presented by a particular man to a particular group with the claim that they were revealed by God, constitute the political charter of the West in much the sense that the Declaration of Independence and the Constitution constitute the political charter of the United States.

Now it is one thing to bring God into politics, and it is quite another to bring in what claims to be divine revelation. If our still-regnant secularism will make no place for God or even virtue in political discourse, imagine its incredulity at an attempt to construe the divinely revealed Decalogue as a political instrument in the narrowest sense of the term, and a foundational political instrument at that. To what still might be styled the modern mind, the claim that a code revealed by God, or pretending to have been so revealed, played a decisive role in founding our civil society and the culture that has sustained it must move beyond paradox toward the absurd.

Such secularism retains its dogmatism and much of its power over our political institutions, especially the judiciary and the media, but since history took it by the throat in the eighties it no longer retains its self-assurance. Nor do men any longer hold it in awe. They are beginning to recognize it as peculiar to a culture whose confidence was shaken when the failure of statism became too obvious to deny. Increasingly, they recognize our secularism as a heritage, or more correctly a curse, of that eighteenth-century attempt at universal secularization which called itself Enlightenment.

In every culture known to history until the Enlightenment, men took the role of religion in civic life as wholly proper and natural. To speak of 'secular society' among the Hebrews of Sinai, where we begin our study, would be unhistorical: these cultural ancestors of ours knew no such animal – no such pure-bred animal, that is. Through the body politic the sacred coursed like the blood of life, and men took it as given that things had to be so.

It is a monumental irony that the dogma of civil secularity sprang, like some recalcitrant bastard, from Christian teaching. The particular teaching is the revolutionary distinction between the sacred and the civil brought out by Jesus Christ in the now-familiar formula: 'Render to Caesar the things that are Caesar's, and to God the things that are God's.'[5] Nor is this the only Christian principle to be retained in some isolated or distorted form as liberal dogma; far from it. One illustration is found in the fact that the men of the West will agree on human rights, though disagreeing on their source.[6] Here we see heresy surviving the only way it can: on the truths it retains.

Every culture known to history except the newly secularized West and its epigones has understood religion to be a necessary part of public life. Until the Enlightenment, or just before, we of the West took it as given that the laws of God inform the just and necessary laws of civil society.[7] Because

[5] Matt. 22:21. The distinction between the two orders, and its implications, are treated magisterially by Joseph Lecler in *The Two Sovereignties* (New York: Philosophical Library, 1952).

[6] See Jacques Maritain, *Man and the State* (Chicago: University of Chicago Press, 1951), ch. 4.

[7] St Thomas represents the standard position of earlier times: 'The measure in which all laws share in right reason is precisely the measure in which they are derived from the eternal law' (I-II. 93. 3).

Although one of the principal characteristics of the Enlightenment was its attempt to divorce a jurisprudence of natural law from theology, this simply pushed to an extreme what had been recurring in history for centuries. Suarez, in *De Legibus ac Deo Legislatore*, gives a list of Catholic authors who saw law in the nature of things without explicitly tracing it, or the things themselves, back to the Creator. But these authors differed from the tradition only in method: taking nature as the basic datum, they argued from it direct to *jus* – what is right as distinct from what is wrong, not a right as distinct from, say, a privilege – while prescinding from God as the author of nature. Because they did not challenge any of the theological foundations of natural law they did not disrupt the Thomistic tradition.

Such disruption came with early Reformation writers, whose theological voluntarism struck at the root-concept of nature. But they still recognized the dependence of law on the will of God, even if they made that will arbitrary. They reflected the voluntarism of the fourteenth-century Franciscan school, including Scotus himself (and which did not begin, as has been asserted, with the nominalism of Ockham).

Juridical voluntarism of this theological cast met a decisive reverse in the writings of a later Protestant, Hugo Grotius, whose Arminian premises rejected theological voluntarism. This enabled him to focus his juristic method on nature. He argued hypothetically and *per impossibile* that the existence of the Author of nature need not enter the question.

only just laws can safeguard the common good, the notion that divine law is the source of civil law is basic to this study.

The particular law scrutinized here is that of chastity, chiefly in so far as it is subject to civil discipline but also where it lies beyond the reach of civil authorities. We shall see how, in each of these two cases, it contributes to the common good.

Method and Terms

Because chastity falls under both laws, civil and divine, it will be treated from both standpoints. Yet we hold that civil law is no less theological in its foundations than that part of the moral law which is beyond the authority of civil law.

That would be reason enough to breach an over-restrictive boundary between the philosophical – in this case political philosophy – and what is broadly termed the theological, but the opening proposition of this work, that the Decalogue is the most basic document in Western political history, makes it actually incumbent on us to step across that line. To recognize an insurmountable barrier between the theological and the political would be a surrender to secularism, itself under siege because of its political failures, less spectacular in the West than in the East but no less significant.

Before getting deeper into this study, we should define a few key terms. We have noted that the word *theological* is used herein to characterize anything that concerns God. By *political* we mean *pertaining to civil society and its governance.* Of *civil society*, we only need specify that it is a synonym neither for the suspect term *secular society* nor for *nation*, which we use in a protean sense to mean *a group that has ties of language*

This set the tone of argument until Rousseau, with his claim that laws 'are but the registers of our wills,' and Hegel, who carried that notion further by divinizing the state.

On the eve of the Enlightenment the most influential author in the philosophy of law was the Protestant Samuel Pufendorf, who, like Grotius, and with a reverential bow to his genius, argued from nature alone. This made it easy for the Extremists (Hébertists) of the French Revolution to proclaim the rights of man while denying the existence of God.

and culture, and often of blood.[8] A nation may, but need not, be organized under a single government (or state, as the apparatus of government is called in modern times). A nation may be divided among governments, while several nations may be ruled by a common government and constitute a single civil society. Yet under whatever government it finds itself, the nation always has strong political implications. It ordinarily outlasts the state that attempts to subsume it or destroy it.

The cultural ties that bind a nation together include religion, though not necessarily a common religion, it is widely maintained nowadays; common reverence for a moral law stemming from a supreme author is thought to suffice.[9]

Men did not always think that way. A cardinal principle for the understanding of political history is that from antiquity right up to and even into modern times, common religion not only has been a characteristic of a nation, even of a body politic, but has also been deemed essential to national or even political unity. Modern experience, or more precisely the

[8] 'There is no more thankless task than trying rationally to distinguish . . . common notions that have arisen from the contingent practical needs of human history,' writes Jacques Maritain at the beginning of his treatment of the distinctions among nation, body politic, and state, and between the more fundamental groups constituting a community and a society (ch. 1 of *Man and the State*). Maritain's treatment, however, remains classic.

[9] Thus George Washington in his Farewell Address: 'Of all the dispositions and habits which lead to political prosperity, religion and morality are indispensable supports. In vain would that man claim the tribute of patriotism, who should labor to subvert these great pillars of human happiness, these firmest props of the duties of men and citizens. The mere politician, equally with the pious man, ought to respect and cherish them. A volume could not trace all their connections with private and public felicity. Let it simply be asked, where is the security for property, for reputation, for life, if the sense of religious obligation desert the oaths which are the instruments of investigation in courts of justice? And let us with caution indulge the supposition that morality can be maintained without religion. Whatever may be conceded to the influence of refined education on minds of peculiar structure, reason and experience both forbid us to expect that national morality can prevail in exclusion of religious principle.'

Note that if such reverence for the laws of the Creator is an integral part of the common good, it follows that chastity is such a part.

modern experiment, is widely taken to show that it need not be so. History, however, has not yet rendered judgment.

As for our own particular focus, the role of chastity in the common good, we shall see that from the very foundation of Israel, itself the foundational nation of Western society, honest genital behavior was perceived as vital to national survival. Then, when we study attempts to institutionalize a different sexual ethos within the Jewish society and again within the Christian society, we shall see that the primeval Jewish and Christian perception of the key role played by chastity within the common good emerges from such historical trials justified.

Our study of crises in the sexual ethos of the West also surveys the sexual license of the late Roman Republic, and the attempt of Augustus to strengthen his newly founded Roman Empire through a restoration of chastity. We halt with the medieval crisis of Christianity, of chastity, and of esteem for bodily existence.

Beyond the scope of this work are later experiments with libertinism stemming from the Enlightenment, such as among the intellectual elites of eighteenth-century France and among our own liberal elites, intellectual and otherwise, from the sixties on. Suffice it to say that the results of such experimentation have not been encouraging.

It must be borne in mind throughout that this survey of ideas and events is not merely historical; it is critical too, surveying history from a philosophical perspective.

Four thematic concepts of this work remain to be defined: chastity, liberty, society, and the common good. We shall treat the common good extensively, and in the process define society. Of liberty we shall give only a spare working definition. Chastity, as a principal subject of this essay, receives fuller treatment here.

By *chastity*, in this work, is meant *the confinement of deliberate genital activity to that shared by husband and wife.* Even within marriage there are moral limits to such activity if it is to remain honest, but because our focus is on civil society, on civic virtue, and on civil law, we do not enter that question except to point out that chastity, as a virtue, is a finely articulated whole, hence no part of it can be abused without collapse of the structure.[10]

Because chastity tempers one of our two basic biological drives, one designed to preserve the self, the other the species, it has classically been considered under the larger heading of temperance. There, as the virtue governing the marriage bed, it shares honors with moderation at table. The latter virtue is in the classical scheme divided into abstinence (from excess of food) and sobriety (in drink).[11]

Immediately we note a special characteristic of temperance, setting it apart from all other virtues. Because it deals with functions necessary to the preservation of the human being and the human race, temperance possesses a worth attaching to what is necessary to our nature. Moreover the pleasures it governs, precisely because they lead men to the most necessary of natural functions, are the sharpest of all.[12]

Another characteristic of temperance, hence of chastity, bears adversely on our enterprise. The relation of temperance to the common good – hence, again, of chastity to the common good – is far less perspicuous than, for example, courage on the battlefield or justice in matters of state. Grateful nations erect statues to statesmen and the brave, not to the chaste.

St Thomas puts it in absolute terms:

> Justice . . . and fortitude concern the good of the multitude more greatly than does temperance, because justice concerns dealings, which are with another, while fortitude concerns the perils of war, which are borne for the common safety. Temperance, however, moderates only the desires and delights of those things which pertain to the man himself.[13]

[10] To urge 'abstinence' upon schoolchildren who are ceaselessly subjected to sexual imagery is a futile if not cynical gesture, a cruel hoax. Correct comportment in sexual matters is possible only through inner discipline, which can scarcely be expected of anyone – least of all the young – in a sex-saturated culture.

[11] I transliterate St Thomas's Latin terms, *abstinentia* and *sobrietas* (II-II. 143).

[12] St Thomas describes them as 'the chief pleasures' (*praecipuae delectiones*), adding that because they are attached to necessary operations, they themselves are 'essential' (II-II. 141. 5).

[13] II-II. 141. 8.

Thus because chastity is seen as concerning the individual, not the commonality, its relation to the common good is obscured.

There are other reasons why the link between chastity and the common good is blurred in the minds of men. One is that chastity, for reasons we shall examine, is tied to religion, which in the modern world has been ruled out of public life. Moreover chastity is the most private of virtues, dealing with the most private of behavior. It is often the subject of the most private of dramas, known only to the protagonist: a man can easily spend a lifetime trying to rein in this instinct lest, like Stephen Leacock's lovelorn horseman, it ride madly off in all directions.

Because chastity is surely the most private of virtues, and may seem to be the most thorny, apostles of sexual freedom can plausibly call it purely personal: if you want to deprive yourself that's your affair, and lots of luck! This kind of argument is only too persuasive to those who find it very hard indeed to temper the sexual drive.

Yet even considering chastity in the dimension of temperance alone, we observe a critical difference between it and temperance at table. Whereas temperance in food and drink deals with a desire and a delight designed to maintain an individual man in being, temperance in sexual affairs deals with a desire and a delight designed to maintain the human race in being. Now to keep humankind alive is clearly for the common good, which vanishes without it. Chastity, regarded as a species of temperance, is essential to that maintenance. Just as gluttony drags a man to the sickbed and the grave, lechery leads a nation to cultural disintegration, which is tantamount to extinction.

Moreover justice, so evidently a part of the common good, plays a powerful role in chastity. Justice concerns dealings with another, and in the act of genital congress three persons are present and affected: the two actors and, potentially yet really, the child. Where the man and woman are not married, they deal unjustly with one another. Where one is married to someone else, or where both are so married, they also do an injustice to the spouse or spouses. The child too is dealt with unjustly: he is brought into the world by parents who are not married to one another and consequently cannot provide him with the home necessary to his proper nourishment, his comfort, and above all his education. Moreover they are more likely to destroy him before birth. (This is our modern plague.)

St Thomas highlights the injustice of fornication when he asks whether it is a mortal sin.[14] (His immediate response, incidentally, is emphatic: 'Without any doubt whatsoever.') His focus here may surprise us. It falls on the father's role in helping the whole child become the whole man. In the work of educating boys and girls alike, St Thomas gives the father priority:

> For it is manifest that the education of man requires not only the care of the mother, who nourishes him, but far more the care of the father, who instructs and defends him, and who causes him to advance in goods both inward and outward.

St Thomas takes that as a point of departure for a sally into marriage as an institution demanded by human nature, and into why sleeping around is unnatural:

> And therefore it is against the nature of man to copulate at random; rather a husband must have a determinate wife with whom he remains not for a middling period but for a long time, or even throughout life. Hence there is naturally found in the males of the human species an anxiety to be sure of their offspring, for the upbringing of offspring is incumbent on them. But such certainty would disappear were there random coupling.

Yet it is not only because of injustice to the child that fornication is seen to be unjust. Because his education is faulty, a man born outside the family is less likely to contribute to the common good than one raised by father and mother. Furthermore he is more likely to be a burden to the

[14] II-II. 154. 2. In speaking here of man, St Thomas uses the generic *homo*, so he is referring to the education of female children as well as male.

larger society because he lacks the supports provided by the family, the most basic, efficient, and versatile support system known. Finally he is more likely to disrupt order and peace. The unchaste act that produces him is a sin against society.

Such disorder and injustice might suffice to show that unchaste behavior is disgraceful, but there are other reasons why a particular disgrace attaches to this sin. Any kind of intemperance degrades a man, as when a glutton is said to make a pig of himself.[15] Obsession with sensual pleasure distracts him from intellectual pursuits, and may even block them out of his mind. When the object itself of such obsessive desire is sinful, hence irrational, the obsession can scarcely enhance intellectual life. Obsession with sensual pleasure deadens a man's appreciation of the beautiful, of things more suited to the rationality of his nature.[16] It radically curtails his freedom: he is called a slave to his passions, and aptly so.[17]

When the passion is lust, the degradation is especially deep. More of men's powers are debased and diverted, or rather perverted, to the working of deceits and other injustices. Shakespeare puts it bluntly:

> The expense of spirit in a waste of shame
> Is lust in action; and till action, lust
> Is perjur'd, murd'rous, bloody, full of blame,
> Savage, extreme, rude, cruel, not to trust.[18]

[15] Intemperance 'is greatly repugnant to the excellence of man,' says St Thomas, 'for it concerns pleasures common to us and to brutes' (II-II. 142. 4).

[16] Intemperance, St Thomas observes, 'is especially repugnant to the luster of man, his comeliness, in as much as the pleasures that intemperance immerses him in show least of the light of reason, which gives virtue all its brightness and beauty' (ibid.).

[17] Sensual pleasures breaking the bounds of reason 'are called especially slavish,' says St Thomas (ibid.).

[18] Sonnet CXXIX. Cf. *Summa Theologiae*, II-II. 153. 5, where St Thomas lists 'the daughters of lust' as 'blindness of mind, lack of thought, headlong haste, fickleness, self-love, hatred of God, attachment to this world, and horror of the future.'

Elsewhere he says the fickleness arising from lust 'totally extinguish[es] the judgment of reason' (II-II. 53. 6, ad 1), adding, 'duplicity of mind also is a certain consequence of lust' (ad 2).

The classic division of lust into its sub-species (or parts, as St Thomas also calls them) lists 'simple' fornication first.[19] The adjective serves to distinguish it from the synecdochic use of the word *fornication* to denote unchastity in general; it also serves to distinguish it from sacrilegious intercourse, wherein one party at least has consecrated himself to God through vow or orders.[20] In fact St Thomas counts such sacrilegious intercourse as a distinct species of lust.[21]

The other species of lust are adultery, incest, seduction (violation of a virgin), rape, and unnatural vice.[22] The last is the worst because not only is it contrary to right reason, as are all kinds of unchastity, but it is contrary to nature to boot.[23] One proof of this, despite the success of efforts to have homosexuality officially declared normal, is that works of clinical psychology detail great efforts to set homosexuality straight, and none whatsoever to correct normality. That may well change, but only as part of the enormously successful campaign of seduction that has been waged in the past quarter-century under the twin banners of tolerance and liberty.

The basic meaning of *liberty* is *the power to choose.*[24] In this work however the word ordinarily means civil liberty, the

[19] II-II. 154. 1. One of the major themes of the Old Testament is that the consequences cited by Aquinas and Shakespeare can come to characterize not just an individual but also a society. We might well read modern history the same way.

[20] See II-II. 154. 10.

[21] Ibid.

[22] Ibid.

[23] St Thomas explains: 'In any genus whatsoever, the worst corruption is of the principle the others depend on. Now the principles of reason are those which are in accordance with nature: for reason, once it has presupposed the things that are determined by nature, disposes of other things in accordance with what is suitable. And this is seen equally in speculation and in operation. Hence as in speculative matters the most serious and disgraceful error concerns those things which are naturally implanted in man, so in matters of action the most grievous and disgraceful action is against things determined according to nature. Therefore, because in vices contrary to nature man transgresses what is determined according to nature concerning the use of venery, it follows that this sin is the most serious in this material' (II-II. 154. 12).

[24] St Thomas calls freedom of will 'nothing other than the power of choice' (I. 83. 4).

absence of external constraint save by laws framed for public order, which enables all persons, classes, and societies within the body politic to achieve their good, whether physical, intellectual, moral, or otherwise.[25]

That good taken in the aggregate may be considered *the common good* itself, but the concept is at once richer and simpler. It must be examined in some depth at the outset if this work is to be comprehensible and constructive.

The Common Good

Scarcely any concern of philosophy can have engendered more perplexity, as measured by prolixity, than the common good. Little wonder! So many various if not disparate elements of the common good swarm before us when we begin to ponder it that we find difficulty picking out its unifying note, its principles. Yet to examine the common good in the concrete is the spontaneous approach. Aristotle's comments on the search for the principles of physical nature are pertinent:

> The natural way of doing this is to start from the things that are more knowable and obvious to us and proceed towards those which are clearer and more knowable by nature.[26]

Aristotle goes on to remark that when we first look at physical nature, 'rather confused masses' present themselves to our view. That is a perfect description of what we see when we first examine the common good. How to cut through the confusion?

It is impossible to do so if we remain on the empirical level. No adequate understanding of the common good can be

[25] Cf. I. 82. 1, where St Thomas distinguishes among the kinds of necessity compatible and incompatible with free will.

[26] *Physics*, I. 1 (184^{a}16). Of course I am not suggesting that the common good is a subject for investigation by physical science, but am merely pointing to the parallel between attempts to draw principles out of the mass of physical data on the one hand and, on the other, the mass of elements in the common good. In fact it is at the outset of his *In Physicae* (I. 1–3) that St Thomas outlines the degree of abstraction proper to each kind of science.

achieved heuristically, that is by examining the 'rather confused masses' of its elements and enumerating them. But the deductive method opens a path straight to the heart of the matter, to the core of the common good.

Basic metaphysics offers the starting point: the nature of the good itself. St Thomas examines this question at the outset of his *Quaestiones Disputatae de Veritate.* In a beautiful and masterful treatment of the transcendentals, he calls the good 'the consonance of being with the appetitive power.' The good is that which all things desire, he continues, recalling Aristotle's definition.[27]

These two integral components of the good, namely being itself and desirability, give us the key to a definition of the common good of a society. The common good as we begin to see it on examining it under this optic is that being, that existing thing, which is common to the members of a society *in so far as they are members,* and which they all desire together. Hence *the common good of a society can be considered the very being of that society in so far as it is desired by its members.*[28] We shall see that they desire this common good as a means to other goods.[29]

Whenever we speak of desire and intent we are talking of the good and the goal respectively. They are really the same thing, for the goal – in the more usual technical language

[27] The quotation from the *De Veritate* is found in I. 1: 'The name *good* . . . expresses the consonance [*convenientiam*] of being with the appetitive power, as is said at the beginning of the *Ethics*: "Good is that which all things strive after."' The citation from the *Nicomachean Ethics* is found in I. 1 (1094^a2).

[28] Cf. Leo Strauss: 'the common good also comprises, of course, the mere existence, the mere survival, the mere independence, of the political community in question' (*Natural Right and History* [Chicago and London: Chicago University Press, 1953], p. 160).

A word of caution on St Thomas's terminology: although he speaks of 'common good, which is convertible with being' ('bonum commune, quod convertitur cum ente' [I-II. 55. 4, ad 2]), thus using the term *common good* as a synonym for transcendental good, he does not in any text I have found apply this expressly to the common good of a society. However, to link the common good with transcendental good is in perfect accord with the thought of St Thomas, as we shall see presently.

[29] Naturally, since the good is 'being [as] perfective of another' (*De Veritate,* XXI. 1).

the end or purpose, and in scholastic terminology the final cause – is never sought except as something good.[30] So it should come as no surprise to find St Thomas putting purpose at the core of the common good. The common good, he says, 'is called a common end.'[31]

How then do particular human actions and their ends or goals fit in with the common good? In what way, to be more specific, are the countless decisions and acts of daily life in a society referrable to and directed toward the common good of that society? In this: that whatever the specific and conscious intent of the agents, all human acts except evil ones work for the common good as an end. Thus they have a commonness of purpose, what St Thomas calls 'a commonness of final cause.'[32]

St Thomas sums it up:

> Actions indeed concern particulars: but those particulars can be referred to a good common, not certainly with a commonness of genus or of species, but with a commonness of final cause. Thus the common good is called a common end.[33]

To grasp this it helps to think in terms of the whole and the parts, with an important caveat that we shall raise later. Much as the whole is the end or purpose common to all the parts and their activity, because they are there precisely to sustain the whole and help it achieve its own purpose, the common good is the end or purpose common to a society's individual members and their actions.[34]

As with the whole and the parts, the well-being of society redounds to the well-being of each member. In fact the

[30] St Thomas observes: 'since the note of goodness consists in this, that one thing is perfective of another as its goal, everything that comes under the heading of a goal comes also under the heading of the good' (*De Veritate*, XXI. 2).

[31] I-II. 90. 2, ad 2.

[32] Ibid.

[33] Ibid.

[34] St Thomas observes: 'The common good is the end of individual persons living in a community, as the good of the whole is the end of each and every part' (II-II. 58. 9, ad 3).

well-being of each depends on the society, civil and familial, in which all live.[35]

Because the good of the part is necessary to the good of the whole, every member of a society is able to refer his own good to the good common to all the members.[36] Hence all members of a society can refer the good of another member to their own good. All share in the individual member's good, and each individual member shares in the good common to all. The existence of the society enables each and all to do both.

Now existence over time and despite obstacles is, by definition, survival. This element of survival is decisive as the *sine qua non* of all other elements in the common good, such as individual acts, if these elements are to remain within it. Unless the society survives, it cannot bestow any further good, that is any benefit, on its members. In so far as they are

[35] St Thomas, in one of the key texts on the common good, takes note of that and adds a second reason. 'he who seeks the common good of the multitude seeks in consequence his own good also, for two reasons: first, because one's own good cannot exist without the common good of the family, or of the city or kingdom. . . . Secondly, because man, since he is part of the household or of the city [*civitas*, often misleadingly rendered, as we shall see, "state"], must consider what is good for him from what is prudent concerning the good of the multitude. For the disposition of the parts is deemed good according to their relation to the whole' (II-II. 47. 10, ad 2).

[36] This is clearest, perhaps, in the case of virtue. No virtue of course is more important to the preservation of the familial society than the special subject of our study, namely chastity.

But prescinding from any particular virtue, when one member of a family is virtuous, this good, seemingly so proper to its possessor, works to the good of all members of the family. The greatest charity we can give those around us is to become better persons.

Prescinding from any particular society, St Thomas observes: 'the good of any virtue whatsoever, whether it composes a man in himself or disposes him to other singular persons, can be referred to the common good' (II-II. 58. 6).

This good of the various virtues, St Thomas notes in the same place, is directed to the common good by what he calls *general justice*. He also calls it *legal justice* in so far as law regulates the common good.

Elsewhere St Thomas points out: 'The justice that directs man to the common good is a general virtue through its act of command, since it governs all the acts of the virtues to its own end, namely the common good. Moreover a virtue, in so far as it is commanded by such justice, receives even the name of justice' (I-II. 60. 3, ad 2).

members of the society, then, they perforce desire the survival of the society.

Because *a society is a group of men brought together in a relation of order established for a common purpose,* it follows that a society can remain in existence only if that common purpose is respected. In practice, this means that a society remains in existence only when the *intention* to pursue and achieve the common aim is maintained, and provided that human misbehavior does not mortally weaken the society.

That practical truth is confirmed from a metaphysical point of view. Society, as *a relation among men,* falls under the category of accident, specifically that of *relatio.* Its unity is not substantial but accidental.[37] It is held in existence by human intent, by the common resolve of men to maintain among themselves that order (built on a foundation of justice both commutative and distributive) which is necessary to the pursuit and achievement of the common goal.

Now that goal, once again, is necessarily seen as good. Because the intention to pursue that good is vital to society's survival, because the aim of achieving that good is a society's very reason for being, the good (as we asserted a moment ago) is integral to the concept of a society in a way that sets society apart from other entities. Society is a sort of permanent common seeking, a permanent common striving after a good.

One might be tempted to argue that society, an accidental entity inasmuch as it is included within the category of *relatio,* is insubstantial and hence perishable. Despite the entirely true conclusion that society is perishable, the argument is false. Not every accidental being is perishable simply from the fact that it is an accident – that is, not every accidental being is more perishable than the substance it inheres in.

[37] St Thomas argues: 'It must be borne in mind that that whole which is the civic multitude or the household family has *only a unity of order,* hence it is not a thing that is one without qualification' (*In I Librum Ethicorum ad Nichomachum,* I. 5; emphasis supplied).

For St Thomas's distinction between, on the one hand, a unity of order and, on the other, a unity of order and composition, see *Summa contra Gentiles,* IV. 35. 7.

Perishability, of course, is a relative term. Although accidents are more likely than substances to change, hence disappear, all material substances are subject to change and can by their nature perish. On the other hand some accidents – the character stamped on the soul by marriage is one, the relations of fatherhood and sonship are others – last as long as life itself, as long, that is, as the human substance. Moreover certain societies, to wit the family and the body politic, grow out of the essential needs of human nature, and the relations that constitute them are in principle as durable as mankind itself.

Yet it remains true that the adherence of will – weak, fickle, inconstant human will – is absolutely necessary to the survival of a society. This brings us to a paradox. Natural as a society may be, growing as such a natural society does out of the inborn needs and yearnings of man, it yet has something of the character of an artifact.[38] Even if men are born into it, it is constantly remade by them, continually renewed and preserved in being by them, through the adherence of their will. In other words, unless men hold to that common goal which is the common good, the society collapses.

Now society is sometimes analyzed according to the traditional four causes of Aristotle: the formal cause, the material cause, the efficient cause, and the final cause.[39] To apply this fourfold principle to society is easy enough when it comes to the material cause: the members of the society, the men, women, and children who make it up. A final cause or

[38] When natural societies are distinguished from other societies the latter are often styled 'artificial.' St Thomas, to the present writer's knowledge, does not use this terminology, and the element of artifact in natural societies may explain why. Another problem with this terminology arises from the indispensability of certain 'artificial' societies for the survival of natural societies. An example would be an army, a society necessary for the survival of the civil society, a natural society.

St Thomas uses the army as an example of 'a multitude gathered for some special business,' and civil society as an example of 'a multitude gathered for all [the needs of] life' (II-II. 48). This distinction corresponds to the one employed in this work between a conventional society and a natural society respectively.

[39] For St Thomas's explanation of the four causes, see *In V Metaphysicae*, II.

purpose of a society is easily discernible also (though requiring expansion and further refinement, as in note 43 below): to enable men to attain the good life, which includes the moral life.

From there onwards it is hard sledding. What is the efficient cause of a society? That is, who must we call its founder or founders? In the case of the familial society, an answer easily comes to mind: the man and woman who, in making themselves husband and wife, create a family. But who founds the larger society? Here, men have had recourse to myth. The most satisfactory answer, human nature, does not fit easily into the category of agent.

Last, and probably hardest, is the question of the formal cause of a society. The variety of answers attests to the difficulty of the question. Some thinkers answer 'A moral bond,' but then fall to disputing what that moral bond is. Is it authority? Or is authority a property stemming from the nature of society?

At one time the present writer supposed the formal cause of society to be the adherence of the will of its members to the common good. This adherence of the will, this love of the members for the society that is theirs, is absolutely vital. But it cannot be pounded into place within a factitious framework of society according to the four classic causes, because society is not a substantial unity and hence is not susceptible to such analysis.

This is a truth pivotal to the understanding of paradoxes that have already arisen in this treatment of society. It is a pivotal truth for the understanding of the errors concerning society that have brought it so much distress, not to say destruction. *Society is not a substantial unity.* Its unity is accidental, a unity of order.[40] It lacks the oneness of a substance, say an

[40] See the remark by St Thomas quoted above in n. 37. For the various kinds of unity, see *Summa contra Gentiles*, IV. 35. 7, and Aristotle, *Metaphysics*, V. 6 (1015^b16–1017^a5).

Aristotle scathingly criticizes Plato's notion in the *Republic* that the political community – the *polis* or city in Plato's terms – should achieve as great a unity as possible: 'Is it not obvious that a *polis* may at length attain such a degree of

animal. Its unity is only *analogous* to that of a substance. *Hence any parallel drawn between society and a substance must be applied with extreme care.*

The most illuminating parallel can be the most dangerous. The rapport between whole and parts casts a strong light on the relation between the common good and the members of society, but when applied without due reservation, as if it were the full reality, it results in statism. (We shall examine this question in the final section of this introduction, 'The State and the Common Good.') And although applying the whole–part analogy to civil society is all too easy, the attempt to apply it to the familial society meets stiff resistance.

Another critical difference between a society and a substance revolves around the role in society of the will, though even here analogy is not out of place. The will to belong to a society depends on *love for self and for other members,* that is on the will for their good, and on *a sense of a common stake* in the society, that is on the understanding of each member that he and those he loves depend on that society for what they need and what they desire. Without that sense, without that love, there might be no society to begin with; without them there will not be one for long.

A society then is seen to be a union of love. What is loved by all is the good of all, the common good.

As for the stake that a society's members have in it, it is the complex of benefits deriving from society as these benefits flow back on them, offering some to all even when this or that particularized benefit is bestowed on a few only, or for that matter on one alone. The love that members of a society bear toward one another makes them happy to see others benefit; but beyond that they sense that the benefit of one redounds, in the right circumstances, to the benefit of all.

---

unity as to be no longer a *polis*? – since the nature of a *polis* is to be a plurality, and in tending to greater unity, from being a *polis* it becomes a family, and from being a family, an individual. . . . So that we ought not attain this greatest unity even if we could, for it would be the destruction of the *polis*' (*Politics*, II. 1 [1261^{a}16–21]).

This is a far cry from the dog-eat-dog model that Machiavelli and his epigones, most notably the ineffable Thomas Hobbes, would impose on civil society. Society is not a zero-sum game, where your loss is my gain. Rather your good tends to work for mine. Beyond that, we see a powerful interlocking dynamism: because we depend on society, all of us desire its flourishing, while its flourishing, indeed its very survival, depends wholly on that desire.

Edmund Burke summed it up with characteristic eloquence. In his historic attempt to win the British government to a policy of conciliation toward the American colonies, he warned:

> Do not entertain so weak an imagination as that your registers and your bonds, your affidavits and your sufferances, your cockets and your clearances, are what form the great securities of your commerce. Do not dream that your letters of office, and your instructions, and your suspending clauses, are the things that hold together the great contexture of this mysterious whole. . . .
>
> Do you imagine, then, that it is the land tax which raises your revenue, that it is the annual vote in the committee of supply which gives you your army? or that it is the mutiny bill which inspires it with bravery and discipline? No! Surely no! It is the love of the people; it is their attachment to their government, from the sense of the deep stake they have in such a glorious institution, which gives you your army and your navy, and infuses into both that liberal obedience, without which your army would be a base rabble, and your navy nothing but rotting timber.[41]

[41] From the 'Speech on Conciliation with the Colonies,' 22 Mar. 1775, in *Edmund Burke: Selected Writings and Speeches*, ed. Peter J. Stanlis (Chicago: Regnery Gateway, 1963), pp. 184–5. Burke continues with words that refer to politicians yet are applicable to philosophers: 'All this, I know well enough, will sound wild and chimerical to the profane herd of those vulgar and mechanical politicians, who have no place among us; a sort of people who think that nothing exists but what is gross and material. . . . But to men truly initiated and rightly taught, these ruling and master principles, which, in the opinion of such men as I have mentioned, have no substantial existence, are in truth everything and all in all.'

A less rhetorical statement of the matter was given by Archbishop Denis Hurley of Durban, now retired. Like Burke, he spoke in the context of a concrete political problem.

> The community instinct and the instinct for survival produce, I think, the toughest and most resistant amalgam in all human experience. There is very little that is rational about it. It cannot even be called emotional. It is the very being of a community determined to go on being and to take whatever measures are necessary to achieve that purpose.[42]

Note how the speaker, for decades a leading actor in the drama of South Africa, draws from that experience the principles he sees at work in that drama, even constituting its dynamic: *the very being of a community determined to go on being, the community instinct and the instinct for survival.*

In citing the resolve of the society 'to take whatever measures are necessary' for its survival, he puts his finger on one of the most important consequences of the society's resolve 'to go on being.' The common good, considered in itself and apart from any particular society, embraces all those elements necessary for the survival of *any* society. The common good of a particular society, whether it be a natural society such as the family or body politic, or a conventional society such as a business corporation or a school (assuming until further examination that a conventional society has a common good properly speaking), will include all those elements necessary for the survival of that *kind* of society and for that *particular, singular* society in its concrete circumstances as well.

When we ask why the members of a society desire its existence; when, going deeper into the matter, we ask what convinces them they have a stake in it, we approach more nearly the particular elements of the common good that appear before us when we examine it empirically. The members of a society know that it enables them to reach their

[42] Remarks on receiving an honorary doctorate at Georgetown University, Washington, DC, 2 Feb. 1987; published in *Origins*, the documentary service of the National Catholic News Service, vol. 16, no. 36.

goals. In the case of civil society, they are aware that without it they and those they love will find themselves lacking means necessary to the good life; in the case of the family, they know that it offers means necessary to an honest conferral of life, to training for an honest life, and to the preservation of life itself. They know that a society such as the family and the body politic, to cite only those which are natural (because intrinsically indispensable), bestows vital benefits, physical, moral and intellectual, on its members.

Thus the common good must include elements designed to foster the well-being of the persons within the society.[43]

[43] Since men form a society because of the good it brings them, since their will – and hence the end that motivates it – not only brings that society into being but maintains it there, since the root of society lies in the inborn need of men for society in order to reach their end, we may reasonably conclude that the purpose and cement of society is the perfection of the person, the achievement of what he is born to be.

However that is not to exclude a higher good still. To enter into this question we must make some distinctions.

Among ends we distinguish three kinds. The two principal kinds of end are proximate and ultimate, the proximate being a means to the ultimate. But an 'ultimate' end may itself be a means to a further end, and thus become intermediate.

The term 'ultimate end,' then, is relative. An end can be ultimate with respect to a given act or intention yet intermediate with respect to further ends.

The only *absolutely* ultimate end is God.

God in fact is the absolutely ultimate end of society as St Thomas observes: 'Men are united among themselves only in what is common among them. And this, most greatly, is God' (*In II Thessalonicenses*, III. 2).

The absolutely ultimate end of the universe is the glory of God, which is achieved through maintenance of the order he put into the world in creating it. St Thomas, in the *Summa contra Gentiles*, asserts: 'the greatest good in created things is the good of the order of the universe' (III. 64. 8).

The absolutely ultimate end of man, then, can be said to consist in integrating his life into the design of the universe; that is what his personal perfection accomplishes *ad extra*. Within the microcosm of the family or the body politic, the role of that same perfection *ad extra* is to integrate the person into the order of that society.

The role of his perfection is also to enable him to enter into union with God in the beatific vision as his absolutely ultimate end *ad intra*.

Over this question a dispute arose in the mid-forties among Thomists. It served to clarify many points, but none more than the fact that confusion obtained among followers of St Thomas on his teachings concerning the common good. The principal publications in this dispute are: Charles De Koninck, *De la primauté du bien commun contre les personnalistes* (Quebec: Editions de l'Université Laval, 1943); Yves Simon, 'On the Common Good,' *Review of*

The well-being of persons is in fact the principal proximate purpose of a natural society. This, along with love of other members of the society, explains the sacrifice of self that individual members, even in great numbers, can be required to make, and often make willingly and heroically, for the common good.[44]

Where a society exists *to do or make something in particular,* or in St Thomas's words 'for some special business,'[45] its common good will include all the means necessary for the fulfillment of that specifying purpose. More important, it will include the object or aim of the society, of its common action. The common good of such a society consists of this: the purpose of the society and the means necessary and suitable to the attainment of that purpose.

Note well however that such a society, which in this essay we term *conventional,* is artificial by nature, so to speak.[46] It is not a society into which men are born, not a society they cannot do without if they are to survive and thrive. It is not a necessary condition for a multiplicity of kinds of action, whether the good which that action aims at is necessary or merely helpful, or even just convenient. Such a society lacks the broad and elastic enabling power of a natural society.[47]

Politics, 6 (1944), pp. 530–633); I. Th. Eschmann, 'In Defense of Jacques Maritain,' *Modern Schoolman*, 22:4 (1945), pp. 183–208; Charles De Koninck, *In Defence of St Thomas* (Quebec: Editions de l'Université Laval, 1945); Jacques Maritain, *La Personne et le bien commun* (Paris: Desclée De Brouwer, 1947).

[44] St Thomas observes: 'each part naturally loves the common good of the whole more than its own particular good' (II-II. 26. 3). Although he is dealing here with the love of God, he explicitly states that this principle can be seen in civic life, where virtuous citizens are willing to suffer terrible loss for the common good.

[45] II-II. 48.

[46] Societies that we term *conventional* are, as we saw in n. 38, more conventionally called *artificial.* We avoid that term here because it can be the occasion of confusion. The state, a natural society because men must live under it in order to thrive or even survive properly, can be given various forms and hence, having the character of an artifact, can reasonably be considered artificial.

[47] Natural societies, as we call them in this essay, are sometimes called *necessary societies* (or *necessary communities*) because they fulfill unvarying needs of human nature. Under this classification, conventional societies are dubbed *free societies* (or *free associations*). There is, within this schema, a third grouping called *relatively*

This leads us to answer a question suggested earlier, as to whether such a society, a conventional society, can really have a common good. It is clear that a conventional society possesses a good participated in by all its members, a good that therefore can correctly be styled common. On the other hand that good, narrow and particularized, is far from the indispensable and variously enabling good of a natural society. Hence the term *common good* is used analogously of the two different kinds of society, the natural and the conventional. In fact the term *common good* is applied at least analogously – some think equivocally – even within natural societies, as should become clear during the progress of this introduction.

But it is in the more severely analogous use of the term in dealing with natural and conventional societies, rarely distinguished, that we find a major reason why the common good can so easily elude political thinkers. To understand the common good a firm grasp of the differences between natural and conventional societies is important, not only because the

---

necessary societies, which would be natural societies not necessary to survival itself, but societies created by birth; *The New Catholic Encyclopedia* (s.v. 'Society') cites the ethnic group as an example.

This classification is however misleading. The presence of intermediate groups – conventional societies – between the family and the state is *necessary* to the health of the body politic and of the family, not to speak of the good of the individual, since otherwise individuals and families would be powerless against the state, and the state would, contrary to nature, assume all authority and responsibility. This or that individual intermediate society may not be necessary to the health of the body politic and of the families that comprise it, but the presence of some intermediate societies is necessary. Without such you will soon have totalitarianism.

A *perfect* society is one that contains within itself all the means necessary to the achievement of its purpose. The only such society that concerns us here is the body politic, or political society, incorporating the state. (The Church is also a perfect society.)

The family, or familial society, is natural (because necessary to the education of human beings) yet imperfect (because, *pace* the Swiss Family Robinson, it needs the larger society in order to attain its end).

As we have seen, St Thomas distinguishes between on the one hand 'a multitude gathered for some special business,' and on the other 'a multitude gathered for all [the needs of] life' (II-II. 48.) Under the latter heading he places the family and civil society, and under the former he gives the example of an army.

common good of a conventional society is different from the common good of a natural society, but also because to overlook the difference is actually dangerous. The common good of a conventional society is a rather simple notion, easy to comprehend at a glance, hence handy as an example in explanation.[48] For that reason the common good of a conventional society tempts the unwary philosopher to import it whole into a natural society.

If the philosopher is led to think that a simple enumeration of particular goods reveals, as in the conventional society, the common good of a natural society, he may find himself on the shoals of individualism, where the common good is reduced to the sum of goods enjoyed by individual members.

Obversely, the philosopher who seeks an overarching principle of the common good may be led by the example of a conventional society to think that a single particular good, such as economic ease or efficient government, constitutes the core of the common good of a natural society, and that all other goods hang on it. In that case he could find himself stranded on the bleak shores of collectivism or statism.[49]

The state, as the organizing agency of the body politic, has a key role to play in the common good. Largely through defense against assault from without and against injustice, violence, and subversion from within, the state must ensure to the members of that society the practical opportunity, through their own actions, to achieve and preserve their personal and familial goods. Nor can the state be indifferent to the availability of particular goods that have no substitute, intrinsic or practical: on the intellectual level we might cite arithmetic, on the moral level such virtues as justice and

[48] St Thomas, in various places, uses the example of an army: its soldiers, its general, and its aim. However, as we have seen, he distinguishes clearly between what in this work are called a conventional society and a natural society. But, again, he does not to the present writer's knowledge use these terms.

[49] This is not just a recent phenomenon. Alexis de Tocqueville writes of the Physiocrats of the mid-eighteenth century: 'private rights were, in their eyes, negligible; only the public interest mattered' (*The Old Regime and the French Revolution*, tr. Stuart Gilbert [Garden City, NY: Doubleday Anchor Books, 1955], III. 3, p. 159).

temperance (even perhaps down to playfulness, since all virtues are irreplaceable and have some public effect), on the political level authority and the honor due it, and on the physical level water or, under present technology, roads.[50] Moreover, into the notion of the common good of civil society must enter a sufficient number of particular goods and their adequacy, not to speak of their quality.[51]

Because the abiding habit of behaving morally constitutes virtue, which is one of the principal constituents of the common good, the morality of the acts by which particular goods are achieved is of vital interest to the common good.

Many of these goods could not even come into being, and I venture that none of them except the free gifts of the natural world could long remain, without that great enabler which is the common good. The intrinsic purpose of the common good is to enable persons to achieve their ends, their own intrinsic purposes determined by their nature.[52]

[50] Such goods, when held in public trust, are called by St Thomas *common things* (*communia*), or *common goods* (*bona communia*); see II-II. 61. 1, cor. and ad 2 respectively.

Caution must be exercised not to confuse any one of such common goods (*bona communia*) with the common good we have been treating (*bonum commune*).

Furthermore, neither the common good nor common goods should be confused with transcendental good. Very rationally but, one is tempted to think, almost perversely, St Thomas calls this transcendental good (or ontological good) *bonum commune*, explaining that it is 'convertible with being' (I-II. 55. 4, ad 2; cf. n. 28 above).

[51] 'The common good consists of many things' (I-II. 96. 1).

[52] Jacques Maritain holds: 'The end of society is neither the individual good nor the collection of the individual goods of each of the persons who constitute it. Such a conception would dissolve society as such to the advantage of its parts, and would amount to either a frankly anarchistic conception, or the old disguised anarchistic conception of individualistic materialism, according to which the whole function of the body politic is to safeguard the liberty of each, thereby giving to the strong freedom to oppress the weak' (*La Personne et le bien commun*, in Joseph Evans and Leo Ward (eds. and trs.), *The Social and Political Philosophy of Jacques Maritain* [New York: Charles Scribner's Sons, 1955], p. 82).

One wishes for a demonstration of this position, if Maritain means to *exclude* from the purpose of society the individual good in any sense. Maritain's argument from consequences can scarcely be taken as a rigorous proof.

The end of society can hardly exclude the good of the individual person, a good that he reaches with society's help by achieving virtue and contemplation

Note once again the self-reinforcing dynamism. The principal intrinsic *personal* purpose is virtue itself, one of the chief constituents of that same common good. But experience teaches that nothing is more conducive to personal virtue than living among the virtuous.[53]

Virtue, especially in the form of justice and charity, is the motor of the gross tendency of a good society to maintain itself over time, just as the lack of virtue, the lack of justice and charity especially, explains the gross tendency of an evil society to fragment further than, by the nature of an evil society, it is fragmented already. A society, whose unity is of order, cannot long survive that subversion of order which is injustice.

The very first injustice possible springs from unchastity, and its effects on the common good are only too visible today.

---

and, through them, God. Maritain appears to concede this in his essay 'The End of Machiavellianism;' see n. 84 below.

The person, however, achieves these goals in cooperation with the other members of the society, or more precisely in communion with them. Man is naturally companionate precisely because the society of other men is in the main necessary to the education and survival of the individual, and unqualifiedly necessary to the survival of the species (cf. *In I Librum Ethicorum ad Nichomachum*, I. 4).

This need of his nature is reflected in his natural longings. To be alone is painful for man, and even the enjoyment of beauty is diminished if it is not shared. St Thomas goes so far as to assert: 'no possession is joyous without a companion' (*In I ad Corinthios*, X. 5). It is true that he elsewhere (I-II. 4. 8, ad 2) qualifies this by observing: 'the saying refers to a condition when the blessings present are not entirely sufficient.' He remarks further that the maxim, which he attributes to Boethius but which is found in Seneca (*Ad Lucilium epist*, 6), is not relevant to the question of whether friends are necessary to happiness, the discussion of which he focuses on God.

[53] Elements of the common good, in order to be common in the strict sense, must be communicable. Virtue, perhaps more than any single element in the common good, illustrates both communicability and the need for communicability within the common good

St Thomas, observing that it belongs to the good to do good ('est boni bonum facere'), notes: 'It is better that a good, bestowed on a thing, be common to many than that it be proper [to that thing], for the common good is always found to be more divine than the good of one alone [see *Nicomachean Ethics*, I. 2]. But the good of one becomes common to many if from one it is distributed among others; this can happen only in so far as one diffuses it to others through one's own action; in fact, if one does not have the power of transfusing it to others, it remains proper to oneself' (*Summa contra Gentiles*, III. 69).

While one might think abortion the first injustice in order of time, bastardy merits that dubious distinction since it is imposed on the victim at conception. In the disorder and privation worked upon the person by his bastardy, and very often worked *by* him as a result, we see a microcosm of the social chaos besetting communities where chastity languishes, and the family along with it.

The aetiology of this pathology is easy to trace. The family is the first school of virtue, and of most of the skills necessary for the survival of the individual person.[54] Deprive the larger society of this irreplaceable source of strength, moral and intellectual, economic and demographic, and the survival of that society is thrown into doubt. Every aspect of what we ordinarily call 'society,' from culture and ordinary civility to the economy and military sufficiency, must suffer.[55]

Here we approach the central theme of our thesis. Chastity, as a virtue absolutely essential to the health and survival of the family, is for that reason absolutely essential to the health

[54] St Thomas points out:

> Since man is by nature a social animal, in as much as he needs many things for his life that he cannot furnish himself unaided, it follows that man is naturally part of some multitude through which help for the good life is made available to him.
>
> Such help is needed for two things. First, for those things which are necessary for life, and without which the present life cannot be led. The domestic multitude of which man is a part helps him in this. For everyone without exception gets from his parents generation and nourishment and education. And similarly individuals who belong to the household family help one another in the necessities of life. (*In Librum Ethicorum ad Nichomachum*, lect. 1)

St Thomas proceeds to explain the necessity for the 'civil multitude' ('multitudo civilis'), that is, the larger society. It is necessary, he says, 'so that man may not only live but also live well.' He hastens to add that living well implies not only the bodily comfort that the trades and arts afford, 'but also what concerns moral matters.'

[55] President Ronald Reagan, introducing a tax reform designed to strengthen the family, called the family 'the bedrock of our society.' He continued: 'There is no instrument of hard work, savings and job creation as effective as the family. There is no cultural institution as ennobling as family life. And there is no superior, indeed no equal means to rear the young, protect the weak or attend the elderly' (State of the Union Address, 28 May 1985; see *Congressional Record*, 29 May 1985).

and survival of the larger society. We contend that chastity is essential to the health and survival of the family, as the common good of the family (that is, as *fides*, one of the goods of marriage). Without chastity the common good, taken in its usual reference to the body politic, grows sick unto death.

The Family and the Common Good of Civil Society

Perhaps because the family cannot provide everything necessary for attaining its end, and, therefore, falls under the heading of an 'imperfect' society, it is only too easily seen as a minor part of what is ordinarily called society *tout court*.[56] Its status as a distinct society in itself, indeed as an indispensable and, therefore, natural society, is often overlooked.

That is why discussions of the common good tend to focus on the body politic and the state. (We shall distinguish between these two entities in due course.) The term 'common good' refers by convention, almost by universal assent, to the common good of civil society. But to infer that no other society has a common good would be an error, and like every error has ill effects, in this case statism or, on a much less serious level, the deprivation of truths about the common good that emerge more clearly from observation of the family than of any other society. Among them are the communicability of good, the role of good as a perfective agent, the constructive and indeed indispensable function of virtue within the common good, and the role of mutual support and of activity in common. But from the point of view of this study the most important lesson to be learned in examining the family is this: that chastity plays an indispensable role in preserving the familial society, and through it society at large. Without chastity, then, the larger society will not be able to carry out its manifold and necessary purposes.

There we find the thesis of this work: that the common good as ordinarily understood – that is, the common good of the larger society – can flourish only if the common good

[56] St Thomas does not make this error. See II-II. 47. 10, ad 2, quoted in n. 35 above, and *In I Librum Ethicorum ad Nichomachum*, I. 4.

of the family is cherished, protected, nourished. But what is the common good of the family?

This is a key question, and a large question, but we already have a large part of the answer. The common good of the family is the common good to be sought and enjoyed by any natural society. This of course is not an essential definition, logically speaking, since it gives the genus without the specific difference, yet the generic meaning of the common good cannot be ignored if the common good of the family is to be understood.

As in any society, the common good of the family is in a basic sense the familial society itself, that is, the relation of order among the members, and the support they give the ensemble and one another. But what imparts to the common good of the family its specific character is the complex of purposes implicit in the foundation of the family.

How are these purposes discovered? This is done not only by examining the institution founded, an investigation that is essential, but also by examining the act of founding and the intention of the founders. The founders of the family are two persons, a man and a woman.[57] They found the family in the act of wedding, the act of consent to a contract (now often called a covenant, perhaps to avoid the legalistic connotations of contract) by which they become husband and wife.[58] They become – if we may import the telling phrase of

[57] We must be careful, in speaking of husband and wife as founders of familial society, to bear in mind that while they are acting as responsible agents (otherwise their union would be no marriage) they are also moved by forces larger than themselves, powers summed up in the term *human nature*. These are not merely the instincts of husband and wife, essential as they are to man's being, but the natural human ends for which man is destined. To these ends the human instincts are at once witnesses and guarantors. Thus, in a sense, the founder of the family, and for the same reasons the founder of the larger society, is human nature itself.

[58] St Thomas calls marriage 'a certain contract' ('quidam contractus') (*In IV Librum Sententiarum*, XXXI. 1. 2, ad 2). Clearly, marriage cannot be dissolved by mutual agreement, or by misbehavior of one of the parties, as can an ordinary contract. In order that there be a true marriage, consummation is not necessary; the use may be forgone but the right may not be denied. Abstention must be freely agreed upon by husband and wife. Cf. III. 29. 2.

Holy Scripture – two in one flesh, and to attain this fleshly union is why they marry.

Here an objection may arise from the traditional principle that the primary purpose of marriage, its chief good, is offspring. To answer that objection, we must examine the principle itself.

This requires a considerable exercise in distinction. The youthful St Thomas carries this out in his *Commentary on the Sentences* when dealing with the question of primacy among the three goods that Christian tradition ascribes to marriage, namely offspring, fidelity, and sacrament. He first distinguishes between the natural order and the supernatural order; in the supernatural order he finds the good of sacrament, and in the natural order the goods of fidelity and offspring.[59] He proceeds in the following article to distinguish between what is primary by being more essential and what is primary by being more worthy. If we consider the latter order, what is more worthy,

> then in every way sacrament is the principal among the three goods of marriage, because it pertains to marriage in so far as it is a sacrament of grace, while the other two pertain to it in so far as it is as it were a service to nature; now a perfection of grace is more worthy than a perfection of nature.[60]

St Thomas next examines primacy according to what is more essential. Here too he distinguishes:

> If however what is more essential is called principal, then a distinction must be made, for fidelity and offspring can be considered in two ways. One way is in themselves; then they pertain to the use of marriage, through which both offspring is produced and the conjugal agreement kept. But inseparability, which the sacrament brings in, pertains to marriage in itself, because from the very fact that through the conjugal agreement the spouses surrender power over themselves to one another *in perpetuum*, it follows that they cannot be separated. And it is from this that marriage is never found

[59] *In IV Librum Sententiarum*, XXXI. 1. 2.
[60] *In IV Librum Sententiarum*, XXXI. 1. 3.

> without inseparability. It is, however, found without fidelity and offspring, because the existence of a thing does not depend on its use, and according to this the sacrament is more essential to marriage than fidelity and offspring.[61]

St Thomas, dealing with marriage as a society that he has described in the previous article as 'in the service of nature,' thus calls indissolubility prior to offspring and fidelity because the marriage remains despite every eventual abuse of marriage. It cannot be voided by any human action.

Yet the other goods of marriage, offspring and fidelity, considered in themselves (and not, as we shall see presently, in the sense of assuming the obligation of fidelity and intending to produce offspring, both of which are essential to the act of wedding), can be voided by adultery and by refusal to procreate and educate children.

St Thomas proceeds to explain the sense in which the goods of offspring and fidelity can never be voided:

> Fidelity and offspring can be considered in another way, according as they are in their principles, as when offspring is taken as the intention of offspring, and when fidelity is taken as the obligation of preserving fidelity. Without them marriage itself cannot exist, because they are brought into being by the very conjugal agreement, so that if anything directly opposed to them were expressed in the consent that constitutes marriage, it would not be a true marriage. So taking fidelity and offspring in that way, offspring is the most essential to matrimony, fidelity second, and sacrament third, just as the being of nature is more essential to man than the being of grace, even though the being of grace is more worthy.[62]

Offspring is the principal good or end of marriage in that at the moment of this society's foundation offspring specifies the marriage as a particular kind of society, namely one aimed at procreating and educating children.

Fidelity takes second place for two reasons. One is that, considered as the loyalty and support and love that the

[61] Ibid.
[62] Ibid.

members of this marital society give one another, it demonstrates the characteristics of any natural society, not of marital society specifically.

The second reason is that, considered as the fidelity specific to marriage, namely the confinement of genital activity within the marriage partnership, fidelity stems from and is dependent on the specific nature of marriage, namely a society designed for the procreation, protection, and maturation of children. Such fidelity is necessary for the proper fulfillment of that design.

Although St Thomas puts sacrament last in the order of what is essential to marriage, he does this on the ground that it is in the supernatural order and therefore less essential to man than the natural goods. Concerning indissolubility, it might be argued that because it stems from both of the other essential goods of marriage, namely offspring and fidelity, it is last in the order of the essence of marriage.[63]

[63] St Thomas, as we have seen, teaches that inseparability is introduced by the sacrament, and that at the same time it pertains to marriage itself because the spouses 'surrender power over themselves to one another *in perpetuum*' through the conjugal agreement (*In IV Librum Sententiarum*, XXXI. 1. 3).

Is there a contradiction here? If inseparability belongs to marriage as a natural institution, how can it be introduced by a sacrament, that is from the supernatural order?

St Thomas presents the objection in another way: 'The sacraments are not of the natural law. But the inseparability of matrimony belongs to the good of the sacraments. Therefore it is not of the natural law' (*In IV Librum Sententiarum*, XXXIII. 2, 1. obj. 2).

He responds: 'Inseparability belongs to matrimony in so far as it is a sign of the perpetual union of Christ and the Church, and in so far as it is in the service of nature ordained to the good of offspring, as has been said. But because the separation of matrimony is more directly contrary to this meaning than to the good of offspring, which, as has been said, it opposes by its consequences, the inseparability of marriage is understood more in the good of sacrament than in the good of offspring, though it can be understood in both. In so far as it pertains to the good of offspring it will be of the natural law, not however in so far as it belongs to the good of sacrament.'

But if 'the creator from the beginning' made husband and wife inseparable (Matt. 19:4), how could the law of the old dispensation have permitted divorce with remarriage, and the law of utter inseparability have returned to the world of men and women only as part of the Christian dispensation?

St Thomas bases his solution to this problem on a distinction between primary and secondary precepts of the natural law (*In IV Sententiarum*, XXXIII. 2).

What, in the light of St Thomas's treatment of the goods of marriage, are we to say of human motives for marriage?

Without entering into that solution, far less rejecting it, we suggest another. It might be argued that the unteachability (more literally 'hard-heartedness,' from the Greek *tēn sklērokardian humōn*) to which Jesus Christ attributes the introduction of divorce (Matt. 19:8 and Mark 10:5) consisted in the weakening of the will and the clouding of the intellect that were consequent on the fall of man. If that is so we can further argue that only the grace of the sacramental order could enable wounded human nature to rise to the standard of indissoluble marriage.

There may well have been a foreshadowing of the sacrament in Our Lord's original words. The Greek of St Matthew's and St Mark's Gospels, *sklērokardia*, which is most literally rendered 'hard-heartedness,' is also found in the Septuagint, the Greek translation of the Old Testament dating from pre-Christian times. In Deut. 10:16 the Septuagint exhorts to circumcision of hard hearts: '*peritemeisthe tēn sklērokardian humōn.*' (The Hebrew actually speaks of cutting away the foreskin of the heart.) In Jer. 4:4 the Septuagint uses the same phrase. It seems quite possible that the Semitic phrase used by Jesus, whose knowledge of the Old Testament is abundantly clear from the Gospels, had to do with the scriptural figure of an uncircumcised heart, a heart whose hardness and impurities had not been cut away.

Now circumcision in the Old Law was associated not only with marital purity (see Gen. 34:14–17 and Exod. 4:25–6) but, as we shall see in ch. 3, with fidelity to Yahweh as well. As a physical act symbolizing a spiritual reality, it foreshadowed those symbols which produce what they symbolize and which are called sacraments.

In order that this explanation stand, it must be agreed that Jesus Christ was addressing his interlocutors not as members of the Jewish nation but as members of the human race. Our Lord's words, it seems to this writer, can be understood that way even though the question put to him dealt with Moses as lawgiver to the Jews. Moses, under this construction, was simply dealing with the universal condition of mankind, not any weakness or malice peculiar to the people under his care.

Supporting this understanding is the fact that divorce was far from a uniquely Jewish institution. Indissoluble marriage is the only civil institution to have been introduced into the world by Jesus Christ. Along with the eradication of slavery and a clear distinction between the religious and civil orders, it remains the distinguishing mark of a Christian society.

Holy Writ itself seems to pose an objection to the Catholic tradition that Jesus restored perfect indissolubility to marriage, for twice in Matthew (5:32 and 19:9) Jesus is quoted as allowing an exception. In the Greek text of Matthew, which is the earliest we possess, the word used for this exception is *porneia*, which is usually rendered 'unchastity' or 'fornication.' But the Dead Sea Scrolls found in the area of Qumran after World War II strongly support the view that *porneia* in the two texts on divorce in Matthew refers to marriage within forbidden degrees of kinship – incest – or even polygamy. See Joseph A. Fitzmyer, 'The Dead Sea Scrolls and the New Testament after Thirty Years,' *Theology Digest*, 29 (1981), pp. 361–3.

How does his analysis fit into life as we live it and see it lived?

Little experience is needed to learn the vivid lesson that children are not foremost in the minds of a man and woman when they marry. They may marry even without the express intention of bringing children into the world.[64] Children rather are taken for granted. If they are excluded from the intention of either party, in the sense either of denying the other the genital act or of so denaturing it that it is deprived of its genital power, then there is no marriage; the man and woman would in the latter case be mere concubines, those who lie together, and in the former mere companions, those who break bread together.

To get a firm grasp on this we must bear in mind that from the viewpoint of purpose, of final causality, children are already present at the wedding. The motive for marriage may not be to bring forth children, but the reason for marriage built into the institution by nature is precisely that, and the obligation and right stemming from that intrinsic purpose must be respected in the act of wedding or there is no marriage. This remains true even if, often enough, the express goal of the man and woman who wed is simply to share their lives as fully as a man and a woman are able; in a word, to become two in one flesh.

What do they in fact find, these two founders and sole actual members of a new society? They first find the union they felt driven to seek, 'the full kingdom of that final kiss.'[65] They become two in one flesh.

[64] Shakespeare sees this clearly. In writing of the desire that carries a man to marriage, he puts a teleological gloss on it:

> From fairest creatures we desire increase,
> That thereby beauty's rose might never die.
> (Sonnet I)

Is there significance in the fact that Shakespeare lays down this principle in his very first sonnet?

[65] Richard Crashaw, *The Flaming Heart upon the Book and Picture of the Seraphical Saint Teresa,* line 101. The poet is, however, speaking of the final ecstasy of this saint.

However, they often, perhaps usually, and I suspect almost always, fail to realize the full meaning of that consummation of their marriage until the first child arrives. Then it dawns on them like thunder. There, in the flesh, lies the two of them. *There* they are two in one flesh.

And there we find a second reason for the claim that men and women marry to become two in one flesh, and a way to understand that the purpose of marriage is offspring. A Catholic tradition understands the Scriptural term *two in one flesh* to mean not only the act of marital congress but the child born as its fruit.[66]

The intrinsic natural purpose of marriage is offspring, though husband or wife or both may be very imperfectly aware of it until that purpose presents itself in a stunning epiphany, the birth of a child. From that moment they know. In that child they see the incarnation of their love. In him they descry their destiny. They live for him and work together for him, finding a mutual reliance, mutual esteem, and mutual gratitude that give their marriage – both the founding act of wedding and the continuing institution of wedlock – transcendentally fuller meaning and correspondingly fuller satisfaction. Where the child is concerned there can be, barring pathology, no jealousy between husband and wife. He is their love incarnate. He is their common joy, their common good, the common aim of their life together.

To put it another way, once the child is born a curious inversion appears. Although marriage, because it is a natural society, is aimed at mutual help and support; although marriage, again as a natural society, is a union of love, such love and such mutual help and support, whatever their

[66] St Thomas, quoting Matt. 19:5, gives the sense of St Jerome: '"And they will be two in one flesh." Jerome: That is, in the flesh of the offspring. And this is the fruit of marriage' (*In Matthaeum Evangelistam Expositio*, XIX).

Commenting in the *Catena Aurea* on the same verse, St Thomas says: 'The reward of marriage is to be made, out of two, one flesh, that is the offspring.'

Alexander Pope observes:

> Nor ends the pleasure with the fierce embrace;
> They love themselves, a third time, in their race.
> (*Essay on Man*, epistle III, iii)

intrinsic worth, now are clearly seen as means to the begetting of the child, and means to his proper upbringing.[67]

Once husband and wife, with the birth of the child, know this truth, they spend the rest of their lives living it. They serve the child, preparing him to serve the larger common good through virtue and knowledge and productivity, and orienting him toward his final goal through piety.

So we find the child to be the primary purpose of marriage, hence its common good.

In the light of the child's role as common good of a marriage, we can enquire further into the meaning of a family. If the child is so central to the act by which a man and woman

[67] In grappling with a theological problem of the sufficiency of the three goods traditionally ascribed to Christian marriage, namely offspring, fidelity, and sacrament, St Thomas, as we have seen, deals at length with their priority. He poses the objection, drawn from Aristotle (*Nicomachean Ethics*, VIII. 12), that marriage is 'not only for the procreation and education of children but for a fellowship of common life for the sake of a sharing of activities.' His response is revealing: 'by *offspring* is understood not only the procreation of offspring but also their upbringing. To this, as to an end, is ordered all the sharing of activities that is found between husband and wife.'

His conclusion: 'and so within offspring, as if within the principal end, the other is included as if coming in second place' (*In IV Librum Sententiarum*, XXXI. 1. 2, ad 1).

Late in his life St Thomas gave this question a somewhat different treatment. In some of the last lines to come from his pen he observed, first, that a marriage is called true when it achieves its perfection (III. 29. 2). He then argued that the 'form' of matrimony is its 'first perfection,' and that this form 'consists in a certain inseparable union of minds binding husband and wife to keep faith with one another unsunderably.'

The 'second perfection' of a thing, he noted, 'consists in the thing's operation, through which the thing in some way attains its end.'

For St Thomas the natural end of marriage is offspring. But within that end he noted two operations: the generation of children, and their education. The former is achieved by marital congress but the latter 'through the other activities of husband and wife by which they accommodate themselves to one another for the rearing of children.'

Thus, in his final word on the subject, St Thomas subsumed mutual help and support on the one hand, and marital congress on the other, under the primary natural good of marriage, the final end of marriage, which is offspring. They are means to the end of marriage.

The logical inference from this should be noted. A refusal, on the part of either party at the moment of wedding, to bestow the right to marital congress would mean that there was no marriage. Would the same hold for a refusal, at the moment of wedding, to bestow the right to help and support which St Thomas also subsumes under the heading of the final end of marriage?

enter into marriage, must we say that a marriage that in fact lacks a child cannot be said to constitute a family? Must a family be husband and wife and children, or can it be the married couple alone?

The answer to the question is found in examining the alternative, a 'married couple alone.' There is no such thing. The very act of marrying implies children as the purpose and perfection of the state created by the act; if, at the moment of wedding, the union is deliberately deprived of that purpose, as in the case of couples of whom even one partner excludes the right to fruitfulness, it is no marriage. Therefore man and wife 'by themselves' constitute a family, since in reality, if only in potency, there is no such thing as man and wife by themselves. When you say husband, you say father; when you say wife, mother.

Now if we consider husband and wife a family, as they are, it is easy to answer the question: what is the common good of the family? The answer is: the child.[68] This is not to say that the marital society itself, the union of husband and wife in fidelity to each other, is not also a part of the common good of the family. But the very establishment of the marital society is necessarily aimed at the procreation and education of children. Moreover the activity of the family, its work, is oriented toward the child. This is due to the dependence of the child, his immaturity, his need for help and his drive toward a state where he is master of himself and can fully participate in the world around him.

The child is in a peculiar way the common good of the family to which he belongs precisely because he is a child. He has not reached the state of knowledge, of physical strength and skill, and of virtue where he can care for himself and contribute fully to the larger society. As we know, his perfecting – his education, that is – is as much a part of his parents' common purpose, their common good, as is his begetting and

[68] We have seen that the term *common good* is used analogously of a natural society and a conventional society. Now we see that the term *common good* is used analogously of the two kinds of natural society, namely the family and the body politic.

birth, and this carries over into the family once he is no longer just implicit in it but has become an actual part of it.

All the child's activities, including play, study, discipline, and training in piety, are aimed at his maturation and what comes with it. These activities, significantly, contribute to the education of his siblings also. It is in this sense, of global orientation toward arrival at maturity, that the child is the common good not only of his parents but of the family he belongs to, including himself.

This emerges most clearly when the family is seen as a unit-member of the larger society, the body politic.[69] Within that larger society the chief purpose of the family – hence, let us always bear in mind, its common good – is to offer it new members, men and women so matured through familial

[69] We do not speak here of *nation,* which according to the persuasive argument of Jacques Maritain 'is not a society' and 'does not cross the threshold of the political realm' (*Man and the State,* p. 6).

Maritain distinguishes between society and community, though he admits that the two terms 'may licitly be used synonymously, and I myself have done so many times' (p. 2). But he maintains that it is more proper 'to assign them to two different kinds of society groups which are actually different in nature' (ibid.).

Maritain explains: 'In order to understand this distinction, we must remember that social life as such brings men together by reason of a certain common *object.* In social relations there is always an object, either material or spiritual, around which the relations among human persons are interwoven. In a *community,* . . . the object is a *fact* which precedes the determinations of human intelligence and will, and which acts independently of them to create a common unconscious psyche, common feelings and psychological structures, and common mores. But in a *society* the object is a *task* to be done or an *end* to be aimed at, which depends on the determinations of human intelligence and will and is preceded by the activity – either decision, or, at least, consent – of the reason of individuals. . . . A business firm, a labor union, a scientific association are *societies* as much as the body politic. Regional, ethnic, linguistic groups, social classes, are *communities*' (p. 3).

Maritain proceeds to claim that although the word *nation* originates from the Latin for birth, 'the nation is not something biological, like the Race' (p. 5). It would be more accurate to say the nation is not *purely* biological, since, as Maritain admits, it is 'based on the fact of birth and lineage.' He adds that it also includes elements of culture and tradition. 'Yet for all that the Nation is not a society; it does not cross the threshold of the political realm. . . . Like any other community the Nation is 'acephalous': it has elites and centers of influence – no head or ruling authority; . . . no common good' (p. 6).

Maritain's treatment of the problem of nation, body politic, and state, and the abuses thereof, is found in ch. 1 of *Man and the State.* It will reward study.

education as to be capable of contributing their full share to its common good.

We can sum up our conclusion: the child, as the fully contributing adult *in fieri*, is the *specifying* common good of the family, that is, the purpose which determines the nature of the family in itself, in the relations of its members to it and to one another, and finally in its own relations to the larger society. This is so for a reason we have examined at some length. The child, his conception and final maturation, is the end of marriage both when marriage is considered as a state stamping its character on husband and on wife, and also when marriage is considered as a society that by its nature includes offspring, whether implicitly or actually, and does so for the common good of the larger society. It is the child that gives purpose to the love of husband and wife, to their mutual help and support. It is in the child that husband and wife find the meaning of all they are to one another.

Now it is quite clear in principle, and all too clear from experience, that dishonest genital behavior is incompatible with the full union of husband and wife, their love, their mutual help and support. Nothing is more corrosive of a society than injustice, and infidelity is an injustice striking at the compact between man and woman that makes them husband and wife. That in turn strikes at the ability of the parents to educate children. In weakening the familial society, unchastity deprives the larger society, the body politic, of its full share of the goods the family supplies, chiefly citizens educated in virtue.

What does the body politic supply the family and its members? Chiefly *access* to other societies and individuals; from them particular goods enabling men to live well are obtained.[70] But such access *hinges on order*, which in turn depends on personal virtue, on a widespread sense of the

[70] St Thomas, explaining why man is social by nature, notes that while the family provides him with things needed for life itself, the 'civic multitude' ('multitudo civilis') provides him with things needed 'for a perfect sufficiency of life, that is, so that man not only may live but may live well' (*In I Librum Ethicorum ad Nichomachum*, I. 4).

stake each member of the civic multitude has in it, and on reasonable laws duly enforced.

Here is where the state enters in most essentially: in writing and enforcing laws. Note however the twofold power of laws. They not only *enforce order through their punitive power* but also *foster order through their pedagogical power.* Laws instruct citizens in virtue.[71]

That includes chastity, safeguard of the family and through the family the child, his education, and everything that the properly educated child, the virtuous man, the dutiful citizen, offers to his fellows, to the family, to the larger society, and to the state. Among the weightiest duties of the state and its magistrates is to establish and enforce laws protecting and fostering the family. This might seem sufficiently obvious in principle, and is abundantly and even painfully obvious from experience, but these fundamentals and the lessons that have brought them home are meeting resistance.

One reason for the strength of this resistance is that the powers of state have in large part thrown their weight behind it. Virtually throughout the West the state has not only abandoned the family to its enemies, but has even joined them. Legislatures are writing laws broadening the definition of the family – or more properly distorting it – to include homosexual unions. Where such laws are lacking, judges are decreeing them into existence.

A more direct assault on marriage comes from no-fault divorce laws, which within fifteen years of the first such law,

[71] St Thomas notes: 'Because every law is so made that it be obeyed by its subjects, it is plain that a property of law is to bring its subjects to the virtue proper to them' (I-II. 92. 1; see also I-II. 92. 2, ad 4).

He proceeds however to contrast the effect on citizens of good laws with laws written for what later came to be called Machiavellian purposes: 'If the lawmaker is aiming at true good, which is the common good regulated according to divine justice, it follows that men will be made simply good through the law. But if the lawmaker's intention bears on what is not good simply speaking, but useful or pleasurable to him, or repugnant to divine justice, then the law does not make men good *simpliciter*, but *secundum quid*, to wit with reference to such a regime. Such good is found however even in things evil in themselves, such as when someone is called a good thief because he operates in a way suitable to his aim' (I-II. 92. 1).

effective in California in 1970, spread to all fifty states. Because of no-fault divorce, marriage has become the only contract in the United States that can be voided by the simple will of one party without evidence of misbehavior on the part of the other. This legal anomaly has constitutional implications, since the US Constitution prohibits any State from passing a 'Law impairing the Obligation of Contracts.'[72]

Such laws making family dissolution a simple and routine matter, joined to legislation and judicial decrees giving homosexual unions equal status and to tax laws giving virtually no relief, not to speak of preferential treatment, to citizens burdened with the task of raising and educating new citizens, hardly foster the family as an institution. They might be seen as attempts to abolish the family.

The struggle to restore the state to its proper role as defender of the family must be counted among the pivotal political dramas of our time, along with the struggle to restore God and virtue to their place in public life, and to restore widespread ownership of property.

In order to understand the role of the state within the body politic, and especially in its relations with the family, we must focus more closely on the state itself.

The State and the Common Good

When dealing with the concept of the state it is vital to distinguish it from the body politic. *The state* is the organizing agency of the body politic. It is that part of the body politic whose task it is to govern.[73] Jacques Maritain explains:

> The State is only that part of the body politic especially concerned with the maintenance of law, the promotion of the common welfare and public order, and the administration of

[72] Art. I, sect. 10. Chief Justice John Marshall commented: 'When any state legislature shall pass an act . . . allowing either party to annul [the marriage contract] without the consent of the other, it will be time . . . to inquire whether such an act be constitutional' (*Dartmouth College* v. *Woodward*, 1819).

[73] This act is called 'government.' However, to call it 'governance' avoids the ambiguity arising from the conventional use of the term 'government' to mean the state itself.

public affairs. The state is a part which *specializes* in the interests of the whole.[74]

Thus, goods that the family and conventional societies require from the body politic are ensured by the activity of the state: order through law, the access to other persons and societies which such order ensures, the shelter of the military, and not only access to common amenities – usually called public utilities – but the guarantee of their adequacy.

Though men may structure the state in widely varying forms from age to age and country to country, the state remains a natural entity. The natural character of the state stems from the indispensable need of the body politic for such an authority if the common good – that is, the purpose and indeed the very existence of the body politic – is to be preserved. Despite many historical distortions, that structuring of the body politic which is the task of the state must rise on natural, imprescriptible bases, reached by reason and summarized in the word 'justice.'

The responsibilities of the state extend, of course, far beyond the maintenance of justice, far beyond the defense of the body politic. As we have seen, the state holds responsibility, in one way or another, for what is called infrastructure.

That is, the state must create, or maintain, or at the very least ensure through oversight, common amenities such as

[74] *Man and the State*, p. 12. Maritain adds:

> the State is not a kind of collective superman; the State is but an agency entitled to use power and coercion, and made up of experts or specialists in public order and welfare, an instrument in the service of man. Putting man at the service of that instrument is political perversion. The human person as an individual is for the body politic and the body politic is for the human person as a person. But man is by no means for the State. The State is for man.
>
> When we say that the State is the superior part in the body politic, this means that it is superior to the other organs or collective parts of this body, but it does not mean that it is superior to the body politic itself. The part as such is inferior to the whole. The State is inferior to the body politic as a whole. Is the State even the *head* of the body politic? Hardly, for in the human being the head is an instrument of such spiritual powers as the intellect and the will, which the whole body has to serve; whereas the functions exercised by the State are for the body politic, and not the body politic for them (p. 13).

transportation systems and water systems, and must guarantee access to them. It also holds a certain responsibility for activities vital to the common good such as commerce and education. The extent of that responsibility may vary from state to state, and often is determined in the concrete by custom, and if not by custom then, for better or for worse, by the prevailing philosophy of state. As for education in particular, principle and experience combine to show that the best case arises where the state ensures certain standards, and the worst where the state becomes the educator.

Access, an important part of liberty, has in modern times been perceived as essential to the common good. In earlier times it was everywhere a function of the state to regulate it by the enforcement of privilege, while nowadays, in Western society, it has become a function of the state to guarantee it to all. Access, joined to technological culture and a thriving economy, creates opportunity, itself an important part of the common good. Access is a function of civil liberty because to be truly free it does not suffice to be able to move unhindered (the early meaning of political freedom, dating to the centuries when the West was gradually abandoning the institution of serfdom); one must have some acceptable place to move to.

It is worth noting that these responsibilities of the state are included in the inventory of goods ordinarily listed in treatments of the common good. Since the state holds responsibility for so vast a field of the common good, since so much authority and wealth, hence power, are ordinarily in the hands of the state, statism, at least in the mild sense of the word, has historically been an abiding temptation.[75]

[75] The limitations of language not only make this temptation all the more plausible, but for anyone philosophically inclined may give even mild statism a nudge toward radical statism, which is totalitarianism. (We shall examine these two kinds of statism in due course; suffice it to note here that they are different in kind, and hence that the terms 'mild' or 'mitigated,' and 'radical' or 'extreme,' are misleading in so far as they imply differences of degree.)

Treatment of the question can be confusing. Aristotle, for example, holds that mankind 'was made by nature more for marriage than for civil society,' explaining: 'and this in the measure that the household is earlier and more necessary than the city' (*Nicomachean Ethics*, VIII. 12 [1162^{a}17]). Yet he declares

The temptation to statism also stems from the problem of terminology that arises, in treating of society and of the common good, from the necessity of using the terms 'whole' and 'parts' (or, which on analysis comes to the same thing and raises the same difficulty, 'members' rather than 'parts'). From this terminology comes the anomaly that while the parts (or members) of a human society are persons, yet, in the words of St Thomas, 'the concept of part is opposed to that of person.'[76]

---

later that the city 'is by nature clearly prior to the family and to the individual, since the whole is of necessity prior to the part' (*Politics*, I. 2 [1253^{a}19]).

Neither Aristotle nor St Thomas, in expatiating on this latter passage, attempts to explain in what sense the state is prior to the family; Aristotle restricts his explanation to the priority of the state over the individual man, and St Thomas follows suit. The explanations of both depend on the role of the part within the whole, St Thomas however being careful to state that individual men '*are compared* to the whole city, as the parts of a man to the man' (*Sententia libri Politicorum*, I. 1; emphasis supplied).

In the following pages we shall deal with the question of how the terms 'part' and 'whole' should be understood in reference to the citizen and civil society. The distinction drawn by Maritain in *Man and the State*, quoted in the previous note, casts light on the specific question of the relationships between man and the state, and between man and the body politic.

The word we render 'city' in the foregoing passages from Aristotle and St Thomas is *polis* in the Greek, *civitas* in the Latin. It is often translated 'state,' although that is an anachronism. The *polis* was for Aristotle a perfect society, as the state is for us (understood as necessarily joined to the body politic, because it is a *part* of that particular body politic for which it holds responsibility). But there are inconveniences in this translation. Sir Ernest Barker notes: 'It is easy to translate the Greek word *polis* by our word 'state;' but the essence vanishes in the translation. . . . The word for 'state' comes to us from the Latin *status*, in its sense of standing or position: it meant, when we adopted it in the sixteenth century, the standing or position of the person (or persons) in authority, so that Louis XIV was etymologically justified in saying *L'état, c'est moi!*' (introd. to his translation of the *Politics* [New York and London: Oxford University Press, 1958], p. lxiii).

Cf. Harry Jaffa's comments on the translation of *polis*, and the meaning of *polis*, in his essay on Aristotle in *History of Political Philosophy*, 2nd edn., eds. Leo Strauss and Joseph Cropsey (Chicago and London: University of Chicago Press, 1972), esp. pp. 65–8.

[76] *In III Librum Sententiarum*, V. 3. 2. The Latin has it: 'ratio partis contrariatur rationi personae.'

Caution must be exercised in applying this principle, as we shall see. St Thomas invokes it here in demonstrating that the soul, because merely a part of the person, could not, when separated from the body in death, constitute the person.

Jacques Maritain warns that for the correct development of the discussion on society we must bear in mind 'the irremediable deficiency of our language.' In his view the 'only possible way for us to express the fact that persons live in society is to say that they are parts of society or compose society.'[77]

To understand how dangerous this necessary terminology can be, we need only advert to the fact that the whole is the part's very reason for being. This, applied to the body politic, can lead to the most totalitarian statism.[78]

The terms employed by St Thomas in dealing with persons within society are as precise as the limitations of language allow. Where in the context of society he introduces the terms 'whole' and 'part' he is likely to qualify them, as when treating the meritoriousness of a human act: 'everyone living in any society is *in some way* a part and member of the whole society.'[79] Once he has made the point, however, he apparently feels free in that same article to use the term without qualification, speaking of 'man, who is master of his actions, even he, in so far as he belongs to another, that is *the community of which he is part*.'[80]

[77] But he adds that this 'does not at all mean that he [the person] asks [*demande*] to be in society in the way in which a part is in a whole, nor does it mean that he asks [*demande*] to be treated in society as a part in a whole' (*La Personne et le bien commun*, p. 51; Evans and Ward, *The Social and Political Philosophy of Jacques Maritain*, p. 85).

[78] Maritain's formula: 'The human person as an individual is for the body politic and the body politic is for the human person as a person. But man is by no means for the State. The State is for man' (*Man and the State*, p. 13).

[79] I-II. 21. 3; emphasis supplied.

[80] Ibid., emphasis, again, supplied. In his treatment of justice as a general virtue (II-II. 58. 5), St Thomas says it 'directs a man in his relations to other men.'

How? In two ways, says St Thomas: 'first as regards his relation with individuals; secondly as regards his relations with regard to others in common, in so far as a man who serves a community serves all men who are contained within it.'

Still refusing to call man a part, St Thomas continues very carefully: 'Now it is evident that all who are contained under any community are compared to the community as parts to a whole.'

The article proceeds: 'but a part as such belongs to a whole; hence any good of the part can be directed to the good of the whole. Therefore the good of any virtue, whether directing a man to himself or to other individual persons, can be referred to the common good.'

It should be borne in mind that when St Thomas points to the opposition between person and part, he is dealing not with society and its members but with soul, body, and person.[81] There it is a question of a substance and its parts. In the other case it is a question of an accident, a *relatio* among substances, and of the substances that are the terms of that *relatio*. Society, once again, has only an accidental unity, a unity of order.

We speak of a temptation to statism, but mark well that statism is of two kinds. Statism properly speaking is totalitarianism. It is a statism both *radical and ramifying*: the state not only attempts to sink its roots into all institutions but even to be the root and branch of all institutions. What we refer to as 'mild' or 'mitigated' statism is really quite a different animal from totalitarianism; hence the terms, strictly speaking, are incorrect. Such statism is reliance on the state for what the state cannot or ought not do. This 'mild' statism has in recent decades in America been called liberalism. The opposite error, now dubbed libertarianism but in the last century known as liberalism, is unrestrained individualism.[82]

[81] His question is whether the soul, separated from the body in death, is the person. On the principle that the part – in this case the soul – is distinct from the whole, he argues that the separated soul is not the person. Here he disagrees with the Master of the Sentences, Peter Lombard.

Dealing with this text, Charles De Koninck observes: 'The whole of any society or of the universe is but an accidental unity. . . . When St Thomas calls the intellectual creature a part of society, he is obviously not using the term "part" in the sense in which it is understood in the article referred to . . . , i.e., as part of an "unum per se"' (*In Defence of St Thomas*, p. 17).

Cf. St Thomas's treatment of society as a unity of order, n. 37 above.

[82] Unhappily, in recent decades there has been little realization among Catholics that their tradition points the way to a wholesome alternative to socio-economic libertarianism on the one hand and, on the other, liberalism as the latter term has come to be understood. This is a polity based on a sense of the common good and of the stake each member of the body politic has in it, on personal virtue and on the liberty that only personal virtue and widespread distribution of property make possible. Widespread ownership allows such liberty to expand by fostering that personal responsibility which is its necessary condition, by providing a check upon government, by rendering government intervention into private life less necessary, and by encouraging a love of liberty among citizens.

Liberty is also enhanced by a strong family life and a proliferation of voluntary organizations. Such organizations render intervention by the state into the body

Ironically, the corollary of radical statism is individualism, not the self-centered and socially irresponsible individualism of economic libertarianism but the lonely and despairing individualism of the person submerged in the mass, stripped of his power to organize and achieve. This individualism, this statism, sees only two components in the body politic: the omnipotent state and the impotent individual.

By right, however, there are many societies within the body politic, and the principle governing their role within that larger society, and governing the roles of the state and the individual as well, was formulated with admirable concision by Pius XI:

> Just as it is gravely wrong to take from individuals what they can accomplish by their own initiative and industry and give it to the community, so also it is an injustice and at the same time a grave evil and disturbance of right order to assign to a greater and higher association what lesser and subordinate organizations can do. For every social activity ought of its very nature to furnish help to the members of the body social, and never destroy and absorb them.[83]

We have argued that basic to the common good is the very existence of the society to which that good is common. This

---

politic patently less necessary by shouldering tasks the state otherwise might feel obliged, or tempted, to take on itself.

Sound family life is essential to the virtue of the citizenry, long recognized as a check on the tyrant. But virtue, plus a widespread and vivid sense of the stake each citizen has in the common good, renders a multiplicity of laws and intervention by the police less necessary. Virtue, therefore, acts as a natural check both on the police, that arm of the state which along with taxation is most easily turned into an instrument of statist oppression, and on a multiplicity of laws, which is onerous to the citizens whether imposed by a statist government or a more rational government.

High taxation goes hand in hand with statism, even of the mild variety, lending itself to unwise or frivolous uses. If taxation is imposed for unjust purposes, it amounts to theft of the fruits of labor of the citizenry.

[83] *Quadragesimo Anno*, 70. Forty years earlier (1891), Leo XIII had warned against submerging the family beneath the state: 'Wherefore, assuming of course that those limits be observed which are fixed by its immediate purpose, the family assuredly possesses rights at least equal to those of civil society, in respect to choosing and employing the things necessary for its protection and just liberty' (*Rerum Novarum*, 20).

conclusion must be accompanied, however, by an awareness that evil means to the survival of the society are self-defeating. The use of evil means necessarily weakens the good, the ability to survive, of the agent, in this case the society.[84]

Yet given the modern philosophy of state, and the state of human nature, the instinct of a political society for survival is very likely to override any scruple as to the means of survival.

We have noted Denis Hurley's penetrating remark that the community instinct and the instinct for survival produce a superbly tough amalgam which he described as 'the very being of a community determined to go on being and to take whatever measures are necessary to achieve that purpose.' In our day the phrase 'take whatever measures are necessary' is likely to be interpreted as indifference to the morality of the means, so widely is *realpolitik* taken for granted, so widely indifference to the morality of means. But such indifference is an error destructive of the common good.

In ancient thought it was practically a commonplace to consider the virtue of the citizenry the chief constituent of the common good, or even identifiable with it. Aristotle called virtue so essential to the common good that without it 'the

[84] Maritain comments in his classic essay, 'The End of Machiavellianism:' 'This common good is at once material, intellectual and moral, and principally moral, as man himself is; it is a common good of human persons. Therefore, it is not only something useful, an ensemble of advantages and profits, it is essentially something good in itself – what the Ancients termed *bonum honestum.* Justice and civic friendship are its cement. Bad faith, perfidy, lying, cruelty, assassination, and all other procedures of this kind which may occasionally appear *useful* to the power of the ruling clique or to the prosperity of the state, are in themselves – in so far as they are political deeds, that is, deeds involving in some degree the common conduct – injurious to the common good and tend by themselves toward its corruption. Finally, because good life on earth is not the absolute ultimate end of man, and because the human person has a destiny superior to time, political common good involves an intrinsic though indirect reference to the absolutely ultimate end of the human members of society, which is eternal life, in such a way that the political community should temporally, and from below, help each human person in his human task of conquering his final freedom and fulfilling his destiny' (pub. in *The Range of Reason* [New York: Scribners, 1952], 134–64; the foregoing passage is taken from Evans and Ward, *The Social and Political Philosophy of Jacques Maritain*, pp. 301–2.)

political association becomes a mere alliance.'[85] Naturally virtue, *ex vi termini*, was seen as always operating within the limits of honest means. With the arrival of modernity and of the *realpolitik* that characterizes it, the role of virtue within the common good, and indeed the role of the common good itself, have been cast into the shade, or at least twisted out of their traditional configuration. That is as much an index of the decline of metaphysics as of the decline in morality.

However, vice has taken such a toll on national life that, certainly in the United States, a vigorous and intellectually based reaction has set in. Despite setbacks, the notion that virtue is vital to the common good has enjoyed a powerful resurgence. That, I expect, will make it so much the easier to carry out the twin tasks of this study. The first is to establish the proposition that the virtue of chastity is essential to the common good, to the survival of our society; the second is to show how closely, in the West, this survival has been bound up with the revealed norms of religion.

[85] *Politics*, III. 9 (1280^{b}7).

PART I

THE FOUNDATION

Chapter 1

ISRAEL, YAHWEH, AND COVENANTAL CHASTITY

The Decalogue is Western civilization's most basic political document. This proposition is our starting-point, for the lasting political import of the Decalogue rests upon a principle that gives this work direction: that moral law is the substance of civil law.[1] Indeed any civil law that clashes with moral law is less law than institutionalized violence.[2]

To say however that morality is basic to civil law does not fully explain how the Decalogue can be the West's political charter, or how in fact it has become such. It only supplies one part of the explanation: the sense in which men of traditional bent will agree that the Decalogue, as *symbol of morality in our culture,* has been the foundation of our culture's political structure, where that structure has been honest. The Decalogue, adopted in the West as the summary of morality, is the ground of the principles that prevailed in Western political thought until the new age ushered in by Machiavelli, principles that to this day public men must publicly profess or be banished from public life.

There is a further reason – we ought not to say *deeper* reason, for there is no deeper foundation to politics than morality – there is a further reason why the Decalogue is the West's political charter. This reason does not depend on the

[1] St Thomas notes that positive law 'has just that much force of law as it has justice' (I-II. 95. 2).

[2] 'Indeed, to the extent that [a human law] departs from reason it is called an iniquitous law; and thus it does not have the character of law, but rather of a kind of violence' (I-II. 93. 3, ad 2).

Decalogue's traditional role as a summary of morality but, quite the contrary, on *the strictly civil character of the Decalogue as promulgated at Sinai.*

Clearly two paradoxes are at work here. One is that the Decalogue, living symbol of the moral law, was uttered as civil law. The other is that the Decalogue lies at the foundation of Western political life in both capacities, that is, as symbol of the moral law, and as civil law.

We argue that it was *as civil law* that the Decalogue, and the Covenant of which it was a part, founded the nation of Israel, itself the foundational society of the West. Western civilization is of course a Christian structure. Like the Church, it is built on Israel. In so far as it remains Christian, Western civilization can be seen mystically as a new Israel, giving hospitality to the old Israel, herself now a mystical nation scattered among host nations.

That the Decalogue was given the Hebrews on Sinai as civil law and not as moral law is far from the received understanding. So far as the present writer is aware, no one else has claimed that it was *purely* civil law. We shall not only have to demonstrate the truth of this claim, but do it against odds. The demonstration must therefore be thorough and painstaking. It will be long, taking up most of the second part of this chapter, headed 'The Basic Provisions of the Covenant.'

The question of how the Decalogue, although cast as civil law, can stand as a symbol of the moral law is treated in the final section of this chapter, 'The Manifold Functions of the Decalogue.' We shall show how the teaching of St Thomas on the Decalogue helps reconcile its civil character with its subsequent, now traditional, moral role. We shall attempt to achieve that reconciliation, showing that the primeval civil character of the Decalogue is not incompatible with the purely moral character it has assumed in tradition, and hence not contrary to our contention that the Decalogue is basic to civil codes in its traditional capacity as the symbol of moral law.

There is a further reason why we shall devote substantial effort to demonstrating that the Decalogue was given in the form and substance of civil law. It is that the civil character of the Decalogue adds force to the central thesis of this work, namely that chastity is a constituent of the common good of civil society.

From the civil character of the laws adopted by the fugitive Hebrews at Sinai it follows that the demand of the Decalogue for chaste behavior was civil in character, hence held a manifest role in the common good of the body politic.

Civil as was the Decalogue in character, nothing could be more divine than the intervention by which Yahweh, entering into covenant with the children of Israel, bestowed on them those Ten Commandments. Nothing could be more religious than the moral decision of the Hebrews to accept the Covenant and shoulder the burden of the Decalogue. Nor could anything convey a more vital lesson to modern, secularized society than the religious character of that historic decision to make the Decalogue the rule of life, for the enduring success of that code stands among the foremost achievements of history.

At first its success was political and societal; then, after the scattering of the Jews, when the political force of the Decalogue was diminished and scarcely discernible, its mystical force came to the fore, supplying the strength both to hold the Jewish nation together and to resist assault from within and without.

Religion overarches this entire history. In this opening section of the chapter we study at some length how divine intervention, religious decision, and religious experience built the foundation and framework of our civilization. Although religion is not our direct concern in this work of political philosophy, the need to touch on it again and again, indeed to delve into it, offers evidence of the role it must play in national life.

The political role of religion makes the civil form and content of the Decalogue all the more paradoxical. But the Decalogue's civil character corroborates in two ways our thesis that chastity is integral to the common good: first, by illuminating the civil character of the Decalogue's prescriptions on chastity, and then by enabling us to hold, even in the present climate of civil secularism, that the Sinai Covenant with its law of chastity maintained Israel in being as a political society until she was scattered among the nations, thus demonstrating the political power of laws protecting family unity.[3] The primeval civil character of the Decalogue is a lemma of our larger demonstration.

Most of the historical and linguistic analysis in these opening chapters, and much of the examination of the Commandments, will seem to bear little if any relation to chastity unless two principles are kept firmly in mind: first, that to demonstrate the role of chastity in the common good it is helpful (though not intrinsically necessary) to demonstrate the civil character of the Decalogue, a novel and lengthy process; and second, that chastity works within legal justice, which orchestrates all the virtues of the individual members of a society toward the common good.[4] No single virtue can be construed as guaranteeing the common good of any society, whether civil, familial, or ecclesial.

Because the Decalogue has assumed a purely religious and moral character, its bearing on the common good of civil society is no longer manifest. That in large part is due to the modern habit of mind that, without reflection, separates

[3] It is more important *quoad nos* than *in se*, since men of the largely secularized West see immediately that a civil law contributes to the common good of civil society. There is no intrinsic reason why a religious law cannot contribute to the common good of civil society.

[4] St Thomas explains: 'It is clear that all who find themselves within a community are compared to the community as parts to the whole. But a part is what belongs to a whole. Hence the good of every part whatsoever can be ordered to the good of the whole. So the good of every virtue whatsoever, whether regulating a man within himself or towards other individual persons, can be referred to the common good, to which justice orders men. And in this way the acts of all the virtues can pertain to justice in so far as it orders a man to the common good. In this regard justice is called a general virtue. And because it is up to law to set in order for the common good . . . , so it is that such aforesaid general justice is called legal justice, because through it a man behaves in accordance with the law, which orders the acts of all virtues to the common good' (II-II. 58. 6).

Legal justice 'is the most splendid among all moral virtues to the extent that the common good outranks the individual good of a single person' (II-II. 58. 12).

the civil from the moral and religious. None the less the Decalogue's modern persona as a living symbol of the moral law bears directly and powerfully on the common good, and illustrates the role of chastity within it. Moreover, we hold that the Commandments, and most specifically those demanding chastity and the worship of the one God, kept Israel in being not only in the land of promise but even during two millennia of dispersal, when the civil nation found survival in its new role as a mystical nation.

We start our demonstrations now, with an attempt to show something more difficult of proof, namely that the Covenant and its Decalogue created the nation of Israel; a corollary will be that the law of chastity, as part of the Covenant, was instrumental in creating Israel. Whether we succeed in this attempt, the reader will judge, but if he judges that we fail he must not for that reason dismiss our distinct and more important claim that the Covenant has maintained Israel in being.

The demonstration runs into a serious difficulty at the outset. Laws, even the most equitable and most provident of laws, do not create a people.[5] St Thomas remarks that law

[5] There is some force to the claim that the Declaration of Independence brought the American nation into existence. Archibald MacLeish held the Americans to be 'the first self-constituted, self-declared, self-created People in the world' (*A Time to Act* [Boston: Houghton Mifflin Company, 1943], p. 115).

On the other hand the Declaration of Independence itself speaks of Americans as 'one People,' and as if they were already such. More than a decade before the Constitution of the United States was drafted and a dozen years before it became effective, the Declaration of Independence refers to 'our Constitution.' Throughout the previous century and more, Americans had conquered a wilderness. In 1774, two years before the Declaration of Independence, Patrick Henry could declare to the first Continental Congress: 'I am not a Virginian, but an American' (speech published in a pamphlet entitled 'I am not a Virginian but an American' by the Veterans of Foreign Wars of the United States [n.p., 1926], p. 4).

But if the Declaration of Independence brought the American nation into being, then a striking parallel with Israel emerges. For that momentous American asseveration opens with an appeal to 'the Laws of Nature and of Nature's God' as entitling Americans to 'separate and equal Station' among the 'Powers of the Earth.' America, then, was born not only declaring independence but declaring dependence. Like Israel at its birth it averred its dependence on the laws of God.

'ought not to be given unless to a people.'[6] True, laws can bring a state into existence; laws can even, on occasion, form a body politic to be governed by that state. But, with the sole exception for which we shall argue, laws have never created a nation. That exception is Israel, that body of laws the Decalogue.[7] How the Decalogue forged the racially diverse Hebrews of Sinai into a politically coherent whole (and, we here argue, a nation as well), and how Israelite polity made of Western civilization an extension of itself, so to speak, are two questions that demand examination if we are to understand the role of the Decalogue in Western politics.

History, with very little coaxing, shows how Western culture became so deeply impregnated with Judaic culture. It shows that one of the two confluents that merge to form the great river of Western culture is Christianity (the other being the classical culture of antiquity). Christianity, for the Christians, is the fulfillment of Judaism.

The answer, then, to the question of how the Decalogue came to the West is simple, though volumes might be written on it. The Decalogue was carried to the West within the Gospel, which left its impress on every dimension of Western society: political and cultural, national and familial, scientific, and of course religious.

To the question of how the Decalogue gave the Israelites political cohesion, we answer that it was through their Covenant with Yahweh.[8] The Exodus account of the birth of Israel is in fact the oldest extant history – as distinct from fable or myth – of the birth of a nation. Because Israel was founded on the Covenant, whose stipulations were the Decalogue, and because Israel is the most successful civil-societal venture in history, as measured by survival,

[6] I-II. 98. 6, ad 2.

[7] In speaking of Israel we mean the nation that arose on Sinai, occupied Palestine, and now finds itself scattered among the peoples of the world.

[8] In rendering the Hebrew *berit* as the Greek *diathēkē*, or testament, the translators of the Septuagint gave us the curiously inadequate term 'testament' to describe our Scriptures, Old and New. 'New Covenant' and 'Old Covenant' would be more precise titles.

the Decalogue with its law of chastity must take its place as the most successful foundational document in history.[9]

The worship of Yahweh, to which worship the Covenant bound Israel, and to which worship the Decalogue was the basic guide, became so closely bound up with the fabric of Israel's life that the distinction between the religious and the civil would hardly have occurred to an Israelite of the millennium preceding the birth of Christ.[10] Yahweh was the sovereign of Israel, its soul, and the rock of its foundation, and he became all these through the Covenant. Israel was conceived through him, and was and remains inconceivable without him.

Yahweh is a personal being unprecedented in recorded history.[11] He has remained utterly singular. The name

[9] We must, in dealing with the Decalogue and the Covenant by which the Israelites accepted it, constantly bear in mind the place that chastity is given in it. On the face of it, then, chastity played and continues to play a role in the survival of the oldest nation in history and in the life of the West, since both are built on the Decalogue.

We must also bear in mind throughout that chastity in the sense of external behavior, like justice, cannot be maintained consistently without that internal disposition, constituted by habit, which we call virtue proper. Yet the Decalogue as given to the Hebrews has the character of a civil document both in form and matter, and hence at its first appearance does not deal directly with internal dispositions. The Roman juridical maxim states the principle succinctly: *De internis non judicat praetor.* Cf. n. 40.

This principle in no way implies disregard for the role of inward acts and dispositions either in that outward behavior which is the concern of civil magistrates, or in the common good, which is the concern of law itself and indeed its sole purpose (see I-II. 90. 2 and 4). Nor does it imply that the ancients failed to see that the moral law, that is, the natural law, lies at the foundation of civil law (see I-II. 95. 2); note, for example, Cicero's celebrated paean to the natural law in the *Republic*, III. xxii.

Throughout these opening chapters we must keep in mind a twofold distinction: one distinguishing the civil from the religious, the other distinguishing the civil from the moral. Neither distinction, however, implies a separation: both the religious and the moral penetrate and inform the civil.

[10] Recall that the distinction between the religious and the civil is a mark of the Christian era.

[11] This is not to rule out the worship of the one God in prehistory. His worship among untouched primitive tribes of the modern world suggests it.

Anthropological studies of this phenomenon are found in Wilhelm Schmidt's twelve-volume work *Der Ursprung der Gottesidee* (Münster: Aschendorffsche Verlagsbuchhandlung 1912–55). Older works on this subject include

'Yahweh' has been taken as bearing immeasurable metaphysical significance.[12] The notion of the one God in a world of national or tribal or local gods was more than novel: it has to be seen as revolutionary.[13]

Yahweh is striking not only in his historical uniqueness, not only in his metaphysical dimensions (eventually explored by theologians), but also in his political relationship to the Jewish nation. Until Israel arose, nations had given their allegiance to some earthly authority, perhaps even (as in Egypt) conceived as a divinity. But in the early history of Israel, Yahweh alone was lord of the nation. For the chosen people, Yahweh, Lord of heaven and earth, was the political head, their king. So firmly embedded in their ethos was this

---

Andrew Lang's *The Making of Religion* (London: Longman Green, 1900) and E. H. Man's *The Aboriginal Inhabitants of the Andaman Islands* (London: Royal Anthropological Institute, 1885).

[12] On the metaphysical import of the terms of Yahweh's self-revelation ('And God said to Moses, "I Am who Am"' [Exod. 3:14]), see Etienne Gilson, 'Maimonide et la philosophie de l'Exode,' *Medieval Studies*, 13 (1951), pp. 223–5. Cf. John Bright, *A History of Israel*, 3rd edn. (Philadelphia: Westminster Press, 1981; subsequent references to this work are to this edition unless otherwise stated), pp. 157–8.

[13] Of course Yahweh was the God of Israel. Israel was his chosen people. Other gods were rivals, but only in the sense that the false worship of them rivalled the worship of Yahweh; in the patristic view, they were demons presenting themselves as gods.

Yet the revolutionary character of the worship of Yahweh would obtain even under the hypothesis – far from proven – that the Hebrews of the exodus originally regarded Yahweh as a merely national god.

Gottfried Quell observes: 'In the main . . . , OT statements concerning Yahweh as Lord already go far beyond the idea that He is just the lord of the land or people and more or less clearly presupppose the prophetic belief in Yahweh as Lord of all.' ('The Old Testament Name for God,' in Gerhard Kittel, ed., *Theological Dictionary of the New Testament*, tr. Geoffrey W. Bromiley, vol. III, p. 161 [Grand Rapids, Michigan: Eeardmans, 1965], p. 161).

Here 'prophetic' is used in the sense of 'proclaimed by the prophets.'

The author declares three pages later: 'The God to whom the canon bears witness is called "Lord" because He is there shown to be the sole exerciser of power over the universe and all mankind, as the creator of the world and disposer of life and death.'

Not only from a theological point of view but also from a philosophical and political point of view, this conception of God as creator and master of 'the universe and all mankind' is integral to the thesis of his lordship, first over Israel and then over all mankind. Cf. Bright, *A History of Israel*, pp. 159–60.

that serious problems arose in Israel when the people sought and obtained a human king.[14]

Before the institution of the kingship, the human leaders of the Israelites were of two kinds, distinct from kings and from one another: prophets and judges. Judges were less judicial magistrates than military captains who exercised the authority necessary to preserve order within and repel threats from without. The kingship resided entirely in Yahweh.

When the Israelites eventually took a king, Yahweh is quoted as saying: 'they have rejected me from ruling over them,'[15] and as telling the Israelites: 'But today you have rejected your God . . . and you have said, "No, you must set a king over us."'[16]

What was it that the Israelites were denying? To what, that is, were they responding 'No'? It was to Yahweh's claim, 'I brought Israel out of Egypt and delivered you from the power of the Egyptians and of all the kingdoms that were oppressing you.'[17]

Here it is crucial to note that in reproaching the Israelites for repudiating him as their king, Yahweh echoed the opening words of his Covenant on Sinai: 'I am Yahweh your God, who brought you out of the land of Egypt, out of the house of slavery.'[18] Manifestly, according to Israelite tradition as found in Exodus, it was through that Covenant that the Israelites took God as their ruler.

They knew full well that this made them unique. This is clear in their demand to Samuel, last of the great judges, to be given a king: 'give us a king to rule over us, *like the other nations*, to judge us;'[19] and, 'We want a king, so that we in

[14] The kingship arose out of military necessity. The tribal confederacy had proven incapable of withstanding Philistine aggression (see Bright, *A History of Israel*, pp. 185–7). What changes this early kingship worked in the political structure of Israel is not entirely clear, but for some problems arising from the early kingship of Israel, see I and II Samuel and the first eleven chapters of I Kings.

[15] I Sam. 10:19. Some translations explicitly refer to kingship.

[16] Ibid.

[17] I Sam. 10:18.

[18] Exod. 20:2.

[19] I Sam. 8:5; emphasis supplied.

our turn can be *like the other nations*: our king shall rule us and be our leader and fight our battles.'[20]

Israelite tradition, then, holds that the Covenant installed Yahweh in the very first position in the governance of Israel. A detailed examination of the polity put into effect through the Covenant is outside the scope of our study, but the political function of the Covenant is within it, as is therefore its civil form, which happens to be that of a suzerainty treaty.[21] Both the civil form and function of the Covenant argue that its laws, the Ten Commandments, were civil in character. That civil character of the Decalogue, if demonstrated, fortifies our contention that that law of the Covenant which demands the chastity of marital fidelity has an important role in the common good of civil society.

The question we are seeking to answer at this point is how the Covenant, in putting Yahweh on the throne of Israel, united the Israelites into a political body. Our later enquiry,

[20] I Sam. 8:20; emphasis supplied.

The eventual acceptance of a human monarchy obviously did not annul the role of Yahweh in the foundation of the Jewish nation. Nor, as Holy Writ testifies abundantly, did it remove from him the title of Lord.

[21] George Mendenhall explains the form of a suzerainty treaty – one between a great sovereign and his vassals – and its implications in two articles republished in *The Biblical Archeologist Reader*, vol. 3 (Garden City, NY: Doubleday, 1970): 'Ancient Oriental and Biblical Law,' and 'Covenant Forms in Israelite Tradition.'

For refinements of this thesis, and arguments against it, see Dennis McCarthy, SJ, *Old Testament Covenant* (Richmond, Va.: John Knox Press, 1972), especially pp. 11–19. Mendenhall replies tartly to such objections: 'In spite of some historical difficulties, or rather difficulties in the sources, the majority of which are shared by extrabiblical sources, the thesis that the Sinai covenant was actually such a suzerainty treaty has proven to be a useful working hypothesis that can well take precedence over other hypotheses until something better arrives. Many of the objections to it constitute defenses of existing presuppositions which are themselves merely accepted and not examined' (*The Tenth Generation* [Baltimore and London: Johns Hopkins University Press, 1973], p. 14).

Father McCarthy goes further: 'Despite many difficulties in detail, the evidence that Israel uses the treaty-form . . . to describe its special relationship with Yahweh, is irrefragable' (*Old Testament Covenant*, p. 14).

Bright offers a clear account of the elements of a classical suzerainty treaty, that of the Hittites, and shows how they are respected in the Covenant of Sinai. See *A History of Israel*, pp. 150–2.

crucial to our thesis, seeks to find how that unity was preserved by Yahweh's Law, especially by the law of marital fidelity.

But were not the Israelites united before the Covenant? Not as they were after it, certainly, and evidence that this transformation was radical is found not only in the historical texts but, I believe, in the utterly unique survival of Israel for three millennia and more.

George Mendenhall offers a description of their earlier condition:

> The clans who left Egypt under the leadership of Moses were of diverse background with perhaps a nucleus who traced their origin back to Jacob. Others are called in Numbers a 'mixed multitude.' In the desert, as also in Egypt, the entire group had no status in any social community large enough to ensure their survival.[22]

[22] 'Covenant Forms in Israelite Tradition,' p. 38. (The citation from Numbers is found at 11:4; instead of 'mixed multitude,' the Jerusalem Bible and the Common Bible give 'rabble,' and Ronald Knox 'a crowd of mixed breed.')

St Thomas takes another position. He says that law 'ought not to be given unless to a people.' In support of this principle he adduces the unexceptionable reason that law is 'a common precept.' The precepts given to Abraham were merely 'domestic, as it were.' Noting Aristotle's dictum that slaves are not a part of a people or state to which law is properly given, and saying that the descendants of Abraham had been freed from slavery and had multiplied to the extent 'that they were a people,' he concludes that law 'could suitably be given them' (I-II. 98. 6, ad 2).

To keep this argument in perspective it must be remembered that St Thomas is here responding to the objection that it would have been more fitting had the Law been given to Abraham. The essence of St Thomas's response is that a law cannot be given to those who do not constitute a people, either because of their civil condition – slavery – or because they are few in number.

It does not seem clear whether his position is irreconcilable with our contention that the Covenant, of which the Law was the central part, made the wandering Hebrews a people. Certainly at Sinai they were no longer slaves, but did their numbers render them a people in a sense different from ours yet fulfilling the condition St Thomas sets for receiving the Law? In the sense that a large crowd, a vast multitude, can be called people (though hardly *a* people)?

If by the Latin term *populus* St Thomas meant a nation, the case is different and we cannot claim that the position adopted in this chapter harmonizes with his. Numbers indeed are a necessary condition for constituting a nation,

John Bright, speaking of the Israelites once settled in Palestine, takes the same position: 'as the Bible itself makes clear, Israel . . . included elements of the most heterogeneous origin who could not possibly have descended from a single family tree.'[23]

In fact the account in Exodus is unequivocal, admitting of little argument and scarcely requiring any. When Pharaoh finally relented, not just permitting the 'sons of Israel' to leave Egypt, but actually ordering them out with no time to provision themselves, 'People of various sorts joined them in great numbers.'[24] The Hebrews of Sinai were not a national unit.

Because the ancient term 'Habiru' was applied widely in the Near East, and beyond, to diverse peoples who could not

---

and even scholars who will not accept the biblical statistics at face value will not deny that the followers of Moses were numerous. But numbers do not suffice to constitute a nation. A certain homogeneity of culture is also necessary, as we have seen. That, according to the argument brought by modern scholars such as Mendenhall and Bright, was lacking in the band that roved the Sinai peninsula under the leadership of Moses, and among those who joined themselves to Israel in Canaan. When Exodus says, 'People of various sorts joined them in great numbers' (12:38), that could well mean that that cultural homogeneity was lacking within this wandering band, and certainly means that the wanderers were not united by ties of blood. Yet there was a core descended from Abraham by way of Jacob, and this is vital to St Thomas's argument since it is that part of the premise of the objection which he admits.

[23] *A History of Israel*, p. 163. In the preceding chapter he argued that those who took part in the exodus 'were themselves a mixed group, by no means all descendants of Jacob. There was (Exod. 12:38; Num. 11:4) a 'mixed multitude,' a 'rabble' with them; by implication, its number was considerable. These were presumably likewise fugitive slaves, perhaps ʿApiru, perhaps even Egyptians (Lev. 24:10). Egyptian names mentioned above might argue for Egyptian blood in Israel. There was also Midianite blood. Moses' father-in-law was a Midianite, and his clan is said to have joined Israel on the march (Num. 10:29–32). Later we find their descendants among Israel (Judg. 1:16; 4:11) as well as among the Amalekites of the Negeb (I Sam. 15:16). Moreover, Caleb, who figures prominently in the tradition and whose clan later settled in the Hebron area (e.g., Josh. 14:13f.; Judg. 1:10–20), is, like Othniel, who occupied Debir (e.g. Josh. 15:16–19; Judg. 1:11–15), called a Kenizzite – i.e., of an Edomite clan (cf. Gen. 36:11, 15). Though not Judahites, Calebites came to be reckoned to that tribe, in whose midst they had settled (Josh. 15:13). This does not exhaust the evidence' (p. 134).

[24] Exod. 12:31 and 12:38.

possibly have had racial connections, but who are always outsiders with a penchant for troublemaking, we can assume that the Biblical term 'Hebrew' implies the same.[25] This is especially so since Exodus puts it into the mouths of Egyptians, and into the mouth of Moses only in speaking to Pharaoh of his own people.[26]

Not only is it certain that the enslaved Hebrews of the exodus were a mixed crew, it is also quite possible that whatever ethnic cohesion may have been found among them was weak. Mendenhall, as we have seen, entertains no doubt on this score, speaking only of a core tracing itself to Jacob. In that case, the perduring unity achieved by the Covenant – including the Decalogue and its laws on chastity – is not merely unique but has been achieved against compound odds.

Mendenhall should be cited *in extenso*:

> The covenant form is essential not only for understanding certain highly unusual features of the Old Testament faith, but also *for understanding the existence of the community itself* and the interrelatedness of the different aspects of early Israel's social culture. Here we reach a clear watershed, so to speak, in historical research. *Do the people create a religion, or does the*

[25] See Albrecht Alt, *Essays on Old Testament History and Religion* (Oxford: Basil Blackwell, 1966), p. 95.

[26] Exod. 12:31 and 12:38. No insuperable obstacle to this understanding of the word *Hebrew* is raised by the etymology given it in Genesis. Even if that etymology is correct – and it smacks of folk etymology since there is no apparent reason to single out Eber from the Hebrew genealogy for the distinction of giving his name to the entire nation – the Egyptian term *Habiru* was close enough in both sound and meaning to be applied to the protagonists of Genesis and Exodus.

The name 'Hebrew' itself indicates that the men under Moses' leadership were united chiefly in their aim of escaping state slavery. In only two places does the Genesis narrative apply the name 'Hebrew' to Abraham or his descendants: where Abram (as he was then called) was caught in the crossfire between invading kings and the king of Sodom, and in the story of Joseph. In both cases, the Hebrews are outsiders. 'Outsider' appears to be approximately the meaning of the term 'Habiru,' known in texts from Mesopotamia to Anatolia to Egypt, and spanning the period from Abraham through the Hebrew exodus. Cf. Bright, *A History of Israel*, p. 94, and Mendenhall, *The Tenth Generation*, ch. 5.

> *religion create a people?* Historically, when we are dealing with the formative period of Moses and the Judges, there can be no doubt that the latter is correct, for the historical, linguistic, and archeological evidence is too powerful to deny. Religion furnished the foundation for a unity far beyond anything that had existed before, and *the covenant appears to have been the only conceivable instrument through which the unity was brought about and expressed.*[27]

For Bright too there is no reason to doubt that at Sinai 'Israel received that law and covenant which made her a people.'[28]

Within 'that law and covenant which made her a people' was the law of chastity, which would preserve family unity and constitute a *conditio sine qua non* for Israel's unique survival as a people.

Now to understand the nature of this covenant, we must note that Yahweh became the suzerain, the political overlord, of the people newly constituted by it. In Moses, to be sure, the Israelites had a leader. Yet they tendered him no oath, contrary to custom in those times.[29] Rather they bound themselves to Yahweh. The manner of binding is crucial: the tie was through obedience to his commandments.

Because the structure of the Covenant was that of a suzerainty treaty (where one party is the overlord, as distinct from a parity treaty, where the parties are equals), Israel bound herself as vassal of the sovereign Lord, and *in exchange for benefits he had given her in the past* returned a promise of obedience.[30]

The absence of any promise on Yahweh's part is essential to the argument that the Sinai Covenant was a suzerainty treaty, hence to the claim that Yahweh took on the role of overlord while the newly constituted nation of Israel took on that of vassal. As in the Hittite suzerainty treaties of an

[27] *The Tenth Generation*, p. 16; emphasis added.

[28] *A History of Israel*, p. 125.

[29] Mendenhall, 'Covenant Forms in Israelite Tradition,' pp. 38–9.

[30] See Bright, *A History of Israel*, pp. 150–2. On pp. 152–5 he discusses, and in the end dismisses, objections to the antiquity of the covenant form in Israel.

earlier age, there was no promise on Yahweh's part of temporal benefits such as had been bestowed in the past – numerous offspring and possession of the land – but merely the *assurance* of God's predilection, and of holiness.[31]

These benefits flow straight from obedience to God's commands. As we shall see repeatedly, they flow not least from that unity of the family which is ensured by obedience to his command to abstain from unchaste acts. They flow naturally and necessarily from conformity to the natural and necessary law of chastity that God created concomitantly with human nature. Indeed, the law of chastity is as much a part of human nature as it is of the Decalogue. The benefits stem from obedience to that law independently of any explicit undertaking on God's part.

For this reason it was scarcely necessary for Yahweh to make promises, promises which would have broken the design of a suzerainty treaty. In other words, it is precisely because the Decalogue is in full accord with the nature of man that no promises were necessary, hence that the Covenant of Sinai could take the shape of a true vassal treaty. The Covenant,

[31] In the words that Yahweh commanded Moses to relay to the fugitive slaves of Sinai there is no promise, only an assurance: 'Say this to the House of Jacob, declare this to the sons of Israel: "You yourselves have seen what I did with the Egyptians, how I carried you on eagle's wings and brought you to myself. *From this you know* that now, if you obey my voice and hold fast to my covenant, you of all the nations shall be my very own, for all the earth is mine"' (Exod. 19:3–5; emphasis added).

Of course 'God's every word of grace is a promise,' in the happy phrase of *The Catholic Encyclopedia*, s.v. 'Promise, Divine, in Scripture.' As far as the Covenant at Sinai is concerned, it is a question of form. The blessing attached to the Fourth Commandment, for example, could have been couched as a promise, but if it had, the form of a suzerainty treaty would have been flawed. This meticulous respect for the formalities of the vassal treaty in such a minute detail strongly confirms the thesis that the Covenant is indeed such a treaty.

As for the holiness of which Israel stood assured in the Covenant, the Israelites of those days understood it as *set apart*, that is, consecrated to the divine. Through the Covenant the Hebrews were set apart from other nations, thereby becoming a nation, and becoming God's chosen nation, God's own people.

It is worth noting that without prompting from archaeology, it was only too easy to overlook the actual structure of the Covenant. Louis-Germain Lévy, for example, in a work full of rabbinical erudition, describes a covenant as 'a reciprocal promise' (*La Famille dans l'antiquité israélite* [Paris: Felix Alcan, 1905], p. 78).

then, becomes a symbol of the wholesomeness of God's laws, of their virtual identity with the natural law.

Thus the very concept of a pact with God is enriched, because linked with the natural law it is linked with the concept of creation. Whereas to the patriarchs, covenant consisted of unconditional promises on God's part, and faith on men's part, now covenant consists of the promulgation of God's law, and the life-giving acceptance of it.[32] To refuse this law – including, we must always remember, the law of chastity – means death for the nation. Hence the man who put it before the Hebrews at Sinai, and who now at the end of the wanderings and in sight of the promised land was renewing it at Moab, could say as a last testament:

> See, today I set before you life and prosperity, death and disaster. If you obey the commandments of Yahweh your God that I enjoin on you today, if you love Yahweh your God and follow his ways, if you keep his commandments, his laws, his customs, you will live and increase, and Yahweh your God will bless you in the land which you are entering to make your own.
>
> But if your heart strays, if you refuse to listen, if you let yourself be drawn into worshipping other gods and serving them, I tell you today, you will most certainly perish.[33]

There follows one of the peak dramatic moments in the Hebrew Scriptures, indeed in human history. Moses puts before them the momentous choice:

> I set before you life or death, blessing or curse. Choose life, then, so that you and your descendants may live, in the love of Yahweh your God, obeying his voice, clinging to him; for in this your life consists.[34]

[32] Bright writes: 'It will be noted that this conception of covenant is markedly different in emphasis from that found in the patriarchal narratives. There covenant consists in unconditional promises for the future, in which the recipient was obligated only to trust. Here, on the contrary, covenant is based in gracious actions already performed, and issues in binding obligation' (*A History of Israel*, p. 155).

[33] Deut. 30:15–18.

[34] Deut. 30:19–20.

It is in this last discourse that Moses declares that through the Covenant Yahweh 'makes a nation of you, and he himself becomes a God to you.'[35]

This immediate political effect of the Covenant – whose stipulations, it must constantly be borne in mind, comprised the Decalogue – is summed up with admirable succinctness by John Bright: 'With that, a new society was founded where none had been before, a society based not in blood, but in historical experience and moral decision.'[36]

But what kind of 'new society'? Clearly a religious society, a sacred society, bound together by common worship of Yahweh. Also a political society, bound together by submission to him as civil ruler.

The 'moral decision' cited by Bright is of course Israel's undertaking to obey the Decalogue, including of course its injunctions to respect the marriage bond. The 'historical experience' is Yahweh's contribution to the Covenant: past deliverance from 'the land of Egypt, out of the house of slavery.'[37]

Under the Covenant, the familial groups and tribes of Israel retained their distinctness and whatever civil authority they had exercised. What the Covenant did to them – perhaps *for them* is an apter expression – was to join them in a sacred federation, often (though more recently with reservations) likened to the amphictyony of classical Greek history.[38]

Mendenhall observes: 'In effect, then, each clan became a vassal of Yahweh by covenant – *and at the same time bound to each other by sacred truce.*'[39]

[35] Deut. 29:13.

[36] *A History of Israel,* 1st edn. (Philadelphia: Westminster Press, 1959), p. 134.

[37] Exod. 20:2; Deut. 5:6.

[38] For Bright's account of the analogy, and the reservations he had begun to entertain concerning it by the time he wrote the third edition of his *A History of Israel,* see pp. 162–3. He does however state earlier in that same edition: 'But that it was during this period [the wandering in the desert] that Israel received her distinctive faith and became a people cannot be doubted' (p. 124).

[39] 'Covenant Forms in Israelite Tradition,' p. 39; emphasis supplied. Mendenhall does not elaborate upon the concept of 'sacred truce,' but common sworn allegiance of the tribes to the sovereign Lord via a single covenant necessarily includes an overriding common purpose.

The sacred federation was of course altered when Yahweh gave way to human kings in Israel's monarchical structure, and the Covenant appeared to lose its full political force. Israel herself eventually was split, exiled, and finally scattered. Yet her unity has been marvelously maintained. The principle of her unity, and the principle preserving her unity, is the Law. Therefore in order to obtain an understanding of Israel's perdurance, we must study the Decalogue.

The Basic Provisions of the Covenant

We now examine each of the Ten Commandments in some detail to show that each of them has a civic function, and bears evidence of having been couched as a civil law. It was within this civil framework that marital chastity was conceived as essential to the cohesion and survival of the new nation, Israel. That that conception was justified is the thesis of this work, and in order to put firm ground under it we shall show that the Decalogue was indeed first promulgated in Israel as civil law, whatever role it may have come to play with the passage of centuries.

We have already attempted to show that the Decalogue, as part of a document civil both in form and in function, shares in that civil character. We now fortify that conclusion with an attempt to demonstrate that the Decalogue reveals itself as civil law by prohibiting outward misbehavior only, not evil intentions in themselves, and by forbidding only that more serious misbehavior which most men are capable of avoiding, and which is dangerous to society.[40]

[40] St Thomas observes: 'Human law is laid down for the multitude of men, the greater part of which consists of men not perfect in virtue. Therefore human law does not forbid all the vices from which the virtuous abstain, but only the more grievous ones, from which most of the multitude can abstain, and especially vices harmful to others, without whose prohibition human society could not be preserved: thus homicide, theft, and the like are forbidden by human law' (I-II. 96. 2).

As a rule, civil law punishes only external acts: cf. n. 9. St Thomas explains: 'man can make laws only about things he is able to judge; on the other hand his judgment does not extend to interior acts, which are hidden, but only to outward actions, which show themselves' (I-II. 91. 4).

The Ten Commandments fall under three heads if divided according to their immediate object.[41] Three deal with the family: the Fourth, Sixth, and Ninth. Four – the Fifth, Seventh, Eighth, and Tenth – deal with the safety of person and property. The first three concern God himself. Yahweh has pride of place.

The First Commandment, 'I am Yahweh your God. . . . You shall have no gods except me,'[42] is a powerfully compact summary not only of Yahwism but, if plumbed, of all acts of the religious man. It is the core of the other nine taken in their moral and religious sense, now traditional.

Because it is the only Commandment lacking a manifest intra-human or civic purpose, it poses at the outset of our examination of the Commandments themselves a challenge to our contention that the Covenant was a civil document that created a civil society.

To men of our times, the challenge may seem more formidable than it really is. The prevailing orthodoxy demands a separation, more or less strict, between the religious and the civil. But in dealing with any ancient society we must keep clearly in view the sharp distinction between the modern mindset and the ancient philosophy of state: the ancients, we have seen, could scarcely admit of a separation between the religious and the civil, or even conceive it. We know that the persecutions that struck Christian communities of the Roman Empire were prompted by the conviction that any religion refusing to be syncretized into the state religion of emperor-worship was a virus threatening the body politic.

Yet the objection might be posed that the First Commandment reaches into the heart of man, and that that is beyond the power of civil law except in so far as the law is a teacher.[43] The objection presupposes the traditional reading of the Decalogue as governing internal acts and dispositions, the mainspring of human action. But if we take the words of the

[41] See I-II. 100. 4. We subdivide the seven cited by St Augustine as relating to one's neighbor.

[42] Exod. 20:2; Deut. 5:6–7.

[43] Again see I-II. 91. 4, as in n. 40.

Commandment at face value, that is, literally and minimally, they refer to public honors.

A further objection might be that civil law ought not to command worship. Prescinding momentarily from the question of whether there should be any recognition by the state of God's role in civil society, we note a historical reason why the First Commandment cannot be out of place in that civil code which we claim the Decalogue to be: *in the society created by this particular code, Yahweh is the civil monarch.* He could scarcely be replaced publicly by another god.

Thus the *prima facie* political reason why the First Commandment holds a rightful place in this particular civil code is that the public recognition of God is the foundation of the agreement by which the Israelites accepted Yahweh as the ruler of Israel. Another reason, ahistorical and applicable to any state that ever existed or will exist, is that the state must acknowledge its dependence upon the Creator.[44]

The Second Commandment, 'You shall not utter the name of Yahweh your God to misuse it,'[45] exercised force within several mansions of society. Its most obvious prohibition is levelled against false oaths, but conjoined to the prohibition of carved idols, which in the Catholic system of division is subsumed under the First Commandment, this

[44] Abraham Lincoln's proclamation of 'a day for national prayer and humiliation' states the principle with the eloquence of one who in youth was a defender of atheism (see Christopher Hollis, *The American Heresy* [New York: Minton, Balch & Co., 1930], p. 148) but now is humbled by 'the awful calamity of civil war:'

> Whereas, the Senate of the United States, devoutly recognizing the supreme authority and just government of Almighty God in all the affairs of men and nations, has by a resolution requested the President to designate and set apart a day for national prayer and humiliation:
>
> And whereas, it is the duty of nations as well as of men to own their dependence upon the overruling power of God; to confess their sins and transgressions in humble sorrow, yet with assured hope that genuine repentance will lead to mercy and pardon . . .' (30 Mar. 1863; in *The Life and Writings of Abraham Lincoln*, ed. Philip van Doren Stern [New York: Modern Library, 1940], pp. 752–3).

[45] Exod. 20:7; cf. Deut. 5:11.

Second Commandment can be credited with uprooting sorcery from Western society, an achievement sometimes attributed solely to the Greek philosophy of nature.[46]

It was probably in business transactions, however, that the Second Commandment played its most salient civil role. A loosely structured society such as the incipient Israelite federation, lacking a detailed code of law or a body of legal precedent, necessarily bestowed on oaths a crucial role in civil affairs, especially commerce. The principle is: the looser the legal structure, the stronger the function of oaths. Such civil importance attached to oaths is compounded when literacy is rare. In contracts, the oath takes the place of the document, God the place of the magistrate.[47]

Although the notion of a people's pact with God has all but disappeared from modern society, the oath remains standing, not as a stately ruin or as a cherished bit of folklore but as a vigorous relic, carefully preserved, revered even where it is not understood, widely utilized by our civic institutions. It is a relic of Yahwism. Should belief in God vanish it will remain in use, though appealing to other mysteries. When a nation, like a man, stops believing in God, it starts believing in anything, if for no other reason than to give solemnity to guarantees.

Even on its face the Third Commandment reveals the civil dimension of the Decalogue, and of worship: 'Remember the sabbath day and keep it holy. For six days you shall labor and do all your work, but the seventh day is a sabbath for Yahweh your God. You shall do no work that day, neither you nor your son nor your daughter nor your servants, men

[46] For the prohibition of carved idols see Deut. 5:8.

[47] During the period we are dealing with, the Late Bronze Age, oaths played a key part in relations among nations. Especially where parties to a treaty could not appeal to a more powerful authority against violations, each party would hold a curse suspended over itself, to fall upon its head should it prove faithless. The Second Commandment threatens such a curse, another indication that the Decalogue was part of a treaty with Yahweh: 'for Yahweh will not leave unpunished the man who utters his name to misuse it' (Exod. 20:7). Cf. Deut. 5:11. Cf. Plato, *Laws*, III (684).

or women, nor your animals nor the stranger who lives with you.'[48]

This Commandment not only ensures the worship of Yahweh, Lord of Israel, but also ensures that no one, not even the slave, not even the stranger in Israel's midst, will be driven into the ground by work. All will be able to rest and refresh themselves. In this Commandment, the Decalogue reveals its benevolence toward those who have bound themselves to it, and toward those subject to them. That benevolence probably has an economic function, since the weekly day of rest restores efficiency. And it certainly gives the nation that minimum of leisure necessary to create and enjoy a culture.

Critical to an understanding of the Decalogue's role in the forging of Israel is the function of culture as a cohesive force within a nation. There is a commonality between culture and nationhood, to the point where they may seem identical. Because culture and worship also have much in common, it should be doubly obvious that this Commandment, like its predecessors, has powerful civic functions.

With the Fourth Commandment, 'Honor your father and your mother,'[49] we come to our special interest, the family. It is often remarked that this Commandment alone carries a blessing: 'so that you may have a long life in the land that Yahweh your God has given to you.'[50] What usually goes without remark, however, is that this blessing *upon a people* – the Decalogue, recall, is addressed to a people – gives assurance of *national* stability and prosperity provided the family's structure is respected.[51] Taken from a purely philosophical

[48] Exod. 20:8–10. Cf. Deut. 5:12–14, after which the Commandment proceeds: 'Remember that you were a servant in the land of Egypt, and that Yahweh your God brought you out from there with mighty hand and outstretched arm; because of this, Yahweh your God has commanded you to keep the Sabbath day.' Once again the Commandment is justified by *remembrance* of God's past favor.

[49] Exod. 20:12; cf. Deut. 5:16.

[50] Exod. 20:12. Again, cf. Deut. 5:16.

[51] Older translations made this clearer by using the 'thou' form, which is how Yahweh addressed Israel in the Covenant. This form of address was used in the Hittite suzerainty treaties on which the Covenant is modeled (see Bright, *A History of Israel*, p. 151).

point of view, the command can be seen as practical advice, and the blessing as a statement of natural consequences.[52] But whether viewed as philosophy or as revelation, *the link proposed between the family and the common good of the larger society is manifest.*

While the preservation and prosperity of Israel are express aims of the entire Decalogue,[53] the singularity of the blessing attached to this first of familial commands must be significant. Its significance surely lies in the link between the family and national survival. We hold that that link, forged by marriage, is kept strong by chastity. This is the thesis of our study, and we shall confront it more directly in dealing with the Sixth Commandment.

What gives the Fourth Commandment and its conjoined blessing special point is that in the Israelite economy the value of persons aged 60 or more was set at a fraction of that of working-age persons.[54] Moreover, among the Israelites aged parents lived in a single unit with their married sons and the children and dependants of those sons. Hence the elderly could easily be an economic burden. The likelihood that the aged parents would seem a burden could well have increased once the Israelites were settled in Palestine and each clan drew its livelihood from a fixed tract of inherited

[52] Recall that there is no real distinction between God's promise and God's blessing (see n. 31, above). The distinction however is not merely verbal. It appears to be the logical distinction found among the attributes of God, called 'minor' because deriving from the weakness of our intellect. In such a distinction, one of the concepts can be directly predicated of the other, and is implicitly contained in the other. See H. Renard, *The Philosophy of Being*, 2nd edn. (Milwaukee: Bruce Publishing Co., 1943), pp. 43–5.

The obverse of *blessing* and *promise* can be found in *curse* and *warning* respectively, and when these come from God the distinction between them is logical also. Thus Moses says: 'See, I set before you today a blessing and a curse: a blessing, if you obey the commandments of Yahweh our God that I enjoin on you today; a curse, if you disobey the commandments of Yahweh your God and leave the way I have marked out for you today' (Deut. 11:26–8).

[53] 'These then are the commandments, the laws and the customs which Yahweh your God has instructed me to teach you,' says Moses. 'Listen then, Israel, keep and observe what will make you prosper and give you great increase' (Deut. 6:1, 3).

[54] See Lev. 27:1–7.

land. From a narrow economic point of view the promise of prosperity might therefore seem inconsistent with the Commandment. But recent attempts of economists to forecast economic decline through dividing resources, presumed to be fixed, by a growing population have proven sterile. Such calculations leave out human ingenuity and all that comes under the heading of the human spirit.[55] But in the calculus of this Commandment they are, it seems clear, taken fully into account.

Like the other Commandments, the Fourth does not explicitly demand an interior act of filial piety and love. This will prove critical to the conclusion we shall arrive at from this examination of the Decalogue: that the Decalogue was framed as civil law. The premise of this conclusion is that civil law neither prescribes nor proscribes inner dispositions of the heart.[56]

We shall see that that principle, heavily qualified, applies to our special interest, the Sixth Commandment, outlawing adultery.

The Fifth Commandment safeguards life: 'You shall not kill.'[57] The civic role of the prohibition of killing might seem so evident as scarcely to merit comment. But it was not respected by the nations surrounding Israel: child sacrifice was practiced among them, and attempts were made to introduce it into Israel despite a warning from Yahweh that it was a profanation of his name.[58] We shall deal with this in the next chapter.

The law of Israel links child murder to unchastity by putting its prohibition in the middle of a list of sexual sins

[55] See the excellent treatment of such prophecies by Julian Simon in *The Ultimate Resource* (Princeton, NJ: Princeton University Press, 1981). The 'ultimate resource' of Simon's title is 'people – skilled, spirited, and hopeful people.' In the light of the history of Israel we might add: virtuous people.

[56] For St Thomas, 'justice deals in outward action' (II-II. 58. 10). He says: 'legal justice . . . is ordained to the common good . . . ; yet legal justice extends to the other virtues chiefly with respect to their outward actions' (II-II. 58. 9, ad 3). Cf. *Summa contra Gentiles*, III. 128, and n. 40 above.

[57] Exod. 20:13. Deut. 5:17 is identical.

[58] Lev. 18:21.

such as incest and sodomy. (We shall see this in the next chapter.) Indeed, a broader definition of chastity, covering the entire process of human reproduction, makes abortion a sin against that virtue.

Abortion is certainly a sin against the future, threatening the survival of the nation that promotes it or even tolerates it. Yahweh repeatedly warned Israel that if she fell into child murder and other unspeakable crimes such as bestiality and sodomy, and even the cursing of father or mother, she would suffer the fate of the nations she had supplanted in the promised land.[59] That Yahweh traces this fate to the weakening of the family is apparent from his inclusion of the cursing of father and mother among the crimes that bring about the dissipation of the nation. Here we see Yahweh the political philosopher, as it were, teaching that in adopting such practices a nation undermines its own foundation, the family. That reason alone would justify prohibiting them by civil law.

Where the Fifth Commandment aims at the protection of life, the Seventh, 'You shall not steal,'[60] has traditionally been understood as aiming at the protection of property. However, modern scholars such as Albrecht Alt and J. J. Stamm argue that it refers to the theft of persons, to kidnapping free Israelite men.[61]

It might first be noted that between the Seventh Commandment in its *prima facie* meaning and the Tenth Commandment, 'You shall not covet your neighbor's house,'[62] there is the same parallel as between the Sixth

[59] See Lev. 18; also 20:22–3.

[60] Exod. 20:15. Deut. 5:19 is identical.

[61] The claim is based on two passages in Exodus and Deuteronomy stipulating the death penalty for kidnaping. The first, Exod. 21:16, is part of a series of apodictic clauses providing penalties for violations of the Decalogue, while the second, Deut. 24:7, specifies that the kidnaped person is a free Israelite. Both passages make it clear that the kidnaping is for enslavement.

In itself, this argument appears to be merely probable, but it gains in strength by relieving the Decalogue of redundancy, as we shall see in examining the Ninth and Tenth Commandments.

For a more detailed account, see J. J. Stamm, *The Ten Commandments in Recent Research* (Naperville, Ill: Alec R. Allenson, Inc., 1967), p. 104.

[62] Exod. 20:17; cf. Deut. 5:21.

Commandment, outlawing adultery, and the Ninth Commandment, which outlaws the coveting of another's wife. Moreover the same problem naturally arises from both parallels: does the Decalogue prohibit a mere act of the will, and hence reveal itself to be a set of purely moral commands, not a set of civil laws? On the face of it, one Commandment prohibits the overt act, the other the intention.

Yet just as the Ninth Commandment, as we shall attempt to show, prohibits not just the intention of adultery but kidnapping another's wife or other dependents for enslavement, so the Tenth Commandment prohibits machinations against the property of another, and appropriating it. This understanding of the Tenth Commandment lends itself to a plainly civil interpretation of the Decalogue, especially when the Seventh Commandment is read as a prohibition not of the theft of property, but of kidnapping free Israelite men for the purpose of enslavement, and when the Ninth is read as a prohibition of kidnapping an Israelite woman or other dependant persons for the same purpose.

'The commandment in v. 17,' says Martin Noth, referring to the verse of the twentieth chapter of Exodus that prohibits the coveting of a neighbor's house, wife, slave of either sex, ox or ass, or any property whatsoever, 'is formulated with a verb which is rendered "covet". But it describes not merely the emotion of coveting but also includes the attempt to attach something to oneself illegally.'[63] He is referring to the verb *hamad.*

This understanding of the Ninth and Tenth Commandments relieves the Decalogue of redundancy, which would be egregiously wasteful in a code consisting of only ten laws. It also fits into our understanding of the Decalogue as a civil code prohibiting only outward acts. Because this is fundamental to our claim that the Decalogue was framed as civil law, we give corroborating arguments from modern scholars.

[63] *Exodus* (Philadelphia: Westminster Press, 1962), p. 166.

Gerhard von Rad observes:

> If in the last commandment the translation of the verb as 'covet' were correct, it would be the only case in which the decalogue deals not with an action, but with an inner impulse, hence with a sin of intention. But the corresponding Hebrew word (*hamad*) has two meanings, both to covet and to take. It includes outward malpractices, meaning seizing for oneself (Josh. 7:21; Micah 2:2, etc.).[64]

J. J. Stamm, who credits Albrecht Alt with demonstrating that this commandment necessarily entails outward action, says:

> the eighth commandment [the Seventh Commandment in the traditional Catholic, that is Origenistic and Augustinian, reckoning] originally had in view not theft in general, but kidnapping (the stealing of persons), and still more accurately, not the kidnapping of any person, but only that of the free Israelite man. The waylaying of dependent persons or those who were not free, such as women, children and slaves, is on the other hand covered by the tenth commandment.[65]

[64] *Deuteronomy*, tr. Dorothea Barton (Philadelphia: Westminister Press, 1966), p. 59.

[65] Stamm, *The Ten Commandments*, p. 104. Under the Tenth Commandment, which in the Augustinian system concerns the goods of another, Alt subsumes the clause dealing with the wife, the Ninth Commandment in the Augustinian system. This subsumption is in accordance with the numeration of Philo and the Greek Fathers, and of the modern Greek and Reformed Churches. That system makes the prohibition of images into a separate commandment, the Second, prohibits the vain use of the divine name in the Third, demands Sabbath observance in the Fourth, requires honor of parents in the Fifth, prohibits murder in the Sixth, adultery in the Seventh, theft (that is, the kidnapping of a free Israelite man, according to Alt's thesis, which we adopt) in the Eighth, false witness in the Ninth, and finally, in the 'Tenth,' all that in the classic understanding had come under the heading of 'coveting.'

Stamm continues with an assertion that supports our contention that the Covenant constitutes a civil charter: 'It is not until this understanding of the eighth [Seventh] commandment has been reached that the inner connection between the five last clauses [six last clauses, in the Catholic system] of the Decalogue is properly illuminated. Beginning with the sixth [Fifth] commandment, they are: his life, his marriage, his freedom, his reputation and his property' (ibid.).

Stamm proceeds to tackle the problem of how the term *covet* came, in the Commandments, to refer to an immanent act only: 'This development starts in the Old Testament itself, that is, in Deuteronomy, which . . . replaces the

With the Sixth Commandment we arrive at the focal point of this work, chastity as the protector of and indispensable condition for the health and survival of the nation and the natural societies of the family and the body politic.

The Sixth Commandment presents itself as a prohibition of adultery, and is just that. It does not attempt to prohibit all sins against chastity. That would be beyond the power of civil law. It does not even outlaw all those crimes of sexual abuse, such as fornication or sodomy, which fall within the ambit of civil law. Whether such crimes are to be outlawed by the penal code is a matter for prudential judgment. As a matter of fact, in our day not even adultery is included in all penal codes. Considering, however, that adultery is an often-fatal assault on marriage, a weakening of the civil order, the wisdom of exempting it from civil punishment cannot be taken for granted. Nor, for that matter, should we give the benefit of the doubt to the refusal to outlaw sexual perversion or even fornication. It runs against the wisdom of the ages.

The fact that sexual crimes besides adultery were not explicitly forbidden by the Sixth Commandment does not impugn our argument. As we shall see in the next chapter, they were prohibited expressly by the more particular laws of the Hebrews, and a civil penalty was attached.

The uniqueness of the Israelite concept of marriage and adultery should be pointed out. At a time when the dominant cultures of Assyria and Babylon saw a woman's adultery as

---

second *lo'-tahmod* 'you shall not covet' by a *lo' tit'awwe*, and thus interprets the preceding verb in a particular direction. The direction is toward mental coveting, for such a coveting is expressed by the verb *hit'-awwa*. As distinct from *hamad*, this means coveting only in the sense of an impulse of the will, without the measures which lead to the realization of the wish being included. This can be seen in passages where (in contrast with *hamad*) the day of Yahweh or the day of the disaster appear as the object of desire (Amos 5:18; Jer. 17:16), objects for whose attainment human means are in any case useless. This is also true of Isa. 26:9: "My soul yearns for thee in the night, my spirit within me earnestly seeks thee."'

Martin Noth, in *Exodus*, pp. 165–6, takes the same position as Stamm, Alt, and von Rad. For reservations concerning the certainty of this view, see G. H. Davies, *Exodus* (London: SCM Press, 1967), p. 167. However Davies does not oppose it.

an assault on her husband's property rights, the Israelites saw it as an evil to be banished from Israel, an offense against the common good.[66] That a man take back a corrupt woman into his house after rejecting her is 'an abomination before the Lord,' bringing 'guilt upon the land which the Lord, your God, is giving you.'[67]

It can scarcely be emphasized too strongly that in Israel, all sins against society (such as adultery) were sins against God, that is, violations of Israel's Covenant with him, against his sovereignty over Israel. Hence, to Israelites there were clear linkages among offenses against the Creator, offenses against nature, and offenses against the common good.

In whatever way the understanding of adultery may have changed among the Hebrews in different epochs, because of changing notions of marriage,[68] it remained constant as a

[66] For a comparison between the view of adultery in Israel and in other countries of the ancient Middle East and in ancient Israel, see Isaac Mendelsohn, 'The Family in the Ancient Near East,' *Biblical Archeologist*, 11:2 (May 1948), 28–40; repr. in *The Biblical Archeologist Reader*, vol. 3 (Garden City, NY: Anchor Books, 1970); in the reprint, the material referred to is found on p. 154.

John L. McKenzie holds that the Hebrews adhered to 'the primitive conception of the wife as the property of the husband' (*Dictionary of the Bible* [Milwaukee: Bruce, 1965], p. 14). He does not corroborate this assertion.

For the Israelite view of adultery as an offense against the nation, see Lev. 20:22 and *passim*.

[67] Deut. 24:4.

[68] The concept of adultery depended on whether polygyny happened to be tolerated. Where polygyny is permitted, says the *Dictionnaire de la Bible*, 'the wife owes her husband complete fidelity, for she belongs to him alone, and if she has guilty relations with another man, she commits adultery; but the fidelity the husband owes his wife is not so strict: the husband does not give himself to her entirely; he reserves the right to take other wives; consequently if he has guilty relations with a woman other than his wife, he undoubtedly commits a crime, because he lacks conjugal fidelity in a certain way; but he does not commit adultery properly so-called, because he does not violate his wife's strict and absolute right' (*Dictionnaire de la Bible* [Paris: Letouzey et Ané, 1895], s.v. 'Adultère').

St Thomas recognizes the distinction, but has strong reservations about the justice of polygyny. In the same chapter of the *Summa contra Gentiles* in which he argues that the need to know who is father and mother to a child demands that a woman have no more than one husband (III. 124), he advances several reasons to show that a husband ought not to have more than one wife. One is that the presence of more than one wife creates dissension; another, that the

metaphor for idolatry.[69] Fornication too was such a metaphor.[70] And throughout the Old Testament period, both

natural concern of the father for his offspring demands it. Then there is the oft-quoted argument: 'Friendship consists in a certain equality. Therefore if a woman is not allowed to have several husbands, because this runs against certitude as to offspring, were a man allowed to have several wives the wife's friendship for the husband would not be that of a free person but like that of a servant. And this is shown by experience, for among men who have several wives, the wives are held almost as servants.'

This should be read in the light of St Thomas's remark in the previous chapter: 'The greatest friendship is seen to stand between husband and wife.' (The Latin can be, and usually is, rendered: 'There seems to be the greatest friendship between husband and wife.')

Polygyny is perhaps the most important example of change in moral customs and moral notions among the Hebrews. Although in the Genesis account of the earliest times there are indications that polygyny was not viewed as normal, among the patriarchs it had wide currency. Nor was the practice always designed to ensure progeny.

Polygyny was conceded by the Mosaic Law, which however tended to limit the custom to bigamy. Yet we can see from later sacred writers that polygyny was considered a makeshift arrangement, for they write as if one wife were present in the home. See, for example, Prov. 5:18–19. Moreover, the oft-repeated alphabetic poem on the perfect wife in ch. 31 of Proverbs hardly bespeaks a polygamous household. This woman is too fully in command. So too the perfect wife of Ecclus. 26:1–4. The same chapter of Ecclesiasticus offers an implicit criticism of polygamy: 'a woman jealous of a woman means heartbreak and sorrow' (v. 6).

By the time of Christ the sacred writers are silent on the question. This is taken as a sign that polygyny had become rare. Yet in the first century of the Christian era, Josephus writes for his Roman and Greek audience that having several wives 'is for us a national custom' (*Jewish Wars*, XVII. I. 2). Cf. *Dictionnaire de la Bible*, s.v. 'Polygamie.'

In the Christian dispensation the perfect equality of male and female – indeed the disappearance of that distinction in Jesus Christ (see Gal. 3:28) – and the deference that husband and wife should show each other (see Eph. 5:21) abolished asymmetrical morality in the command against adultery. Rather Jesus Christ appears to have turned the asymmetry in the other direction, putting a heavier burden on the man than on the woman: 'You have learnt how it was said: You must not commit adultery. But I say this to you: if *a man* looks at a woman lustfully, he has already committed adultery with her in his heart' (Matt. 5:27–8; emphasis supplied). (Not, of course, that this prohibition must be, or ever has been, understood as applying only to males.)

As for polygamy, Jesus could scarcely have been more forceful in his condemnation of even the serial variety (see Matt. 5:32 and Mark 10:2–12).

[69] The book of Hosea offers probably the outstanding example, as in 2:5–10, where the 'lovers' of the adulterous wife are the Canaanite gods of fertility. We shall examine this in the next chapter.

[70] See, for example, the startling claim in Wisd. 14:12 that the invention of idols was the very origin of fornication, and the assertion in Mic. 1:7, echoing

sexual misbehavior and idolatry were seen as threats to national survival. We shall see in the next chapter how they were linked.

In contrast with the concision and apparent unambiguity of the Sixth Commandment, 'You shall not commit adultery,'[71] a curious aura of reduplication surrounds the Ninth Commandment, 'You shall not covet your neighbor's wife.'[72] We have treated this question already, but shall point out here that the greatest commentator on the Law appears to have held that the Ninth Commandment is not merely a prohibition of lustful desire. For if Jesus Christ held the Ninth Commandment to be a prohibition of lustful desire alone, why did he feel obliged to explain the meaning of the Sixth Commandment by saying it prohibited not only the physical act but lust in the heart also? 'You have learnt how it was said: You must not commit adultery. But I say this to you: if a man looks at a woman lustfully, he has already committed adultery with her in his heart.'[73] And if it is objected that Jesus repeated many things clearly contained in the Old Testament, then attention must be drawn to the adversative: '*But* I say. . . .'

Linguistic analysis, as we have seen, makes a strong case that the Ninth Commandment prohibits not the deliberate entertainment of lustful desire but an active attempt to put another man's wife within one's own power.[74] This understanding is of course in full accord with the claim made in this chapter that the Decalogue is civil law, since civil law deals primarily in overt acts, and only secondarily in inner dispositions. Adultery can be and traditionally has been a civil offense, but no man can be put on trial for lusting in his heart.

Hosea, that idols were built with the earnings of prostitutes. The reason will emerge in the following chapter.

[71] Exod. 20:14. Deut. 5:18 is identical.

[72] Exod. 20:17. Deut. 5:21 is ordinarily given an identical form in translation, but we shall have to compare the Hebrew of the two versions.

[73] Matt. 5:28.

[74] Treatment of this is found in Stamm, *The Ten Commandments*, pp. 101–7. We summarize the argument in dealing with the Tenth Commandment.

The reading of the Commandments that is provided by linguistic analysis enables the entire Decalogue to fulfill the requirements of civil law, and to have a direct and manifest civil effect. It supports our central thesis that chastity is vital to the common good. Yet evidence of quite a different kind, not requiring linguistic analysis but simple attention to the plain sense of the words, also supports the claim that the Decalogue was originally a civil code. It comes from the only Commandment we have not yet examined, the Eighth: 'You shall not bear false witness against your neighbor.'[75]

Taken literally, the Eighth Commandment, despite the traditional understanding, forbids only false witness, not lying.[76] On the one hand the Commandment does not forbid an immoral practice that no civil authority could punish, since it is too widespread, admits of minor degrees of malice, and is difficult to prove in most instances; on the other it does forbid an immoral practice that is at once more liable to proof, relatively rare, and highly important for public order.

[75] Exod. 20:16; Deut. 5:20.

[76] J. J. Stamm says: 'Ludwig Koehler has drawn attention to the surprising fact that the Decalogue does not contain any prohibition of lying. As is known, it has often been thought possible to fill up this omission in the ninth commandment. This is the case in Luther's Shorter Catechism, where the commandment is brought into connection with lying, calumny and slander. This certainly does not correspond to the original meaning, since this, being bound to a particular situation in Israelite life, is much less extensive and universal' (*The Ten Commandments*, p. 108).

Stamm, attributing 'this omission' to 'a particular situation in Israelite life,' continues: 'The matter involved in the ninth commandment [the Eighth Commandment by the traditional Catholic reckoning] is . . . reputation, and this was much more directly preserved by the concrete prohibition of false witness than by a general proscription of the lie. In addition to this, the court of law was the situation in which truth and falsehood were of particular importance' (p. 109).

Here Stamm overlooks the effect that the civil character of the Decalogue necessarily has on its component laws. As we argue, that character makes it impossible for the Decalogue to prohibit lying as such.

We shall also see with what caution and acumen St Thomas handles the question of the omission from the Decalogue of a prohibition of lying as such. His treatment is all the more impressive given the absence of archaeological evidence in his day that the Decalogue was framed as civil law.

The vital civic importance of honest testimony is seen in the legal provision that a person could be put to death on evidence brought by only two witnesses.[77] Jesus Christ himself recalled: 'in your Law it is written that the testimony of two witnesses is valid.'[78] Some authors hold that under Israelite law the accused bore the burden of proving his innocence.[79]

The limited scope of the Eighth Commandment offers very strong support to our claim that the Decalogue was framed as civil law. If it were purely moral law, it would certainly prohibit the destructive sin of lying as such, a sin that not only destroys the trust necessary if men are to live peacefully and prosperously in any society, from the family to the nation to the family of nations, but also destroys clarity of mind and a sense of realism, the very ability to distinguish the factual from the fictional. Even the Egyptian *Book of the Dead* prohibits lying.[80] Why, to repeat a pivotal question, is ordinary lying not among the acts prohibited by the Ten Commandments? Our answer is: the limitations of civil law prohibit that prohibition.

The Eighth Commandment, in the present writer's view, offers the clearest indication that the Decalogue was designed as civil law in Israel. The Commandment, despite a tradition not of centuries but of millennia, is not on the face of it a prohibition of lying in general.[81] It is highly particularized, focusing in language and, we must conclude, in intent upon the testimony of witnesses at judicial hearings.

We now are in a position to review the civil functions of each Commandment of the Decalogue. We find that:

[77] Deut. 17:6.

[78] John 8:17.

[79] For example, Stamm, *The Ten Commandments*, p. 111, quoting von Rad, *Deuteronomy*, p. 59: 'The burden of proof in legal proceedings was placed to a large extent on the accused. He was obliged to prove his innocence in the face of the accusation.'

[80] Ch. 125.

[81] Of course Christian tradition conceives the Eighth Commandment as carrying a prohibition of ordinary lying. But St Thomas states plainly: 'false witness is a certain specification of lying' (II-II. 118. 8, ad 3).

- The First Commandment puts Yahweh at the head of the nation of Israel, as her ruler. Further, it enjoins the duty of every civic body, but particularly the historically unique nation of Israel, to orient all its activities toward God and his service.
- The Second safeguards the oath and all that depends on it to this day. At the same time it declares the dependence of society both on personal integrity and on the sacred.
- The Third safeguards the health of the worker, and through it enhances productivity.
- The Fourth safeguards the elderly and unproductive, and solidifies the familial structure.
- The Fifth safeguards life and personal safety.[82]
- The Sixth safeguards marriage, and through it the family and all that the family bestows on the nation.
- The Seventh safeguards not property but personal freedom.
- The Eighth safeguards the judicial mechanism ensuring public order, and safeguards all material and moral goods – indeed life itself – that may be at risk in judicial hearings.[83]
- The Ninth, like the Seventh, safeguards personal freedom, but for free Israelite women.
- The Tenth safeguards the household, the Israelite's property in servile persons, chattel, and movable and real property.

[82] Stamm observes that the word used in the Decalogue for killing, *rasah*, is employed in Holy Writ only to mean either killing a personal enemy, or unintentional killing. Thus it is not, in Stamm's view, confined to murder, but becomes what he calls 'killing inimical to the community' (*The Ten Commandments*, p. 99).

He continues: 'If one wanted to find a concise expression for the rendering of the commandment, then "You shall not commit manslaughter" could be considered. But that is not really adequate. It will therefore be better to keep to the accustomed "You shall not kill" which now has to be clarified along the lines that the life of the Israelite was protected in this way from illegal impermissible violence' (ibid.).

Under this reading the Fifth Commandment too fits our concept of the Decalogue as civil law. Stamm concludes: 'The commandment thus takes its place in a community in which capital punishment exists and war is permitted or even sometimes commanded' (ibid.).

Alt, but not every subsequent student of the question, has accepted this reading.

[83] It might be noted that Stamm puts a different construction on this Commandment; he thinks it protects reputation. See *The Ten Commandments*, p. 104.

For two chief reasons this reading of the Ten Commandments reinforces our original claim, based on the treaty form of the Covenant, that the Decalogue is a civil charter:

- The first is that under this reading the Decalogue prohibits overt acts only, not intentions.[84] That is, it prohibits coveting not in the sense of desiring but in the extended sense of conspiring, or of taking steps as part of a plot, or of actually attempting. Mere intentions, it can scarcely be repeated too often, are beyond the power of civil law to proscribe or prescribe.
- The second reason is that under this reading the Decalogue forbids only those more grievous vices which most people are capable of avoiding, and which are so injurious to society that it cannot be preserved if they abound.[85] A corollary is that adultery, prohibited by the Sixth Commandment, is such a vice, a vice destructive of society.

That corollary will certainly surprise those who deem sexual activity a purely private affair, who deny that sexual behavior has any bearing on the common good, and who consequently would deny to civil authority any power to enforce upright conduct in this field. For this most perduring and most influential of all civil codes, this charter of Western civilization, aims at preserving not only the family but also, through the family, the nation itself by outlawing, as a crime, the sin of adultery.

Still, the civil character of the Decalogue constitutes a mighty paradox, carrying problems of its own. We attempt to deal with them here.

The Manifold Functions of the Decalogue

Because the Decalogue was the core of God's Covenant with Israel, its task was to bind the Israelites to God, and through that to bind them to one another. Individually and as a people, the Israelites were held to God by a tie properly

[84] I-II. 91. 4.
[85] I-II. 96. 2.

known as religious. The very word *religion* is probably derived from the notion of binding.[86]

That bond held in two dimensions, securing both religious unity and politico-national unity.[87] The history of Yahweh-governed Israel demonstrates this truth very clearly from beginning to end, that is from Moses to Samuel, but even during the monarchical period and beyond. Moreover, as we have seen, the Covenant was in the form of a political treaty, specifically a suzerainty treaty between a subject people and its sovereign lord.

Could the Covenant have maintained the form of a political treaty while its stipulations remained exclusively religious in the sense that they only bound the people to God and stated the moral obligations, private and public, of the religious man? This is highly doubtful. In any event, the history of Yahweh-governed Israel shows that the Covenant did not work that way.

The implication of this answer most relevant to our study, namely that the chastity demanded by the Covenant is also a civil demand necessary for the common good of the larger society, will also be examined.

The Covenant is framed neither to state nor to imply a purely internal moral obligation. We have seen that even the First Commandment, despite its manifestly sacred content, despite its overt function of binding the Israelites to God, and despite whatever merely internal moral effect it may have exerted upon the people, was political. Its political character can be seen most clearly in the light of the political character of the agreement to which it was integral, indeed central. It made of God the Lord of Israel, the ruler of this newly founded people.[88]

[86] The Latin verb is *religo*. Cicero gives a different etymology in *De Natura Deorum*, II. xxviii. 72.

[87] In that epoch of Israel's history, the nation and the body politic were identical.

[88] This argument may seem anachronistic in view of the widely held claim that the ancient Hebrews did not distinguish between internal moral law and external civil law, for if the Hebrews did not draw such a distinction, then they could not have understood the distinctly civil character of the Covenant.

A common characteristic of the other Commandments under this civil understanding of them is that they deal strictly with matters that are capable of governance by civil law. Despite appearances, despite tradition, despite the absolutely decisive role they have since played in moral life throughout Western civilization, they do not on the best reading touch immediately on matters that civil law cannot control.[89]

It is ironic that in concluding our demonstration of this we use principles stated with admirable clarity and concision by St Thomas: ironic because far from considering the divinely bestowed Covenant to be civil law, the Angelic Doctor actually put all civil law under the heading of 'human law.'

Naturally we expect civil law to be written by human beings, but St Thomas seems to suggest a further reason for calling civil law human law. It is that civil law must be framed to accommodate the weaknesses of human beings. In a key passage, which we have seen before, he says:

> Human law is laid down for the multitude of men, most of whom are not perfect in virtue. Wherefore human laws do not forbid all vices, from which the virtuous abstain, but only the more grievous vices, which the majority can avoid, chiefly those which hurt others and without whose prohibition human society could not be maintained: thus human law prohibits murder, theft, and suchlike.[90]

However, they could have been ignorant of the distinction and yet have understood what the Covenant demanded of them well enough to consent to it.

Still, it is improbable that any Hebrew could have framed its stipulations – the Commandments – in meticulously civil form without understanding how the civil differs from the moral. The alternative is a literal understanding of the scriptural account of how the Commandments were delivered: 'Then God spoke all these words' (Exod. 20:1).

[89] See I-II. 93. 3, ad 3. St Thomas takes it for granted that civil law is 'human law;' he does not raise the question whether law given by God, hence divine, can be civil. However he divided the Old Law into the moral, the ceremonial, and the judicial; this last was close to our civil law. See I-II. 99. 4.

[90] I-II. 96. 2. St Thomas's classification of civil law under the heading of human law indicates that he does not conceive the Decalogue – which is divine law – as civil law.

The 'suchlike' of St Thomas would include false testimony, as does the Decalogue, but not lying. It would – or could, and probably should – include adultery, as does the Decalogue, but not every kind of unchastity. It could include all the acts expressly prohibited by the Decalogue, but could not include all the acts which tradition – viewing the Decalogue as the summarizing symbol of all moral law, not as civil law – has seen as prohibited by the Decalogue. The conclusion looms large: the Decalogue, as given to Israel at Sinai, was civil law.

Was the Decalogue given to the Israelites as civil law *only*? From the purely historical viewpoint, yes; from the providential viewpoint, no. That highly qualified and I fear mysterious answer becomes clearer when we consider the function of the Decalogue by the time of Jesus Christ, and its history in Israel after the scattering of that nation.[91] Within the Jewish diaspora the civil role of the Decalogue was of necessity much diminished, but among Jews and Christians alike it has retained binding power as the revealed symbol of all moral law, and it remains to this day one of the most powerful forces of history.

This is a paradox. As we shall see, St Thomas supplies the key to it, though he stops short of turning that key and opening the paradox to full view. Still, he applies his principle in a way utterly alien to the rationalist approach that has infiltrated some currents of Catholic thought – even Thomistic thought – since Descartes.[92] Now that thinkers of our time have investigated the manifold functions of symbol, they are better able than those of the nineteenth century to find their way out of the desert of solipsistic logic that

[91] There had been several scatterings of the Jewish people before the third and final revolt of the Jews. The emperor Hadrian, after putting down that revolt, erected a temple to Jupiter on the site of the temple of Yahweh, and banned circumcision. See Meyer Reinhold, *Diaspora* (Sarasota, Fla.: Samuel Stevens & Co., 1983), especially the preface and ch. 25.

[92] Etienne Gilson held that the Cartesian-Kantian critique, which is the core of modern rationalism and scepticism, had its effect even on thinkers who claimed St Thomas as their master. See *Thomist Realism and the Critique of Knowledge*, tr. Mark A. Wauck (San Francisco: Ignatius, 1986).

Descartes created when he destroyed the validity of sense perception and with it the utility of symbol. They are better able to understand in what manner the Ten Commandments have altered their significance over the ages.

The historical paradox of the Decalogue as law couched in terms governing public life only, yet eventually and universally accepted as a summary of mankind's entire moral obligation, internal as well as external, in both public and private life, seems bound to have gone unnoticed by the closest students, the deepest minds, for many centuries. This was for lack of the archaeological information that has drawn it to our attention. But having the paradox before our eyes and understanding it at work are far from the same thing.

How can the Decalogue be a summary of the moral law if it omits even one basic provision of that law, such as the prohibition of *all* kinds of unchastity, or the prohibition of *all* kinds of lying? Or, to revert to our discussion about the limitations of civil law, how can a set of ordinances framed as civil law offer complete guidance for moral behavior?[93]

[93] Jesus of course makes it clear that he regards the Commandments as the rule of the moral life. His reply to the young man who asked him how he could gain eternal life is unequivocal: he must keep the Commandments. See Matt. 19:16–19; Mark 10:17–20; Luke 18:18–20.

John L. McKenzie, observing that Jesus 'cited some of the ten, not in the usual order nor completely,' makes the unexplained claim: 'These passages suggest that even in gospel times the Decalogue had not acquired the set form and importance as a charter of fundamental morality it acquired in later Christianity' (*Dictionary of the Bible*, pp. 187–8). Yet he notes that many older biblical critics, denying that the Decalogue went back to Mosaic times, 'regarded it as a summary of the ethical teaching of the prophets of the 8th–7th centuries' (p. 187). Under either hypothesis the Decalogue became at some point a summary of basic morality.

Walter Harrelson represents the traditional view of the Ten Commandments: 'They simply let the community, and each individual within the community, know what kinds of human conduct are in principle ruled out, not allowable, not to be entertained at all' (*The Ten Commandments and Human Rights* [Philadelphia: Fortress Press, 1980], p. 13).

Pope John Paul II calls the Ten Commandments 'a summing up of all that the Creator engraved in men's hearts before he established it in the Decalogue.' (Address of 12 May 1985 to Catholic social organizations in Utrecht, the Netherlands. Published in *Origins*, 15, 1 [May 1985], p. 16; tr. from the Dutch by NC News Service.)

Obviously St Thomas does not set out to answer that question, which did not call for attention until the discovery by modern archaeology that the form of the Covenant was meticulously and exclusively civil, and along with that discovery, the discovery by modern linguistics of nuances of meaning that allow all the laws of the Decalogue to be construed in a civil sense. Yet the treatment that St Thomas gives the Decalogue, not least his careful terminology, indicates full awareness on his part that an attempt to *deduce* the entire moral law from the Decalogue would meet with failure.

St Thomas's refinement divides moral precepts according to the degrees of clarity with which they present themselves to natural reason. Some are so perspicuous that they 'need no promulgation.'[94] These St Thomas calls 'first general principles.'[95] He cites the avoidance of evil[96] and love of God and neighbor.[97] Such are contained in the Decalogue 'as principles in their proximate conclusions.'[98] In other words, the Decalogue's precepts are just one step away from these principles, which can also be considered 'as it were the ends of the Commandments.'[99]

The Commandments themselves, St Thomas continues, belong to those moral precepts which are 'more determinate.'[100] The point (*ratio*, in St Thomas's term) of these 'more determinate' precepts can be easily grasped by even an uneducated man.[101] None the less, 'they need to be stated because human judgment, in a few instances, happens to be led astray concerning them.'[102]

A third group of moral precepts consists of those 'whose point is not so evident to just anybody, but only to the wise;

[94] I-II. 100. 11.
[95] I-II. 100. 3.
[96] Ibid.
[97] I-II, 100. 3, ad 1, and I-II. 100. 11.
[98] I-II. 100. 3.
[99] I-II. 100. 11; more literally, 'of the precepts.'
[100] Ibid.
[101] Ibid.
[102] Ibid.

these are moral precepts superadded to the Decalogue, and given by God through Moses and Aaron.'[103]

It is not to our purposes to confirm that every explicit precept of the Decalogue is in fact more evident than every precept attached to it. What is critical here is St Thomas's term *superadded.* The further moral precepts that are traditionally linked to each Commandment are not, if we are to take St Thomas at his word, *deduced* from that Commandment. Rather they are *added,* indeed *superadded,* to it.[104]

To the first Commandment's prohibition of false worship, St Thomas, citing Deut. 18:10–11, adds the prohibition of child sacrifice, witchery, and necromancy.[105] This linkage is entirely reasonable since all these crimes constitute false worship. To the Second Commandment's prohibition of

[103] Ibid. Modern scholars consider these additions to be for the most part rabbinical.

[104] Ibid. St Thomas continues: 'But because those things which are manifest are principles of knowing those which are not manifest, the other moral precepts superadded [*superaddita* in the Latin] to the Decalogue are led back to the precepts of the Decalogue by way of a certain addition to them.'

To *superadd* is to add from without, and the same meaning is conveyed by the other terms St Thomas uses when speaking of adjuncts to the Ten Commandments: *per modum cujusdam additionis, additur, adjungitur* (the last meaning 'is attached'). This last term, like *superadd,* brings out clearly that the addition is from without; it is not addition from within, such as that which is found in distinguishing the transcendentals from being, and among themselves, or such as the addition from within that adds to our explicit knowledge from our implicit knowledge through syllogistic reasoning.

The Latin *reducuntur,* rendered above as 'are led back,' can also be translated 'are reduced to.' But in that case, the phrase must not be taken to mean that the further precepts can be boiled down, so to speak, to the Commandments. The precepts are not, according to the mind of St Thomas, logically deducible corollaries of the Decalogue. (Reduction, in its logical sense, is a method of rearranging the middle term of a syllogism to make the syllogism more readily understood. The classical reduction rearranges syllogisms of the second, third, and fourth figures into the first figure, which is considered to be the clearest, hence most perfect, of the four figures.)

The term *principle* need not, in Thomistic parlance, mean a logical source or premise in which other truths are contained virtually; it can mean a foundation or, as the root implies, a starting point. Cf. Roy J. Deferrari *et al.*, *A Lexicon of St Thomas Aquinas* (Washington, DC: Catholic University of America, 1949), p. 885.

[105] I-II. 100. 11. All the additions to the Decalogue that are cited here are taken from this article.

perjury, in the broad sense of a false oath, St Thomas adds the prohibitions of blasphemy and of false teaching (surely in matters religious). And in like manner he proceeds through the rest of the ten, making exceptions only of the last two: 'To the remaining two precepts, however, no others are attached, because through them every evil desire, universally, is forbidden.'[106]

Of most direct relevance to our thesis concerning the bearing of chastity on the common good of civil society is, of course, the Sixth Commandment itself, the prohibition of adultery. Adultery has been condemned in all societies. Of necessity the understanding of it, and the formal condemnation of it, have varied with the various forms and concepts of marriage adopted in each society. It is no stranger to civil law.[107]

Yet civil law has also prohibited other sexual offenses, which attack the family, offenses not cited in the Decalogue. That in itself does not mean that the Decalogue was not civil law. To show that the Decalogue was civil law it suffices to show that all its provisions are in the nature of civil law, not that all possible provisions of civil law, or even all the key provisions of civil law, are explicitly a part of it.

St Thomas cites as 'superadded' to the prohibition of adultery some principal violations of chastity: prostitution, fornication, and perversion (both homosexuality and bestiality). Once again: this language makes it clear he is *not deriving* a particular moral prohibition from the Commandment, but rather views that prohibition as *attached* to the Commandment from outside it.

This Thomistic *principle of addition* offers an answer to the question of how the Decalogue, though given as civil law,

[106] Here St Thomas gives these Commandments the meaning universally attributed to them until modern philology uncovered the probability that they prohibit outward acts, a discovery clinched some decades later by inferences from archaeological discoveries.

[107] As of June 1990, adultery was reported to be a criminal offense in twenty-seven of the US states and the District of Columbia ('Adultery – It's Not Just a Sin,' *Washington Times*, 29 June 1990, sect. E, p. 1).

could come to signify the whole of the moral law. Precepts of the moral law are *attached* to the Commandments, not deduced from them. All deceitful speech is attached to false witness, all unchastity to adultery, all fraud to theft. The particular becomes a symbol for the general.

We shall point out in the next chapter how Holy Writ does this, attaching particular laws to the Decalogue in the five books of the Old Testament known collectively to the Jews as 'the Law.' We shall focus on the laws of chastity, which have worked for the preservation of the Jewish family and, through it, the unique survival of Israel. We shall study the Jewish family, preserved by those laws. And we shall study the titanic battle of the prophets against the gods of sexual license, a contest that stood until the Maccabean Revolt as the most decisive in history for the future of mankind.

Chapter 2

THE LAW

When the Hebrews arrived in the Land of Promise they found that it indeed flowed, as Yahweh had assured them, with milk and honey.[1] But even as it yielded such plenty, Palestine was constantly threatened by drought and disaster. Situated as it was on the southern fringes of the moist westerly winds, its rainy season was unreliable, and famine could follow a winter drought.[2]

There is little reason for surprise then that the inhabitants the Israelites encountered in that region, the Canaanites, resorted to magical rites, sacrifices, and incantations in hopes of propitiating the mysterious forces they believed to control the climate, hence their destiny.[3] The children of Israel instead put their hope in God alone, giving him that absolute trust which finds witness in the Psalms. Here they were unique, so far as we know, among the peoples of antiquity.

[1] Exod. 3:8, 17 *et passim.*

[2] See W. F. Albright, *The Archaeology of Palestine* (Harmondsworth: Penguin Books, 1949), p. 255.

[3] The Canaanite *Epic of Baal* portrays the recurring drama of drought in mythic form. Baal, god of the yearly rain-season and of vegetation, undertakes battle with the god of death but dies before the battle can be joined. The god of artificial irrigation tries to take his place, but lacks the stature. Baal is rescued from death by his sister-consort, Anat, and returns to the earth during the winter rainy season. El, father and ruler of the gods, sends the god of death back to the underworld to rule the dead. This cycle is repeated yearly. See Lawrence Boadt, CSP, *Reading the Old Testament* (New York: Paulist Press, 1984), pp. 219–20; also W. F. Albright, *From the Stone Age to Christianity* (Baltimore: Johns Hopkins Press, 1946), pp. 175–7.

Pagan Worship, Sexual License, and Child Sacrifice

Yet the religion of the Canaanites seeped into Israel without cease. It worked at the foundations, seemed at times to saturate the structure, and even rose to swirl violently around the worship of God Almighty, as if to sweep it away, and him with it. Canaanite religion had a powerful advantage over the austere code of Moses, with its emphasis on fidelity to God and family. It was an orgiastic cult, its rite one of sacred prostitution. Through ritual re-enactment of the union of Baal and Anat, so the Canaanite belief ran, men could help bring about a plentiful harvest. Thus the rite took the form of an institutionalized and indeed sacralized unchastity. Where Yahweh demanded mastery of the sexual drive, the gods and goddesses of Canaan urged surrender to it.

There was a still more sinister side to Canaanite worship: ritual child sacrifice.

Thus the prophets found themselves pitted against the orgiastic and even murderous cult of Canaan. Their struggle against it constitutes the pivotal drama of Jewish history until the last great onslaught of pagan worship and sexual license, which swept across Israel from another culture entirely and was overcome by the Maccabean Revolt.

It is our thesis that Israel, which has survived military ruin, economic destitution, national exile, and political upheavals, which for two millennia has survived political destruction, could not have survived defeat in her prophetic resistance against superstition. The reason is that that superstition was not only an assault on the worship that forged the nation of Israel but, as an assault on chastity, was an assault on the family.

Only when we grasp the nature of that superstition can we begin to understand its tenacity. Only when we grasp its nature can we understand the ferocity of the prophets in fighting it. As a religion of sexual abandon and child sacrifice, it struck two lethal blows at the family, one at its root and the other at its fruit. The struggle of the prophets must be seen as a defense of Israel through defense of the family, a struggle motivated

Sounds like 2005. Whoring (AIDS & STD'S) + abortion, foster care,

in great part by disgust, outrage, and horror at the vile practices that were attacking the family and its most innocent and defenseless members. At the same time the attraction and tenacity of the fertility cult stemmed from surrender to the sexual drive.

The archaeological and linguistic advances of the twentieth century enable us to read the prophets and histories of the Old Testament with renewed confidence in their reliability, and new confidence in our ability to understand them. Through those scholarly advances the fertility cult has come to be far more fully understood, and along with it the historical accuracy of Holy Writ. Although problems remain, we are able to view the struggle of the prophets with fresh insight and appreciation.[4] Prophetic condemnations that once seemed violent are seen now as commensurate to their object. Prophetic expressions that formerly rang of the arbitrary and hyperbolic are now known to be targeted and measured. Prophetic metaphors that savored of abuse are now seen to be sober, indeed scarcely removed from the literal. At the same time, seemingly innocent phrases, such as 'high places' and 'beneath leafy trees,' now take on overtones of ritual prostitution and human sacrifice.[5]

We can glance at a few examples. Jeremiah, reminding Israel of what had happened when she shook off the demands of the Covenant, quotes Yahweh:

[4] Samuel H. Dresner writes: 'With a better understanding of the nature of these pagan cults, we may gain a fuller appreciation of the unremitting struggle of the biblical prophets to root out what the scholars have labeled, almost euphemistically, "polytheistic idolatry." Only in this context do we understand why the Bible uses the verb *zona* – "to whore after" – when referring to foreign gods; the verb is not used only metaphorically. We know that the scriptures do not countenance idolatry, but we have not adequately known why. And we have not known why, because we did not appreciate the character of the threat posed by the pagan cults' ('The Return of Paganism?,' *Midstream*, June/July 1988, p. 33).

[5] Other terms used by the prophets in speaking of the fertility cult do not have the same sinister overtones, but are taken from the vocabulary of the cult itself, namely wine, wheat and oil, rain, trees, and flax. See *The New Jerome Biblical Commentary* (Englewood Cliffs, NJ: Prentice Hall, 1990), s.v. 'Hosea,' p. 218.

> 'It is long ago now since you broke your yoke, burst your bonds and said, "I will not serve!" Yet on every high hill and under every spreading tree you have lain down like a harlot.'[6]

Ezekiel too quotes Yahweh:

> 'You have even – it is the Lord Yahweh who speaks – taken the sons and daughters you bore me and sacrificed them as food to the images. Was it not enough for you just to be a whore? You have slaughtered my children and handed them over as a burnt offering to them . . . To crown your wickedness – trouble for you, it is the Lord Yahweh who speaks – you have built yourself a mound and made a high place at every crossroads. At the beginning of every road you have built a high place to defile your beauty there and to give your body to every comer.'[7]

We are certain now that this language, while clearly figurative because used in an apostrophe to Israel in the image of a woman, describes actual practices in which Israelites were engaged in imitation of their Canaanite neighbors: sacred prostitution, and the ritual slaughter of their own children. Until the third decade of the twentieth century, rationalist scholars refused to credit such scriptural accounts of ritual child sacrifice among Jews and Canaanites, despite abundant confirmation by both pagans and Christians of the early centuries.[8] Archaeological confirmation of these Christian and pagan claims could not be produced. However, in 1921 the first such evidence came to light in the African city of Carthage, capital of a far-flung neo-Canaanite empire on both shores of the western Mediterranean and its islands as well. Because Carthage was a daughter-city of the great Phoenician city of Tyre and heir of the Phoenician-Canaanite culture, there could be little doubt that evidence of child sacrifice in Carthage pointed to the

[6] Jer. 2:20.

[7] Ezek. 16:19–21; 23–5.

[8] See W. F. Albright, *Yahweh and the Gods of Canaan* (London: Athlone Press, 1968), p. 204. The French historian Aline Roussell observes a similar resistance in our own day despite the archaeological discoveries made since World War I: see her *Porneia: On Desire and the Body in Antiquity*, tr. Felicia Pheasant (New York and Oxford: Basil Blackwell, 1988), p. 114, n. 23.

same practice in the mother-culture.[9] This decisive discovery in Carthage was of a stele portraying a priest holding an infant in the manner of a lamb about to be sacrificed.[10]

Confirmation was soon to come. Abundant and pitiable evidence of child sacrifice in the form of tiny charred skeletons was found in Carthage itself and among the ruins of Phoenician colonies of the western Mediterranean.[11] There were no fewer than four such sites in Sardinia alone, and others in Sicily and in the North African littoral, whose inhabitants called themselves 'the African Canaanites.'[12]

The Punic custom of sacrificing children, so abhorrent to the Romans, was none other than the Canaanite custom that had been ensconced in Israel by Queen Jezebel, daughter of a king of Tyre and Sidon.[13]

However, any search for archaeological evidence of Canaanite religious practices in these chief cities of Phoenicia

[9] The Phoenician name of Carthage, Kart-hadasht, means 'New City.' Indeed, the adjective that was applied to anything Carthaginian, 'Punic,' comes from the word *Phoenician*.

The word *Phoenician* itself is thought to derive from the Greek word for red-purple, *phoinix*, while a Hurrian word for that same color, *kinahhu*, may be the origin of the word *Canaan*. The Phoenicians were famous in the ancient world for the production of purple dye, a very expensive and highly prized commodity made from shellfish found along the Phoenician coast.

[10] See Albright, *Yahweh and the Gods of Canaan*, p. 204. Phoenicia began its political and commercial decline in the eighth century BC. 'Henceforth the religion of Tyre was doomed to increasing loss of influence, while the closely related religion of the aboriginal Canaanites of Palestine had probably become virtually extinct as an independent factor' (W. F. Albright, *Archeology and the Religion of Israel*, 3rd edn. [Baltimore: Johns Hopkins Press, 1956], p. 161). Phoenician culture along with, naturally, the Phoenician-Canaanite religion, was to rise again with the growing power of the daughter-city, Carthage, which according to tradition was founded in 814 BC.

[11] Sabatino Moscati in *The World of the Phoenicians*, tr. Alastair Hamilton (New York: Frederick A. Praeger, 1968), observed that no shrines for the sacrifice of children, known from the biblical term for such places as *topheths*, had been uncovered in Spain, 'unless the shrine at Cueva d'es Cuyram [on the Balearic island of Ibiza] was one' (p. 236). This shrine was dedicated to the goddess Tanit, linked in archaeological finds to child sacrifice.

[12] Albright, *From the Stone Age to Christianity*, p. 214. As late as the fifth century of our era, St Augustine testifies, the peasants of Carthage, speaking Punic, called themselves Canaanites (*Patrologia Latina*, XXXV, col. 2096).

[13] The story of Jezebel, and the prophet Elijah's campaign against the Baalism that she introduced, is found in I Kings.

has been interdicted, in Sidon by the modern city that stands on top of it, in Tyre by valuable Hellenistic and Roman remains. Far more telling was a lack of archaeological evidence of religious practices in the archaeologically accessible Canaanite homeland, whose major cities dotted the Phoenician coast of little more than one hundred miles, in modern Lebanon. Nor was such evidence found inland within the shifting borders of primitive Canaan.

As late as December 1965 a foremost authority on Phoenician history could write that material on the Phoenicians of the eastern Mediterranean was 'scanty and uncertain,' while it was 'almost too vast' within Carthaginian territories.[14]

Before a decade had elapsed this anomaly abruptly vanished. Archaeologists of the University Museum of the University of Pennsylvania, during excavations into a tell on the Phoenician coast near modern Sarafand from 1969 to 1974, found what scholars such as Ernest Renan had suspected would be there: the Phoenician city of Sarepta.[15] In a Phoenician shrine in Sarepta they found evidence linking Canaanite and Punic religious practices. This evidence, an ivory plaque inscribed with a dedication to Tanit and presumed to have been set in a putative wooden statue of that goddess, and a glass disc bearing the celebrated 'Sign of Tanit,' was the first to demonstrate Canaanite worship of that chief goddess of Carthage, long thought to be an exclusively African divinity.[16]

[14] Moscati, *The World of the Pheonicians*, p. xvii.

[15] The reasons for choosing the site, the methods employed, and the discoveries themselves are described in fascinating detail by James B. Pritchard in *Recovering Sarepta, a Phoenician City* (Princeton, NJ: Princeton University Press, 1978).

Pritchard observes that the name *Sarafand* 'has long been recognized as similar to the ancient Sarepta,' and the modern spelling 'could easily be a corruption of the older' (p. 7).

[16] Pritchard writes, 'Our Sarepta inscription contains the first unequivocal occurrence of Tanit in the Phoenician homeland in the East, but there were some hints, even before its discovery, that she might have had a Phoenician origin. A stela of remembrance discovered in Athens as long ago as 1795 mentions a certain Abdtanit [Servant of Tanit] as a Sidonian. But when an inscription containing the phrase "Tanit in *lbnn*" was found in Carthage in 1898, scholars . . . found it impossible to read the name as the Syrian Lebanon. And

Now Tanit had been associated with child sacrifice since 1925, when her stelae were found in Carthage along with the burnt bones of little children. James B. Pritchard writes:

> With the appearance in Canaanite Phoenicia of the goddess Tanit, who is linked with child sacrifice in the West, the several condemnations by Hebrew writers of those who 'burn their sons and their daughters in the fire' (Jer. 7:31–32, 19:3–6; II Kings 23:10) take on new credibility as a description of a widespread cultic practice in the Levant.[17]

Little wonder that the Jews in the Nazareth synagogue were outraged when Jesus, declaring that no prophet is accepted in his own country, reminded them:

> There were many widows in Israel, I can assure you, in Elijah's day, when heaven remained shut for three years and six months and a great famine raged throughout the land, but Elijah was not sent to any one of these: he was sent to a widow at Zarephath [Sarepta], a Sidonian town.[18]

A striking parallel emerges between the struggle of the prophets to eradicate Baalism from Israel and the struggle of Rome to destroy Carthage, its rival for mastery over the Mediterranean. There is an even more striking convergence between them, for just as the triumph of the prophets over Baalism meant the survival of the Jewish faith, and was the condition for the fulfillment of Yahwism in Jesus Christ, so Rome, having triumphed over Baalism in the Carthaginian empire, became the chief vehicle for the spread of Christian belief, a role that Carthage seems unlikely to have been able to play had she defeated Rome and ruled instead of her over the Mediterranean basin.

---

in 1964–5, M. Dunand discovered at Eshmun, near Sidon, an ostrakon of the fifth century [BC] containing a list of names, among which was Gertanit. But such well-known scholars as Dussaud, Lidzbarsky, Roellig, Gsell, and Charles-Picard had assigned Tanit to an African origin rather than to a Phoenician one' (ibid., p. 107).

[17] Ibid.

[18] Luke 4:25. The story of Elijah's miraculous generosity to the Canaanite widow who gave him food and shelter is told in I Kings 17.

Speculation aside, archaeological evidence of child sacrifice among the 'African Canaanites,' joined to the evidence uncovered at Sarepta, excludes reasonable doubt that the prophets of Israel, and pagan and Christian authors for that matter, were speaking the plain truth.

No longer, then, could anyone doubt that Isaiah, addressing Israelites as 'you sons of a witch . . . , offspring of the adulterer and the whore,'[19] was addressing them as followers of the fertility cult when he declaimed:

> Lusting among the terebinths,
> and under every spreading tree,
> sacrificing children in the wadis
> and in rocky clefts.
>
> The smooth stones of the wadis, these are your share,
> these, these your portion.
> To these you pour libations,
> bring oblations.[20]

The phrase 'spreading tree' is used in the Old Testament in one sense only: in allusion to sites of fertility rites. As for the 'smooth stones,' they were probably symbols of the male fertility deity.[21]

In the prophetic effort to rescue Israel from sexual immorality, the Covenant is conceived as a mystical marriage between Yahweh and Israel. Israel is the adulterous wife.[22] The words of the prophet Hosea make it clear that Israel's figurative adultery is her literal apostasy to the fertility gods of Canaan.[23] However, she will be reconciled to Yahweh:

> When that day comes – it is Yahweh who speaks – she will call me 'My husband;' no longer will she call me 'My Baal.' I will take the names of the Baals off her lips; their names shall never be uttered again.[24]

[19] Isa. 57:3.

[20] Isa. 57:5–6.

[21] See J. L. McKenzie, *Second Isaiah*, Anchor Bible series (Garden City, NY: Doubleday, 1968), pp. 157 and 158.

[22] Hos. 2.

[23] Hos. 2:13.

[24] Hos. 2:16–19.

This prophecy of Israel's return to the Covenant was fulfilled. That return has proven to be the secret of her survival.

But cultic prostitution had invaded even the Jerusalem Temple itself, and the practice of child sacrifice had reached the royal house of Judah. King Manasseh

> did what is displeasing to Yahweh, copying the shameful practices of the nations whom Yahweh had dispossessed for the sons of Israel. He rebuilt the high places that his father Hezekiah had destroyed, he set up altars to Baal and made a sacred pole as Ahab king of Israel had done. . . .
>
> He built altars to the whole array of heaven in the two courts of the Temple of Yahweh. He caused his son to pass through the fire.[25]

To prevent and punish such misbehavior, highly detailed legislation was attached to the Decalogue. Yet at times the superstition grew so rank in Israel that it crowded out the very memory of those laws. A case in point is offered by the events leading up to the reforms of King Josiah, Manasseh's grandson.

Hezekiah, Manasseh's father and Josiah's great-grandfather, had 'put his trust in the God of Israel.'[26] He had been a reforming monarch, and the scriptural list of his accomplishments shows how widespread idolatry and superstition had been in the kingdom of Judah: 'It was he who abolished the high places, broke the pillars, cut down the sacred poles and smashed the bronze serpent that Moses had made, for up to that time the Israelites had offered sacrifice to it.'[27] The 'sacred poles' were the asherahs, wooden stakes dedicated to the Canaanite goddess Asherah, who was a popular object of veneration among Israelite devotees of the fertility

[25] II Kings 21:2–6.

[26] II Kings 18:5.

[27] II Kings 18:4. The serpent was made by Moses at Yahweh's command, so that those who looked on it would survive the bite of 'fiery serpents' (Num. 21:8). The book of Wisdom calls it a 'saving token,' saying that whoever turned to it 'was saved, not by what he looked at, but by you, the universal saviour' (Wisd. 16:6 and 7). However it had become an object of idolatry.

cult.[28] The 'pillars,' when paired with such stakes, were probably symbols of the male.[29]

But half a century later, when Josiah moved to abolish the Baalism that his grandfather Manasseh had restored, a book of the Law was found by workmen purging the Temple of its pagan furnishings. So little did this restorer of Yahwism know of the Law that its prescriptions rang strange in his ears. But its condemnations terrified him. As if in a panic, he destroyed and desecrated all the places and buildings sacred to the pagan rites, including 'the furnace in the Valley of Ben-hinnom, so that no one could make his son or daughter pass through fire in honor of Molech.'[30]

The More Detailed Commandments

We now examine prescriptions of the kind that inspired Josiah to his radical reform. They are the more particular prescriptions of the Law, commandments attached to the Decalogue.

[28] In Ugaritic mythology Asherah is the consort of El, father of the gods, while Baal's consort is Anath. But in the Old Testament Asherah appears as Baal's consort.

Some scholars hold that none of the scriptural references to the asherah, or sacred stake, upholds a distinction between Yahwism and fertility worship; the Deuteronomic condemnations would under this theory be later additions. For an account of this view see Mark S. Smith, *The Early History of God* (New York: Harper, 1990), pp. 80–1. Smith holds that the asherah 'was associated historically with Yahweh and not with Baal' (p. 84). This is a puzzling claim in view of Judg. 6:25, where Yahweh orders Gideon to 'pull down the altar to Baal belonging to your father and cut down the sacred post at the side of it.' The passage is cited by Smith himself (ibid.). He also examines scholarly opinions that biblical and other evidence point to Asherah as the consort of Yahweh in early Israel, and that the asherah was simply a symbol within the cult of Yahweh without signifying a goddess (pp. 88–94).

[29] See the *Eerdmans Bible Dictionary* (Grand Rapids, Mich.: Eerdmans, 1987), s.v. 'Pillar.'

[30] II Kings 23:10. The 'god' Molech (or Moloch) that appears in biblical translations is considered by most scholars to be a misinterpretation of the Hebrew. Albright says: 'In 1935 Otto Eissfeldt . . . showed convincingly that *molek* was a sacrificial term and not the name of a Canaanite divinity. Punic *molk* and Hebrew *molek* . . . are in fact the same word, and both refer to a sacrifice which was, for Phoenicians and Hebrews alike, the most awe-inspiring of all possible sacred acts – whether it was considered as holy or as an abomination' (*Yahweh and the Gods of Canaan*, p. 205).

In view of Israel's prophetic campaign to protect the family from the corrosion of unchastity, most especially as institutionalized in the fertility cults of Canaan, we need not be surprised that they deal in very large part with chastity and the preservation of the family.

Modern scholars, basing themselves on linguistic and historical analyses, see the scriptural additions to the Decalogue, or most of them, as accruing over centuries. These scholarly positions are far from definitive, and in certain regards remain hypothetical, yet the general conclusion that most additions to the Decalogue were made over a centuries-long period seems well established.[31]

Virtually all the precepts and regulations of Jewish law are found in the first five books of Holy Writ, known collectively to us as the Pentateuch. To the Jews they were known simply as the Law, or 'Torah.' The book of Genesis deals with primordial history, introducing us to the history of salvation, the thread that holds all Scripture together – indeed all history together. Exodus deals with the flight of the Hebrews from their Egyptian oppressors, and with the Sinaitic Covenant. Leviticus deals almost entirely with laws and regulations. Numbers, taking its name from its preoccupation with statistics, continues the narrative of the wanderings of the Hebrews until they begin their settlements; its Hebrew name means 'in the wilderness,' which conveys that latter aspect of the book. Numbers also adds laws dealing with the settlement of the Promised Land. In Deuteronomy, a series of discourses by Moses serves as the vehicle for civil and religious laws.

The very pole of all law in the Old Testament, of course, is the Decalogue. All other laws group themselves around it, and align themselves with it. Most of these laws are found in clusters, or codes. Among those which stand alone, some, such as the law of circumcision, are isolated because they arose to meet some historical circumstance. We focus here on those

[31] For a concise account of the investigations and conclusions of biblical scholars concerning the composition of the Pentateuch, see Neil J. McEleney, *The Law Given through Moses* (New York: Paulist Press, 1960), pp. 9–28.

which are clustered together, all of them of course oriented toward the Decalogue. They are found in Exodus, Leviticus, and Deuteronomy.

The oldest of these clusters is the Yahwist Code of the Alliance, in Exodus 20:22 to 23:19. This supplies more particularized laws to the new nation of Israel, founded through the Covenant. Attached to this code is the Ritual Decalogue (Exod. 34:11–26), which regulates feasts and sacrifices in an agricultural society, although it is found in a book dealing with the wanderings of the Hebrews in the desert. (This anomaly is one reason why the Pentateuch is judged to consist of documents dating from various ages.) Parts of it are repeated in Deuteronomy 12 to 16, but in a form more suitable to a commercial society consisting of various classes. Another collection is the Law of Holiness, found in Leviticus 17 to 26. The Law of Holiness reflects the concerns of the priestly class of the southern kingdom when refugee priests from the north flocked to Jerusalem in the eighth century BC. Tensions between northerners and southerners, significant at that time, were erased after the fall of the southern kingdom of Judah in 586 BC, a century and a half later; then, both during the exile and after the return, the Law and its collections of moral and ritual precepts, whatever their source, became the unifying force of Israel, and its conserving force.

Our claim, of course, is that the ubiquitous laws demanding chastity were vital to the survival of Israel, and more basically to her unity, which is practically the definition of survival.[32] We here survey, briefly, the Pentateuch's more particular laws regulating sexual conduct.

It is significant for our thesis that the Code of the Alliance in Exodus, thought to be the earliest of all these collections and even attributable to Moses himself,[33] lays down specifics for the regulation of marriage. Presupposing a society in which a man might have more than one wife, it stipulates that if the

[32] For proof of the metaphysical identity of being and unity, see Aquinas, *De Veritate*, I. 1.

[33] See McEleney, *The Law Given through Moses*, p. 15.

master of a slave girl whom he had destined for himself grows to dislike her,

> he must let her be bought back. . . . If he takes another wife, he must not reduce the food of the first or her clothing or her conjugal rights. Should he cheat her of these three things she may leave, freely, without having to pay any money.[34]

Justice toward a wronged woman is demanded:

> If a man seduces a virgin who is not betrothed and sleeps with her, he must pay her [marriage] price and make her his wife. If her father absolutely refuses to let him have her, her seducer must pay a sum of money equal to the price fixed for a virgin.[35]

Bestiality is regarded with such horror that not only is the offender put to death but the beast as well.[36]

Virtually at the outset of the Law of Holiness, in chapter 18 of Leviticus, this code presents a detailed list of forbidden marriages, based on consanguinity or affinity, and condemns adultery, child sacrifice, sodomy, and bestiality. The inclusion, among manifestly sexual crimes, of the Canaanite custom of sacrificing children can be readily linked to our own day, when children are sacrificed to sexual liberty, and this unspeakable crime is sanctioned by law, even underwritten by taxes.

Yahweh is quoted as warning the Jews that such behavior means national instability:

> Do not make yourselves unclean by any of these practices, for it was by such things that the nations that I have expelled to make way for you made themselves unclean.
>
> The land became unclean; I exacted the penalty for its fault and the land had to vomit out its inhabitants.[37]

[34] Exod. 21:8, 10–11. It is worthy of note that the text presumes that the slave can hold property. This, and the power of contract, were denied to slaves under American law, making it a 'peculiar institution' (as it was known among the slaveholding classes) because slaves were deemed persons in misbehavior and punishments but not in the right to a share of the fruits of their labor or in the power of contract.

[35] Exod. 22:15–17.

[36] Exod. 22:19 (also Lev. 20:15–16).

[37] Lev. 18:24–5.

A warning against prostitution hints at the same punishment for the land and the people in it: 'Do not profane your daughter by making her a prostitute; the land will not be prostituted and filled with incest.'[38] So sacred is the priesthood that death by burning is reserved for a priest's daughter who prostitutes herself.[39] So sacred is the priesthood, and so precious is sexual purity, that the two are linked in what might be thought an exaggerated way: no priest may marry a woman not a virgin, even a respectable widow.[40]

In Deuteronomy, whose Greek name means 'Second Law,' we find, as we might expect, a statement of particular laws, such as those on marriage and sexual conduct, but also a restatement of the Decalogue itself. That comes within a new recounting of the events at Mount Sinai (called Horeb in Deuteronomy).

However, there is a deeper understanding, a firmer grasp, so to speak, of Yahweh's self-revelation at Sinai. This is seen in the concern that Yahweh's utter and incomprehensible spirituality not be betrayed through any physical image.[41] It is seen in the exhortation to obey Yahweh's Law 'with all your heart, with all your soul,' because it is not an arbitrary set of regulations, but is drawn from the depths of man's heart and soul, 'for your good.'[42] This is summed up in the dramatic last exhortation of Moses to obey the Law: 'Choose life!'[43]

It is as life-giving that the Decalogue has become a symbol of the moral law, indeed stands as the symbol *par excellence* of what is to be done as intrinsically right and what is to be shunned as intrinsically wrong.

A striking difference between the law of primitive Israel and the laws of modern Western states lies in punishment. Violations of the First and Third Commandments could bring

[38] Lev. 19:29.
[39] Lev. 21:9.
[40] Lev. 21:13–14.
[41] Deut. 4:15–19, *et al.*
[42] Deut. 6:5 and 10:13 respectively.
[43] Deut. 30:19.

death.[44] So could kidnapping for enslavement.[45] What chiefly concerns this study is the kind of punishments reserved for offenses against chastity and, more generally, against the family. Adultery, as treason to the family, is punished by death; the interloper dies also.[46] Certain degrees of incest, too, merit death.[47] Sodomy brings death to both sodomites,[48] while bestiality, as we have seen, is so abhorrent that not only is the offender to die, but the beast as well.

The most horrendous of the crimes against the family was ritual child murder, with the sacrifice of the infants to a divinity. That the Law of Israel considered this a crime against the family is quite clear, and is illustrated by the fact that this particular law is surrounded by prohibitions against sexual sins.[49] More than a dozen kinds of incest, plus adultery, precede it, while sodomy and bestiality follow it.

But the reason given by the Law for prohibiting child sacrifice uses language redolent of the Covenant: this would 'profane the name of your God. . . . I am Yahweh.'[50] The prohibition of this unspeakable crime against children, hence against the future of the nation, is tied to God's sovereignty over Israel, and to that worship of him alone which was and remains the distinctive note of Israel's common purpose. Thus this law protecting the youngest members of the family found itself embedded in a politico-religious matrix.

The punishment for child sacrifice was death.[51] This should scarcely be a surprise, yet the sacrifice of children for convenience is sanctioned by the abortion laws of most Western nations.

[44] E.g. Exod. 22:17 and Lev. 20:27, against sorcery, and Exod. 35:2, against work on the sabbath.

[45] Exod. 21:16; Deut. 24:7.

[46] Lev. 20:10. For the concept of adultery in Old Testament times, see Ch. 1, n. 68.

[47] E.g. Lev. 20:15, 16.

[48] Lev. 20:13.

[49] Lev. 18:21.

[50] Ibid.

[51] Lev. 20:2.

What must come as a huge surprise to the modern mind, however, is the death penalty for sins against the Fourth Commandment. The respect due parents is widely understood to this day, but hardly anyone expects civil punishment of any kind, far less death itself, for failures in that regard. Yet listen to the Law of Israel: 'Anyone who strikes his father or mother must die.'[52]

Nor need the blow be deadly to merit death; it must only strike father or mother. This law immediately follows distinctions of penalties for death-dealing blows, depending on malice. But for striking a parent no extenuations are offered. The act merits death.

Even for cursing father or mother death is prescribed, in Exod. 21:17. This of course refers to cursing in the strict and now almost forgotten sense, not to a thoughtless or hot-headed use of blasphemous language against a person. A formal curse, among the Israelites, was a matter of great moment, an act of hatred diametrically opposed to the honor that Yahweh exacted from children toward parents.

Moreover the death penalty for cursing father or mother is restated in Lev. 20:9, along with the comment: 'Since he has cursed his father or mother, his blood shall be on his own head.'

In Leviticus this crime is set at the head of a list of sexual crimes and their punishments: death for adultery, for certain degrees of incest, for bigamy with daughter or mother, for sodomy, and for bestiality. The lesson is easily understood: all these violations of the moral code strike at the family. These prohibitions and punishments, designed to protect the family, were further designed to protect the nation.

That they were designed to protect the nation is seen in the fact that the law itself explained these prohibitions in terms of national stability: 'You must keep all my laws, all my customs, and put them into practice,' says Yahweh immediately after stipulating the punishments for child sacrifice, sorcery, cursing father or mother, adultery, incest, and bestiality. 'You must

[52] Yahweh speaks thus to Moses in Exod. 21:15.

keep all my laws, all my customs, and put them into practice: *thus you will not be vomited out by the land where I am taking you to live.* You must not follow the laws of the nations that I expel to make way for you; they practiced all these things and for this I have come to detest them.'[53]

Thus the same would happen to the Israelite nation were it to fall into the hideous practices that provoked the Lord to drive the Canaanites out of their land. These Canaanites are the ritual child-murderers, the practitioners of bestiality, the sodomites.[54]

Yahweh is repeating the warning he uttered to Israel in forbidding these unspeakable vices:

> But you must keep my laws and customs, you must not do any of these hateful things, neither native nor stranger living among you. For all these hateful things were done by the people who inhabited this land before you, and the land became unclean. If you make it unclean, will it not vomit you out as it vomited the nation that was here before you?[55]

Thus for such crimes the same punishment is to be meted out to all nations indiscriminately, Israel included. That punishment is dispersal, which in the ordinary course of history means disappearance. The universality of this punishment indicates that it is inflicted not by divine intervention but by nature, God's vicar (in the Chaucerian phrase).

There is another crime for which the nation will suffer dispersal and disappearance. It is the worship of false gods. But as we have seen, it is not quite another crime: in the case of Israel it involved sexual aberrations and the sacrifice of infants.

Yahweh warns that terrible punishments will befall the nations for this crime, the last and worst being this: 'I will scatter you among the nations.'[56]

[53] Lev. 20:22–3; emphasis supplied. Yahweh then refers ('I have told you already') to the same warning he had given in Lev. 18 when he outlawed incest, child sacrifice, adultery, sodomy, and bestiality.

[54] Lev. 18:21–4.

[55] Lev. 18:26–8.

[56] Lev. 26:33.

Moses, recalling the Covenant, told the Israelites:

> When you have begotten children and grandchildren and you have lived long in the land, if you act perversely, making a carved image in one shape or another, doing what displeases Yahweh and angers him, on that day I will call heaven and earth to witness against you; and at once you will vanish from the land you are crossing the Jordan to possess. You shall not live there long; you shall be utterly destroyed.[57]

Moses also warns the Israelites:

> Be sure that if you forget Yahweh your God, if you follow other gods, if you serve them and bow down before them – I warn you today – you will most certainly perish. Like the nations Yahweh is to destroy before you, so you yourselves shall perish, for not having listened to the voice of Yahweh your God.[58]

A pattern of punishments emerges in the Pentateuch. If the nation abandons God and turns to idols, it will be scattered and will perish. If the nation falls into crimes against the family, including not only sexual perversions and ritual child murder (which are both connected, in the historical context, with the worship of false gods) but even the cursing of parents, the nation will be scattered and, presumably, die.[59]

A citizen of our day could hardly fail to notice the contrast between the God-centered, family-based, cohesive society created by the Covenant and, on the other hand, the secularistic, hedonistic, atomistic society around him. More

[57] Deut. 4:25–6.

[58] Deut. 8:19–20. Cf. also Deut. 30:15–20; this is among the clearest warnings of Moses that the life of the nation hangs upon the nation's fidelity to God. See also Deut. 32:46–7.

[59] There is a curious and seemingly inconsistent note in the punishments prescribed by Yahweh. Not all the crimes that bring death to the nation bring death to the perpetrators. For example, only childlessness – more like a curse than a penalty – is reserved for a man who marries his brother's wife (Lev. 20:21). The law against marrying a brother's wife (presumably when the brother was still living, since there was an actual obligation to marry a brother's widow) would clearly have its own function in maintaining the cohesion of the family and the larger society, although the forbidden act is not a heinous crime of the sort that might merit death.

remarkable still is the self-righteousness of contemporary society: the ostentatious moral tone of the established amorality, the almost religious zeal for irreligion.

Is the curse of the Covenant hanging over modern society? Does the doom foretold in the Covenant await us?

The obverse of this question is less mystical and more amenable to verification. It is this: did the promises of the Covenant hold true? More specifically: did Israel, obeying, survive?

The answer to this last question is *yes*. But it is a *yes* surrounded by qualifications and even mystery. Israel did not always obey; far from it. Her infidelity brought forth the wrath of the prophets. She was scattered among the nations: believing Christians, and I suppose believing Jews, will see in that the wrath of God. Speaking philosophically, we might not be entitled to pronounce her expulsion from the land and her dispersal a punishment for failure to obey the Law. Yet as philosophers we are entitled to conclude with those contemporary observers, the prophets, that disobedience to the commands of virtue played a role in the loss of the land. We are entitled as well to examine the mystery of her survival amid that dispersal, and to conclude that she has survived through whatever obedience she has given the Law.

We know that Israel did not survive as a state.[60] Yet the survival of Israel as a people through two millennia of dispersal, and even despite the loss of the Hebrew language, is all the more mysterious for that.

Our task is not to delve into the mystery of Israel, a theological question. Nor is it to attempt a sociological investigation of the Jewish people, though in the following section we shall sketch the Jewish family as described by the Scriptures, the form of the family prescribed by the Scriptures, and the present state of investigations into the Jewish family in the diaspora. Our undertaking is not to explain why the Jewish nation was deprived of its land and dispersed, nor even to attempt a full explanation of how the Jews have survived two

[60] We prescind from the modern attempt to revive Israel as a state, as from many other questions of Jewish history.

millennia of dispersal. Yet to give that survival an explanation, however secular, that excludes Israel's covenantal bond to Yahweh, that excludes her fidelity to the Covenant, would be inconceivable. Especially inconceivable, in an explanation of Israel's survival, would be the exclusion of the Covenant's demands for preserving the family. Of key importance here is the Covenant's demand to honor one's parents, and its demand to confine genital activity within marriage.

The Jewish Family

The core of the Covenant, charter of Western civilization, can be seen as a double helix with two intertwined strands sustaining one another in a constant upward thrust. One is worship of the one God, and obedience to him. The other is the family, held in being by that obedience and that worship, and in turn preserving those sources of its own preservation: for within the family are nurtured the principles of the Covenant, which are the Ten Commandments and the vast panoply of moral precepts attached to them.

What is this family, characterized thus by obedience to the Covenant? What is this carrier of cult and culture?

The best sourcebook on the Jewish family remains Holy Writ. In it are found prescriptions for family life honored to this day, prescriptions that give the Jewish family its distinctive character. They have ensured the survival of the Jewish family and with it the survival of the Jewish faith.

Published studies of more recent family life among the Jews are few, to judge by complaints of Jewish scholars. Paula Hyman, in a work that she and Steven M. Cohen edited, *The Jewish Family: Myths and Reality*, begins her introductory essay thus: 'There has been a great deal of mythmaking but remarkably little scholarship about the Jewish family.'[61]

Benjamin Schlesinger, who published a seemingly exhaustive bibliography of English-language works on the Jewish

[61] 'Perspectives on the Evolving Jewish Family,' in Paula Hyman and Steven M. Cohen (eds.), *The Jewish Family: Myths and Reality* (New York and London: Holmes & Meier, 1986), p. 3.

family, recalls: 'In my first search for source material in English I found very little available, especially socio-psychological studies of modern Jewish family life.'[62]

Yet Professor Schlesinger persisted in his search, and with the help of a grant assembled a bibliography of 429 scholarly works and almost 200 novels and collections of stories about Jewish family life. This search took him two years, and to libraries on two continents. With the help of this vast documentation, he published a survey of the Jewish family from biblical times to the present.

He concludes that the Jewish family has been governed by four basic principles derived from the Talmud, itself of course derived by definition from Holy Writ:

> The first is referred to as *taharath mishpacha* (purity of the family) and is founded on a sane, wholesome appraisal of the sexual relationship in human affairs. Sex is seen as a force for good in life, a gift of God to be cherished, ... and used only under the guidance of love to fulfill divine purposes in life: namely, to propagate the human race, to perpetuate the Jewish people and thereby the teachings for which Israel continues its mission among the nations, to strengthen and deepen the companionship of husband and wife, and to promote their physical and psychological well-being.[63]

This *taharath mishpacha*, or 'purity of family,' in Professor Schlesinger's rendering, is a broad description of what we have been calling *chastity*.

He continues:

> Beyond family purity, a second Jewish value is *gidul uboneth* (the obligation for effective child-bearing and child-rearing). An imperative of Jewish living is scrupulous care for the physical, social, educational, and religious needs of the child. This is a central parental responsibility; other people or agencies only assist. Parents are always the child's most impressive teachers, and are obligated to set an example. . . .

[62] *The Jewish Family: A Survey and Annotated Bibliography* (Toronto: University of Toronto Press, 1970), p. xi.
[63] Ibid., p. 6.

> Every facet of the child's education is a parental concern and demands close attention, not the least important being the child's moral and religious training.[64]

The next principle cited by Schlesinger as governing Jewish family life is obedience to Yahweh's command at Sinai: honor your father and your mother. He writes:

> A third value can be called *kibud av vo-em*, or filial responsibility. . . . the child has concomitant obligations, particularly the duty to honor and respect his father and mother as long as they live – indeed as long as the child lives.[65]

As Professor Schlesinger proceeds to a description of the fourth factor governing Jewish family life, it assumes the characteristics of the common good of the family.[66]

> The fourth value of family life is *shalom bayith*, or family compatibility. On the one hand, the home is intended to give each individual in it the opportunity for the fullest development and expression of his personality so that the greatest measure of personal happiness may be achieved. On the other hand, there is a group happiness of equal importance to be considered – a sense of community, solidarity, and unity, of which all family members constantly must be mindful, and upon the attainment of which their finest qualities of heart and mind and spirit need to be concentrated.[67]

Schlesinger concludes: 'These values enabled the Jewish people to survive.' It need scarcely be said that this is our thesis precisely.

Not all Jewish thinkers have appreciated the function of religion, both worship and teachings, in the survival of the Jewish people. Perhaps the outstanding example is Simon Dubnow, because of the fate that befell him and the irony of it in view of his own teachings. This highly regarded historian saw the religion of Israel as a means to the survival of the Jewish

[64] Ibid.
[65] Ibid., p. 7.
[66] See the Introduction above.
[67] Schlesinger, *The Jewish Family*, p. 7.

nation only so long as Israel remained shorn of the ordinary means of national self-defense, or only so long as Israel was surrounded by a hostile society. He argued that the faith of Israel had outlived its usefulness in the nineteenth century, when the secularization of Western society enabled the Jews, themselves secularized, to live as a permanent minority within the broader society, a society no longer ridden by the hostility born of a religion that had separated itself from Judaism and was therefore hostile to it.

The irony arises because Dubnow lived to see the rise of a ruthlessly secular society under Nazism, and died under it. This champion of what has been absurdly called peaceful co-existence (corpses co-exist) fled Nazism but, failing to elude its long arm, died its victim.[68]

Something like Dubnow's thesis can be found among the leadership of American Jewry. It is widely held that by the mid-thirties American Jewish leaders, believing or unbelieving, had reached a consensus that the interests of American Jewry would best be served by a secularized society. Yet nowadays some of the most articulate and effective spokesmen for the sacred within the civil are Jews. Some of them, of course, speak from tradition. Others, to adopt the terminology of a distinguished Jewish observer, have been 'mugged by experience.'[69]

Secularization is alien, indeed radically hostile, to the Jewish ethos. As a nation set apart, the Jews are sacred in that primitive sense of the term. The birth of their nation consisted in consecration to God. Not only is their origin steeped in the sacred, but so is their survival.[70] And nothing in their history, nothing in the dynamism of their survival, is more sacred than the family.

[68] See *Encyclopaedia Judaica* (New York: Macmillan, 1971), s.v. 'Dubnow, Simon.'

[69] This memorable phrase, now practically consecrated in our speech, was coined by Irving Kristol.

[70] The concept of Israel as sacred, or set apart, can be seen in the request of the Jews of medieval Rome to the papal authorities that they be set apart, indeed sequestered in their own community with its own laws, enforced by themselves. It has found more recent expression in the *shtetl* of Eastern Europe, and nowadays in the communities of Hasidic Jews in the United States. (For a survey of the

If we take the history of Israel in the most literal sense, it is the history of a man and his family.[71] The tribes of Israel, which constituted the nation's primeval political units, took their names from sons that the patriarch ('father-who-rules') Israel, also named Jacob, produced by his four wives. Going farther back in Hebrew history, we also find the origins of this nation in a man and his family, the patriarch Abraham.

Archaeology has failed to produce a record of Israelite family life anywhere nearly so abundant and informative as it has of family life among other nations of the ancient Near East. Holy Writ remains our most important source by far. From the sacred writings, whether dealing with law or with genealogy, with what was expected of husband and wife and children or with what actually happened in marriages, we can piece together a picture of the Jewish family of old.

A cautionary note is in order. Such a picture is surely incomplete and, strictly speaking, is quite likely a somewhat anachronistic composite because drawn from elements that, while existing at one time or another, may never have existed together, at a given time. The various books of the Old Testament, it is thought, were written across a period covering almost a millennium, from the ninth century BC to the first. Different literary genres are represented among them, even

---

latter, see William Shaffir, 'Persistence and Change in the Hasidic Family,' in Cohen and Hyman (eds.), *The Jewish Family*, pp. 187–99.)

The dangers of close association with the surrounding Gentile society were made clear to the Jews of Europe in the wake of the French Revolution. With Jewish enfranchisement came assimilation and the absorption of so many Jews into the general population that fears were expressed for the survival of European Jewry.

[71] Rabbi Dresner remarks: 'To understand Jewish history is to appreciate the priority given throughout to the Jewish family. For one of Israel's most important guiding principles is: Whatever is supportive of the family is to be favored. Whatever is harmful to the family is to be opposed. Once we recognize the axiomatic nature of this principle, we can better perceive Judaism's attitude to practices that were seen as disruptive to the family, such as pre-marital and extra-marital sexual relations, homosexuality, and divorce' ('The Return of Paganism?,' p. 35).

within individual books; hence not all aspects of family life presented by them can be taken in a single sense. Historically, these books deal with a changing and, we might think, deepening sense of morality. Sociological conditions among them also change. What obtains as law or custom or expectation in one epoch may not so obtain in another. Moreover, some of the historical books from which we draw our picture of Jewish family life were written centuries after the event, as they themselves recall from time to time. (For example, the book of Judges ends with the comment: 'In those days there was no king in Israel, and every man did as he pleased,' while the book of Ruth comments, in explaining how a bargain was struck: 'Now in former times it was the custom in Israel. . . .'[72])

Yet so long as Israel lives, Jews will search Holy Writ for guidance in their family life. They will find inspiration, consolation, counsel that is sound and law that is highly particularized. They will find dire warnings from the God of Israel against the hedonism that had actually been elevated into the sacred among the nations that surrounded their forebears. They will find a struggle to the death against false philosophy and false sexual morals. So long as Israel lives, devout Jews will search Holy Writ for the principles that give permanence to the passing, not least their marriages.

As structured by law, the family begins, or, to recall our caveat, is at one or another epoch supposed to begin, with a marriage contract. There is no need to try, as some have done, to deduce this from the existence of marriage contracts that modern archaeology has uncovered in other Near Eastern cultures contemporary with Israel. Holy Writ is explicit enough:

> Then he turned to her mother and asked her to fetch him writing paper. He drew up the marriage contract, how he gave his daughter to Tobias according to the ordinance in the Law of Moses.[73]

[72] Ruth 4:7.
[73] Tobit 7:13.

Thus the marriage contract is accepted as part of the early tradition of the Jews, dating to the foundation of the nation.[74]

The question of who might marry whom is treated with some particularity in the Pentateuch. The degrees of consanguinity that preclude marriage are spelled out in Leviticus and Deuteronomy. (The later dispensation of Israel did not permit everything that had been practiced in patriarchal times, as when Abraham married his half-sister Sarah; see Gen. 20:12.)

As for divorce and remarriage, they are treated in Deut. 24:1–4. On grounds of what in Hebrew is called *ervah*, rendered variously 'impropriety' or 'impurity,' the husband may simply repudiate his wife. The precise nature of this ground for divorce, if it had a precise nature in biblical times, is not known. It could have been a physical defect or illness rendering the wife repulsive to the husband. In Jer. 3:8, adultery is cited, but later, in rabbinical interpretation, it is given broader meaning.

The writ of divorce perdured, for it continues to be mentioned in the Old Testament, as in Isaiah[75] in the eighth century BC and Jeremiah[76] a century later, up to the New Testament. Jesus Christ confronted the Pharisees on this question, declaring that Moses had allowed men to divorce only because they were hard-hearted.[77] Divorce, strictly so-called, is not known in the patriarchal period: the only instance we find in Holy Writ amounts to a repudiation of a concubine in favor of a wife.[78]

[74] See the talmudic tractate *Ketubbot*. The marriage contract, or *ketubah*, has proven to be a rich source of documentation on Jewish life from at least medieval times. Because it is written for a solemn occasion, and must be signed by two witnesses, this document is taken as an accurate account of the information it offers, which includes chronology, geography, the locations of Jewish communities, genealogy, Hebrew calligraphy, numismatics, Jewish art, the economic situation of Jews, and even the history of costumes and household furnishings.

[75] Isa. 50:1.

[76] Jer. 3:8.

[77] Matt. 19:3–9.

[78] Gen. 16:1–16; 21:9–21.

The Law of Moses gives the wife no right to repudiate her husband. Josephus calls Salome's repudiation of her husband contrary to Jewish law,[79] yet, perhaps because of his own marital situation (he dismissed his wife, the mother of three children, because her manner grew displeasing to him), would allow a man to divorce his wife for any reason whatsoever.[80] However, by the time of Jesus Christ, the renowned teacher Shammai had demanded that the only ground for divorce be adultery.[81] This position was taken in the next generation by Gamaliel, who at the same time yielded to the wife a right to divorce her husband.[82]

Yet the history of ancient Israel displays fierce family loyalties, reflected most powerfully in revenge against anyone who has wronged a member of the family. The 'avenger of blood,' or *goel*, was a fixture of Jewish family life. Ordinarily he was the closest relative of the victim.[83] But the *goel* had obligations beyond revenge: a close relative was also obliged to come to the aid of family members in distress, such as one who had sold his property or even himself to relieve poverty.[84] The *goel* also had other duties toward his charges, specified by written tradition.[85]

The story of Ruth exemplifies the role of the *goel*, in this case the cousin of her late father-in-law. The young widow asks him to exercise his right of redemption over her and marry her, in order to provide issue for her late father-in-law. The elderly *goel* carries out her wish, thereby becoming an ancestor of David and, through him, of Jesus Christ.

When the Israelites were at last able to abandon their wanderings and settle in Canaan, they confronted a new problem of how to portion out the land; they met it by means

[79] *Antiquities* XV. 7. 10.

[80] Ibid., IV. 8. 23.

[81] *Jerusalem Sotah*, 16. 2, cited in *Dictionnaire de la Bible*, s.v. 'Divorce.'

[82] *Ketubbot*, 77a, also cited in *Dictionnaire de la Bible*, s.v. 'Divorce.'

[83] See Gen. 4:15, Deut. 19:12.

[84] Lev. 25:47–9, for slavery, and 25:25 for property.

[85] The Talmud, according to Louis-Germain Lévy (*La Famille dans l'antiquité Israélite* [Paris: Felix Alcan, 1905], p. 106), holds that among Israelites only the proselyte has no *goel*. He cites *Baba qama*, 109a.

of the family and the larger societies stemming from the familial institution, namely the clan and the tribe.[86] The family took part in the allotment of land.[87] This allotment was carried out 'in the assembly of Yahweh.'[88] Thus the Israelite family, and through it the Israelite nation, found an annealing force in the synergism of land and religion.

Yahweh however remained lord of the land. 'Land must not be sold in perpetuity,' he decrees, 'for the land belongs to me, and to me you are only strangers and guests.'[89] He proceeds to link the continuity of family proprietorship to his own possession of the land: 'You will allow a right of redemption on all your landed property. If your brother falls on evil days and has to sell his patrimony, his nearest relation [*goel*] shall come to him and exercise his right of redemption on what his brother has sold.'[90]

Violations of the law of land ownership, and unjust dispossession of family lands, provoked the fierce denunciations of the prophets, from Isaiah and Amos and Micah in the eighth century BC to Jeremiah and Nehemiah in the sixth.

But the land was not to remain in the possession of Israel. That source of family cohesion was to be taken from the Jews. What remained to them was religion, and nothing has strengthened the Jewish family more, or made the family a more powerful force for the preservation of Israel, than its role as a matrix of worship and of education in religion.

The Passover ceremony is undoubtedly the archetype of Jewish family worship. It is the first family ceremony we know of to be commanded by Yahweh, and remains the central religious ceremony of Jewish family life. It brings out very clearly the family's role as a center of worship, and the father's role as leader of familial worship. Nothing can strengthen the father's role in the family more than his authority as leader of

[86] See Num. 33:53–4, and 36:2–9. Cf. Josh. 13–21.
[87] See Jer. 37:12.
[88] Mic. 2:7.
[89] Lev. 25:23.
[90] Lev. 25:24–5.

common worship, teacher of God's law, and model of upright behavior.

(From Holy Writ one can easily construct a syllabus of the education a devout Jewish father would give his children. Such a syllabus, to be sure too detailed and burdensome for home education, has been the work of centuries and comes to us under the name *Talmud*.[91])

At the moment of Yahweh's self-revelation as He Who Is, he tells Moses that he is to describe him to the Hebrews as 'the God of your fathers.'[92]

In pre-exilic Israel, the period we know best, the father may have fulfilled the functions of a priest.[93]

The pre-eminent role of the father in Israelite law, Israelite religion, and the Israelite psyche is seen in death as well as in life. To die is to rejoin one's fathers.[94]

According to the Talmud, every man has an obligation to leave a posterity.[95] No better blessing could be given than numerous posterity: 'You will be more blessed than all peoples. No man or woman among you shall be barren, no male or female of your beasts infertile.'[96]

So central to the Israelite psyche was progeny, so tragic was death without issue, that a surviving elder brother was required to marry the widow of a childless brother.[97] The child of such a levirate marriage was called after his fictive father, not his biological father.[98]

[91] For a description of how such instruction is given in modern times, see Norman Linzer, *The Jewish Family* (New York: Human Sciences Press, 1984), pp. 120–30.

[92] Exod. 3:16.

[93] See Job 1:5.

[94] Cf. Gen. 15:15. To die is also to go to one's kinsmen, as in Gen. 25:8, 17.

[95] See *Yebamoth* 65a. Louis-Germain Lévy observes: 'Biblical vocabulary has no term for bachelor; in talmudic Hebrew the word *panouy* is used' (*La Famille dans l'Antiquité Israélite*, p. 174).

[96] Deut. 7:14. It is worth noting, for purposes of our study, that this highest of blessings follows on obedience to the Ten Commandments.

[97] Deut. 25:7–10.

[98] See Ruth 4:10. The child need not take his putative father's name except in the patronymic.

Running through the Hebrew Scriptures is a strong current of reverence for life, a reverence tied irrevocably by revelation to the worship of Yahweh and obedience to his Law. The parting words of Moses to the people of Israel sum it up:

> I call heaven and earth to witness against you today: I set before you life or death, blessing or curse. Choose life, then, so that you and your descendants may live, in the love of Yahweh your God, obeying his voice, clinging to him; for in this your life consists, and on this depends your long stay in the land which Yahweh swore to your fathers Abraham, Isaac and Jacob he would give them.[99]

The blessings cited by Moses demonstrate the value the Hebrews placed on life and increase and nourishment:

> Blessed will be the fruit of your body, the produce of your soil, the issue of your livestock, the increase of your cattle, the young of your flock. Blessed will be your pannier and your bread bin.[100]

Set aside by the Hebrews as most suitable for the worship of Yahweh – the sacred, recall, was originally the 'set aside' – were symbols of life at its strongest. The firstborn of men and animals belonged to the Lord, as did the firstfruits.[101] Also deemed worthy of sacrifice to the Lord were the most basic nourishments of life, such as oil and flour.[102] On the other hand, everything savoring of death and corruption was banished from the altar.[103]

The rigor of the Hebrew laws governing marriage and the relations between the sexes stems from that same reverence for life, and serves, as we have seen, to guarantee numerous offspring and their safeguarding and education. But in ancient Israel, to preserve the family was to preserve the political

[99] Deut. 30:19–20.

[100] Deut. 28:4–5.

[101] Examples are abundant, among them Exod. 13:12, and *passim* in Exodus, Numbers, and Deuteronomy; also Ezek. 44:30.

[102] Gen. 28:18 and 35:14

[103] Lev. 11:11 and *passim*; Deut. 14:21.

structure, founded as it was on the family and rising from the family to the clan to the tribe. When the kingship finally arrived it, too, became a family matter. Family permeated the political structure of Israel from top to bottom.

What was life in an Israelite family? Despite a theory that matriarchy prevailed among the Hebrews, it is clear from the Hebrew Scriptures that patriarchy obtained from the earliest ages and remained at least the ideal.[104] At the very beginning, Yahweh tells the woman that her husband will rule her.[105] The birth of a male child is preferred, and only the firstborn male is consecrated to Yahweh.[106] Although man and woman are both created in God's own image, and hence are of equal intrinsic dignity, the notion of a woman's social and economic inferiority runs throughout the Old Testament.[107]

[104] Among the arguments cited to support the theory of matriarchy among the Hebrews are:

- the care employed in the Hebrew Scriptures (Gen. 44:20; Judg. 8:19) to specify the maternal line;
- the recurrence of the expression 'my mother's house' in the Scriptures (Gen. 24:28; S. of S. 3:4);
- the fact that women had their own tents (Gen. 31–3; Judg. 4–17);
- the etymology of the Hebrew word for clan or people (*oummah*), which comes from the word for mother (*em*).

On that level of argumentation, possibly the most conclusive counter-argument is that the word for family itself, *beth ab,* means house of the father. Moreover the word for the father's brother, *amm,* was used to speak not only of paternal parenthood but parenthood in general. 'The relative par excellence,' remarks M. J. Lagrange, 'is the paternal uncle, the father's brother, whose name crops up so often in Arab proper names. It's the same word that in Hebrew designates the people, the tribe, folk [*les gens*] of the same race' (*Etudes sur les religions sémitiques* [Paris: Lecoffre, 1903], p. 114, cited by Lévy, *La Famille dans l'Antiquité Israélite,* p. 131).

But the most persuasive and, in the long run, conclusive argument is the spirit of patriarchy that coruscates from the Hebrew Scriptures. Woven throughout Holy Writ, warp and woof, is the authority of the father.

[105] Gen. 3:16.

[106] For the preference for a male child, see Gen. 35:17; for the consecration of the male child to Yahweh, see I Sam. 1:11.

[107] 'God created man in the image of himself, in the image of God he created him, male and female he created them,' says Gen. 1:27. But in economic terms Leviticus values a woman at 60 percent of the money value of a man (27:3 and 4).

Woman was created as 'a helpmate' for man.[108] She is the source and fountain of life, to be cherished by her husband, while the adulteress is to be shunned:

Drink the water from your own cistern,
fresh water from your own well.
Do not let your fountains flow to waste elsewhere,
nor your streams in the public streets.[109]

Warnings against an evil woman's wiles are plentiful enough in Holy Writ, but the father in Proverbs warns his son that the blame will be his own:

Correction and discipline are the way to life,
preserving you from the woman subject to a husband,
from the smooth tongue of the woman who is a stranger.
Do not covet her beauty in your heart,
or let her captivate you with the play of her eyes;
A harlot can be bought for a hunk of bread,
but the adulteress is aiming to catch a precious life.
Can a man hug fire to his breast
without setting his clothes alight?
So is the man who consorts with his neighbor's wife:
no one who touches her will go unpunished.[110]

A worthy wife, if a man is lucky enough to find her (say, the good wife of the alphabetic poem in Proverbs), is to be valued beyond pearls.

Her husband's heart has confidence in her,
from her he will derive no little profit.
Advantage and not hurt she brings him
all the days of her life.
She is always busy with wool and with flax,
she does her work with eager hands.
She is like a merchant vessel
bringing her food from far away.
She gets up while it is still dark,
giving her household their food,
giving orders to her serving girls.[111]

[108] The term stems from a misunderstanding of a so-called ghost word, Helpmeet, deriving from the early 'an help meet for him' (Gen. 2:18).

[109] Prov. 5:15–16.

[110] Prov. 6:23–9.

[111] Prov. 31:10–15.

The verses that follow make it clear that the women of Israel took their own initiative in business affairs, and stood far above servile status:

> She sets her mind on a field, then she buys it;
> with what her hands have earned she plants a vineyard....
> She finds her labor well worth while;
> her lamp does not go out at night.[112]

Because of her practical business sense she has little need to worry about the future, but 'can laugh at the days to come.'[113]

Although her hard work and practical sense mean that her charges – husband and children, and perhaps elderly parents, servants, and slaves – are clothed against the elements,[114] and though she 'keeps good watch on the conduct of her household,'[115] she is not engrossed in her own circle. Rather she 'holds out her hand to the poor, and opens her arms to the needy.'[116]

Her kindliness and good counsel are the crowning touch: 'When she opens her mouth, she does so wisely; on her tongue is kindly instruction.'[117] Little wonder that in Holy Writ, wisdom is a woman!

Although the wife's subjection to the husband is ordained by Yahweh as punishment for the first sin, such a wife, through her loving industry and kindly wisdom, restores the original order, when God made her to be man's helpmate.[118] Such a wife, joined to a husband who sets a price on her beyond pearls, makes of marriage what the Church's preparation for marriage used to call it, an antechamber of heaven.

In the following chapter, which opens Part II, we shall examine how, at one critical juncture, the demands of chastity that preserved the family also preserved Israel herself. We shall

112 Prov. 31:16, 18.
113 Prov. 31:25.
114 Prov. 31:21.
115 Prov. 31:27.
116 Prov. 31:20.
117 Prov. 31:26.
118 Gen. 3:16 and 2:18, respectively.

see how the attachment of the Jews to chaste marriage prevented the absorption of Israel into the very culture that eventually joined forces with the Church to help create Western civilization. We shall see the role, in that same preservation of Israel, played by the worship of the one God. It is our contention that without Israel's resistance to this alien culture, without her attachment to the family and to the chastity that preserves the family, not only could she not have survived, but the West could not have been born.

PART II

THE STRUCTURE

Chapter 3

ISRAEL: CHASTITY IN DEFENSE OF THE NATION

Of the uniqueness of Israel there can be little doubt. Secular history sees it in that nation's survival, a phenomenon paralleled perhaps but never equalled either in duration or in obstacles overcome.[1] Millennia of dispersal, and before that centuries of schism, exile, and political subjugation, have shown themselves powerless to dissolve Israel. She has survived repeated persecution, subtle or brutal, and even a titanic effort at extirpation by a totalitarian state. In entire regions, such as western Europe, assimilation has diminished her numbers and, to be sure, her fervor, but a critical remnant has perdured and flourished.

The secret of that survival was Israel's Covenant with God, as we have just seen. Now we shall see how it was put to the test in the only attempt known to recorded history against Israel's faith in God.[2]

[1] Arnold Toynbee, to the present writer's knowledge, is the only recent historian to challenge this established reading. He pairs the survival of Jewry with the survival of the Parsees, a community of Persian origin in India. But the Parsees are a close-knit community centered in one country, whereas the Jews have been scattered to the four corners of the earth.

Toynbee however did recognize that the Hellenistic assault, which the Jews survived, constituted a violent disruption: 'The Jews and Parsees are manifestly fossils of the Syriac Society ... before its normal development was suddenly and violently interrupted by the intrusion of the Hellenic Society in the wake of Alexander the Great' (*A Study of History*, 2nd edn. [London: Oxford University Press, 1935], vol. 1, pp. 90–1).

[2] Cf. Elias Bickerman: 'the first and only attempt made in all of history to destroy the Jewish faith in the One and Eternal God' (*The God of the Maccabees* [Leiden: E. J. Brill, 1979], p. 9).

It came in the second century BC in the guise of the utmost the world had to offer of beauty and grace, of learning and wisdom. It threatened to sweep away not only the Covenant but with it the two essential institutions that the Covenant safeguarded: the family, protected by the Commandment prohibiting marital infidelity, and true worship, protected by the Commandment prohibiting polytheism.

This two-pronged attack was led by a successor of Alexander the Great. He was the so-called Seleucid king in Antioch, who ruled an empire running from Asia Minor to the marches of India. His weapon was Greek culture, and the hostility that many Jews felt for it is seen in the pejorative use of 'Hellenism' in this sacred history, where moreover the term is found for the first time in all of known history.

Greek culture is so integral to what we now call the West that at first glance the hostility of pious Jews to Hellenization may seem purblind and bigoted. Greek civilization was the glory of antiquity, illuminating for the world the worth of friendship, of piety, of bodily health, sound medicine, and philosophy. But within the wisdom of Greece was belief in the abeternity of the world, and disbelief in a creator. Within the Greek dedication to health was near-worship of the body and its pleasures. Within Greek piety was the worship of many gods, while within Greek friendship there often lurked passions outlawed not only in Israel but in Greece itself. We shall show how the Jews resisted these, especially Greek sensuality and Greek polytheism.

Resistance was led by a family of pious Jews eventually known as the Maccabees, and from them takes the name history has given it: the Maccabean Revolt.

Had the Maccabean rebels failed, the Covenant would have failed. Had the Maccabees failed, and the Covenant with them, our world would have been so different that we can scarcely speculate on its character. The historic achievement of their revolt was not political independence, which proved ephemeral, but rather the preservation of Judaism through the rejection of Greek polytheism and sexual license.

If Greek hedonism and Greek gods had succeeded in seducing Israel, our civilization would have been no less different than had Carthage, with its ritual child sacrifice, sunk Rome twenty-two centuries ago, or had the Albigenses, with their principled hatred of marriage and procreation, indeed of all material creation, swamped the Catholics eight centuries ago. The Maccabees kept Judaism in being, thus enabling the West to be born.

Hellenization and Homosexuality

The role of homosexuality in provoking the Maccabean Revolt is unexplored territory, left virtually untouched even by specialists. This is a curious oversight since the Hellenization of Israel was launched by erecting a gymnasium, and the homosexual taint of the Greek gymnasium is a commonplace of history.[3]

The gymnasium of the Hellenizing Jews in Jerusalem looms over the Maccabean drama much as the high citadel of the Antioch-based Greeks loomed over the city itself. But the citadel represented merely a foreign military presence, the kind of thing the Jews had tolerated for almost four centuries from the return of Babylonian exiles in 538 BC,[4] whereas the gymnasium represented the cultural invasion that within a decade roused the Maccabees to rebellion. Why historians have failed to raise obvious questions about homosexuality in the Jerusalem gymnasium remains a mystery, although we shall attempt an answer in this chapter.

[3] There is no mention of this in the New Testament, which of course comes down to us in Greek and was written, chiefly, for an audience conversant with Hellenic culture. In fact the word *gymnasion* is not found there.

On the other hand St Paul uses the verb from which *gymnasion* is taken. '*Gumnaze de seauton pros eusebeian*,' that is, 'Train yourself spiritually,' he urges his disciple Timothy (I Tim. 4:7).

The *Reallexikon für Antike und Christentum* offers two chief reasons why the gymnasium 'must have seemed abominable to many Christians': its association with the cult of gods and heroes, and the pederasty found in it (vol. 13, Stuttgart: Anton Hieresmann, 1986, s.v. 'Gymnasium').

[4] See W. O. E. Oesterly, *A History of Israel* (Oxford: Clarendon Press, 1948), p. vii.

Neglect of the revolt itself is even more of a mystery. Secularizing historians might be constitutionally incapable of penetrating its significance, but scholars who happen to be believing Christians or Jews? Ironically it was Arnold Toynbee, a historian unburdened by belief or indeed by any conscious partiality toward Western civilization, who came near the nerve.[5] He observed that the Jews had withstood a sudden and violent invasion of Hellenism 'in the wake of Alexander the Great.'[6] However, for that achievement, and their consequent survival, Toynbee repeatedly relegated the Jews to the category of 'fossils.' The truth of course is quite otherwise: the Jewish society that repulsed Greek culture through the Maccabean Revolt was the very earth from which Western civilization grew.[7]

How titanic a feat was the Jewish repulse of Hellenism can be gauged by the power of the adversary, by the almost universal victory that that adversary achieved.[8] Although Alexander the Great led his armies eastward, the Greek culture he set on the march conquered Rome, mistress of

[5] For a critical account of Toynbee's conceptions about Western culture, see Douglas Jerrold, *The Lie about the West* (New York: Sheed & Ward, 1954).

[6] *A Study of History* (London: Oxford University Press, 1935), vol. 1, p. 91.

[7] Toynbee dealt with Western civilization from a detached vantage point. Enjoying as he did immense prestige in the middle third of the twentieth century, he may be responsible for much of the current scepticism about our Judaeo-Christian culture. He summarized his criticisms in broadcasts sponsored by the British Broadcasting Corporation, the Reith Lectures, published as *The World and the West* (New York: Oxford University Press, 1953).

[8] Five centuries after this first attempt of Hellenism to subvert true faith in God, the Hellenist culture of the Roman Empire made its last attempt at such subversion. This attempt – extremely powerful, tenacious, and almost successful – was the Arian heresy. Arianism adduced the most subtle and plausible philosophy of antiquity, the neo-Platonism of Alexandria, as a solution to three aporia of Christian theology: first, to reconcile the creation of the world – more specifically the act by which God created the world – with the immutability of God; second, to reconcile the humanity of Christ with his divinity; and finally to reconcile the unity of the divine nature with the plurality of divine persons. Of course in all three cases there was less a reconciliation of the terms than an abolition of one of them: the plurality of persons was simply wiped out, the divinity of Christ was denied, and the creation of the world by God was replaced by the production of the Logos-demiurge, who in turn created the world.

the West, and through her her vast empire and eventually the barbarian nations that then teemed beyond its borders. Greek philosophy, rhetoric, and art constituted the most powerful cultural force known in the West until the arrival of Christianity, unless we except Roman administration and law, which acted as a carrier for Hellenic culture and eventually for Christian teaching.

It was not the cultural glories of Greece that the Maccabees detested, so the term 'Hellenism,' though used in one of the sacred histories, has tended to obscure our understanding of the Maccabean Revolt. Rather, these faithful Jews detested Greek hedonism and Greek polytheism, the two chief weapons wielded by Israel's Greek masters in their *kulturkampf* against her. Through syncretic polytheism, which pretended to honor Yahweh by dragging him into the pantheon, the Greeks and their Jewish allies attacked Israel at the summit, worship of the one true God; through homosexual hedonism they attacked Israel at the base, the family.

A thousand years of history had readied the Jews for this double assault. We might even think they had a sense of *déjà vu*. Century after century, their prophets had fought to defend family life against the sexual abandon and child sacrifice of the Canaanites, and to uphold worship of the one God against Canaanite polytheism, linked ritually as it was to prostitution. In those struggles, the prophets had openly confronted kings, and had demanded national repentance. This time however a foreign tyrant employed the tremendous machinery of state in a programmatic effort to impose such worship and such mores by force.

Collaborators and Resistance

In this effort he had the connivance of the Jewish high priest, hence ethnarch of the Jews, who actually took the initiative in bringing a Greek gymnasium to Jerusalem. The leaders of the resistance, too, were men of the priestly class. When they resorted to arms they drew their support and their soldiery chiefly from peasants and ordinary townspeople.

Resistance first arose in Jerusalem itself. We are told of savage repressions: beginning in 167 BC the Greek forces butchered 'an immense number' of Jerusalemites, sold thousands into slavery, tore down Jerusalem's encircling walls, and garrisoned a citadel with the king's men, called Antiochians after the seat of the Greek king at Antioch.[9]

Shortly after this Judas Maccabeus, the immensely able leader who was to give his nickname – whatever it meant – to his family, his followers, and the revolt itself, 'withdrew with about nine others into the wilderness, and lived with his companions in the hills like wild animals.' He and his companions did this, the Second Book of Maccabees explains, 'to avoid contracting defilement.'[10]

What defilement, specifically?

The Greek king, Antiochus IV Epiphanes, had embarked on an unprecedented campaign to weld all the nations of his empire into 'a single people,' ordering that everybody renounce 'his own customs.'[11] The pagan nations beneath the king's rule obeyed, 'and many Israelites chose to accept his religion, sacrificing to idols and profaning the sabbath.'[12] The list of profanations proceeds through the sacrifice of pigs and the worship of idols to 'leaving their sons uncircumcised, and prostituting themselves to all kinds of impurity and abomination.'[13]

Thus the first hint at homosexuality: 'prostituting themselves to *all kinds* of impurity and abomination.' A hint only,

[9] It is II Macc. 5:26 that speaks of an 'immense number' of those slaughtered. Josephus puts the number led into captivity at 10,000 (*Antiquities of the Jews*, 12. 5. 4), while II Macc. 5:14 claims 40,000 were sold.

[10] II Macc. 5:27, Jerusalem Bible tr.

[11] I Macc. 1:41 and 42, Jerusalem Bible and Anchor Bible (vol. 41) trs. respectively. Arnoldo Momigliano observes: 'Such direct interference in the ancestral cults of a nation was unheard of in the Greek-speaking world from immemorial times' (*Alien Wisdom* [Cambridge: Cambridge University Press, 1975], p. 100).

Antiochus was anxious to unify his empire against the designs of Rome, against the irredentism of Greek-ruled Egypt, and against the Parthian threat.

[12] I Macc. 1:42–4, Jerusalem Bible tr.

[13] The quotation is from I Macc. 1:48, Jerusalem Bible tr. The other profanations are cited in verses 45–7.

and far from conclusive even when associated with the sexually significant symbol of circumcision, but, when combined with other, more lucid evidence that we shall examine, it becomes part of a cumulative case that the Greek polytheists and their Hellenizing allies tried to woo the Jewish upper classes away from Yahwism through homosexuality.

This characteristic of the Seleucid campaign, employment of a degenerate sexual ethos as a weapon, is shared by several subsequent attacks on Judaeo-Christian civilization.[14] It is a characteristic of modern secularism.

As for the storm that raged around circumcision during the Maccabean Revolt, moderns will be profoundly puzzled by it. Jews took terrible risks for the sake of this symbol. An unspeakable death was reserved for the mother. One sacred author tells us she was hurled from a high place with her child tied around her neck. It is a punishment unrivalled, we might think, for anguish in a woman, and remains the starkest evidence of the Greek king's fierce resolve to extirpate the loyalty of the Jews to the one God.[15] That

[14] Edmund Burke writes to a young Frenchman in 1791: 'The passion called love has so general and powerful an influence, it makes so much of the entertainment, and indeed so much the occupation, of that part of life which decides the character forever, that the mode and the principles on which it engages the sympathy and strikes the imagination become of the utmost importance to the morals and manners of every society. Your rulers were well aware of this; and in their system of changing your manners to accommodate them to their politics, they found nothing so convenient as Rousseau. Through him they teach men to love after the fashion of the philosophers: that is, they teach to men, to Frenchmen, a love without gallantry – a love without anything of that fine flower of youthfulness and gentility which places it, if not among the virtues, among the ornaments of life. Instead of this passion, naturally allied to grace and manners, they infuse into their youth an unfashioned, indelicate, sour, gloomy, ferocious medley of pedantry and lewdness – of metaphysical speculations blended with the coarsest sensuality' ('Letter to a Member of the National Assembly,' from *Selected Writings and Speeches*, ed. Peter J. Stanlis [Chicago: Regnery Gateway, 1963], p. 515).

[15] II Macc. 6:10; cf. I Macc. 1:60–1. Josephus's account speaks of the crucifixion of the parents, with the circumcised sons hanging from their necks (*Antiquities of the Jews*, 12. 5. 4).

Although every translation of II Macc. 6:10 that I am aware of, including the Vulgate, refers to hurling the mother headlong from a height, a cognate of the Greek verb is also used in Scripture to mean crucifixion.

loyalty, along with purity of marriage, was what circumcision symbolized.[16]

To maintain that same loyalty, many Jews defied the king's decree that they abandon another seemingly arbitrary provision of the Law, prohibiting certain meats. 'They chose death in order to escape defilement by foods and in order to keep from violating the Holy Covenant.'[17] This too will puzzle our contemporaries.

Accounts of the martyrdoms of the 90-year-old Eleazar and of a mother and her seven sons are given us.[18] St Eleazar, as he is called in the Catholic calendar, spat out the pork that had been forced into his mouth, rejected a kindly meant suggestion to pretend to eat the forbidden meat, and was bludgeoned to death. The mother and sons, nameless in the scriptural account, are joined with St Eleazar by the liturgy under the single title 'the Holy Maccabees.' The sons, one by one, while the others watched and exhorted them to steadfastness, were whipped, mutilated, and then fried to death. Last to die was the mother. We are told that she and her sons resisted the pleas and threats of King Antiochus himself, present at the daylong ordeal.

Martyrdom and Dogma

With these nine – the only saints of the Old Testament to be commemorated in the liturgy throughout the Catholic Church – the martyr enters history.

Nor is that the only important first offered us by the Maccabean Revolt. In the mother's exhortations to her sons we find two doctrines never before mentioned in Holy Writ: personal immortality, and creation out of nothing.

[16] Rabbinic tradition gives us the legend of Abraham sitting at the door of hell and saving Israelites from entering. However, those who have been sexually immoral (even though circumcised) he causes to descend (see *Talmud Eruvin*, 19A; cf. Midrash Genesis Raba, 48.8, Albeck edn.).

[17] I Macc. 1:63, Goldstein tr.

[18] II Macc. 6:18–31 and 7:1–41 respectively.

Significantly, these dogmas emerged in Scripture precisely when the Hellenizing Jews, led by the high priest himself, were introducing into Jerusalem a Greek-style gymnasium. The centuries-old institution of the gymnasium, Plato tells us in the *Lysis* and the *Euthydemus*, was a center for the teaching of philosophy.[19] Quite possibly the philosophical seductions of the Greek gymnasium were just as dangerous in their own way as its hedonism. Greek philosophy knew nothing of creation or of a Creator, and offered no certainty about personal immortality. Yet Scripture is silent about any link between these two dogmas and any philosophical dangers posed to Israel by the Jerusalem gymnasium.

However, Scripture offers ample if subtle evidence of that other danger from the gymnasium: homosexuality.

There was hardly any need to speak of it. In the ancient world the all-male athletic club known as the gymnasium was notorious as a nesting-ground for pederasty. Socrates himself was susceptible to it, as we learn in the *Charmides*.[20] The lovers of boys came to the gymnasium in crowds, as Plato notes in that dialogue and in the *Euthydemus*.[21] Some notion of the tenacity of pederasty in the gymnasium can be gained from the four-century interval between Plato and Plutarch, who mentions it in the *Erotikos*.[22]

Hence the gymnasium, with its sexual seductions, was bound to arouse alarm when it came to Jerusalem and attracted 'the noblest young men' of Israel.[23] The Greek of

[19] *Lysis*, 205[a–b] and *Euthydemus*, 273[a], respectively.

[20] *Charmides*, 155[c–d].

[21] *Charmides*, 154 and *Euthydemus*, 273[a], respectively.

[22] *Erotikos*, 751[a]. It must not be thought that homosexual behavior was without its opponents in Greece. Plutarch notes that the Athenian lawgiver Solon, two centuries before Plato, had tried to regulate pederasty (*Erotikos*, 751[b]; cf. the same author's *Life of Solon*, 79[a–b]).

Despite the widespread notions that Plato condoned homosexual behavior, or was indifferent to it – notions that derive from his occasional ambiguity on the subject – he does in fact declare against it (as in *the Laws*, 841[d]).

Although Plutarch cites the view that there is 'only one genuine love, the love of boys,' he is clear and forceful in his condemnation of it. Yet he notes in the same passage: 'You will see it in the schools of philosophy, or perhaps in the gymnasia and palestrae' (*Erotikos*, 751[a]).

[23] II Macc. 4:12, New American Bible tr.

II Maccabees – bear in mind here that Greek is the original language of II Maccabees – underlines the reason for alarm with a pun: '*hypotassōn hypo petason*,' which literally means 'subduing [these noble young Jews] under the *petason*,' the broad-brimmed hat of Hermes worn by naked Greek athletes.[24] But in the Church's traditional Latin translation, St Jerome renders this 'in lupanaribus ponere,' that is, 'to put in brothels.' No contemporary commentator known to the present writer has taken this cue from the fourth-century translator.

That the sacred historians themselves say nothing explicit about homosexuality ought not to surprise us. The ancients knew very well that homosexuality was associated with the gymnasium, whose very name comes from the word for naked. Moreover, pious Jews were reluctant to speak of such matters.[25]

Yet the sacred writers were able to get their point across to an audience familiar with Greek customs. The author of II Maccabees, plainly outraged at the newly introduced 'usages contrary to the Law,' may not specify what they are, yet to his otherwise guarded language there is an extremism that indicates the unspeakable. The Hellenizing high priest Jason – ethnarch of this vassal people and a typical Hellenizing name-changer whose given name was Joshua – 'set no bounds to his impiety.'[26] In the gymnasium that he brought to Jerusalem a 'craze for Hellenism and foreign customs'[27] reached the *akme*, the height or utmost.

Given such terms, and given the ancient world's lack of illusions about the gymnasium, contemporary readers would

[24] Jonathan Goldstein renders this: 'making the education of the noblest adolescent boys consist of submission to the broad-brimmed Greek hat' (Anchor Bible, vol. 41A).

[25] Two centuries after the events here studied, there came this counsel from a Jew as jealous of tradition as the author of I Macc.: 'As for lewd conduct or promiscuity or lust of any sort, let them not even be mentioned among you; your holiness forbids this' (St Paul, Eph. 5:3). Yet elsewhere, when need arises, the author of this injunction himself specifies such sins!

[26] II Macc. 3:13, Jerusalem Bible tr.

[27] II Macc. 4:13, New American Bible tr.

be expected to understand what that utmost was, what those Hellenistic customs were, what that boundless impiety might be.

The writer of I Maccabees, on the other hand, depends less on indignation and the language of outrage, yet gets his idea across to the attentive reader. We give a highly literal translation to bring out as fully as possible all that he implies:

> In those days, there departed from Israel sons opposed to the Law, and they persuaded many, saying: 'Let us go and establish a covenant with the Gentiles around us. Since we separated from it [the covenant we had] with them, many evils have found us.' And the proposal grew good in their eyes; and some of the people became desirous of approaching the king, who gave them authority to effect the judgments of the Gentiles. And they built a gymnasium in Jerusalem according to the customs of the Gentiles.[28]

Obviously, the Jewish Hellenizers were fed up with the isolation from the non-Jewish world demanded of Israel by the Mosaic Covenant at Sinai. But they were also restless beneath the Covenant's demand for sexual purity. The phrase 'to effect the judgments of the Gentiles' would include adopting the sexual mores of the Greeks. This emerges more clearly from the phrase 'a gymnasium in Jerusalem *according to the customs of the Gentiles.*'

Reference to the customary sexual mores of the Greek king's world becomes even clearer as the chronicle proceeds:

> They covered over the mark of their circumcision and abandoned the holy Covenant. They joined themselves to the Gentiles and sold themselves to evil.[29]

[28] II Macc. 1:11–13. The word here rendered *judgments* can also mean commandments or righteous deeds, and may be used sarcastically here. The word rendered *customs* is a substantive form of the adjective meaning lawful, hence also *commandments* or *what are deemed lawful.* Again sarcasm may be intended.

[29] I Macc. 1:14–15.

Examination shows that each of these four phrases savors of sexual misconduct:

- . . . *sold themselves to evil.* In the context of the gymnasium, a male-only club, the phrase points to the homosexuality that for centuries had been associated with that institution. The illustrious English Jesuit Thomas Corbishley takes the phrase to mean 'were prostituted.'[30]

  This is quite plausible, considering that the Greek *ponēron,* here used for 'evil,' is used by the Septuagint in the Joseph narrative when the lad 'brought his father evil reports' about his brothers' behavior while they were tending flocks.[31] (In this case not only homosexuality but also bestiality, a not infrequent practice in agricultural societies, is a possibility.)

[30] In *A New Catholic Commentary on Holy Scripture,* ed. R. C. Fuller (London: Nelson, 1969), s.v. '1 and 2 Maccabees,' p. 745. Father Corbishley also notes: 'The practices hinted at in the words . . . remind us of one of the great moral dangers of the new tendencies. The Greeks were notoriously given to unnatural vice.' He is one of the very few modern commentators to cite homosexuality in the context of the Maccabean Revolt.

Allan Bloom is another. In a brilliant chapter on Plato's *Symposium* in his posthumous *Love and Friendship* (New York and London: Simon & Schuster, 1993), he observes: 'Not long after the *Symposium* was written, the contact of Jewish boys with Greeks and Greek practices caused a crisis in Judaism, echoes of which can still be heard' (p. 437).

St Jerome showed himself aware that homosexuality was a provocation of the Maccabean Revolt (see p. 144 above). Whereas no modern commentator seems to have taken Jerome's broad hint, the fifteenth-century polymath Nicholas Oresme did, holding that II Macc. 4:14 is a rebuke to the high priest for introducing the Greek gymnasium and thus exposing Hebrew youths to 'odious' and 'bestial' practices of the Greeks. Oresme is cited to this effect by Ernest L. Fortin in the introduction to his translation of Thomas Aquinas's *Commentary on the Politics of Aristotle* (Washington: Catholic University of America Press, 1997), reprinted in vol. 2 of Fortin's collected essays, *Classical Christianity and the Political Order* (Lanham, Md.: Rowman & Littlefield, 1996); the citations and locus are in n. 58.

[31] The Greek of I Maccabees uses the adjective *ponēron* – wicked or evil – substantively, whereas the same adjective found in the Septuagint version of the Joseph story, when the lad 'brought his father bad reports' about his brothers' behavior while they were tending his flocks (Gen. 37:2), modifies *psogon* (accusative in the text), or blameworthiness, in a passage that could well refer to a kind of sexual misconduct too shameful for Hebrew modesty to specify. I thank Dr Edward Macierowski for this reference.

- . . . *joined themselves to the Gentiles.* In the Greek, this has a strong connotation of sexual union.[32] The verb, *zeugizein*, means 'to yoke in pairs,' a graphic metaphor for such union. It is used that way in a love-passage of second-century BC Alexandria, hence in a Greek roughly contemporary with that used in our text, a text that very possibly, like the Septuagint, was rendered from Hebrew into Greek in that same city.[33] It also has a nuptial connotation, which explains the translation employed in the New English Bible, 'intermarried with Gentiles.'
- . . . *abandoned the holy Covenant.* For a Jew, to abandon the Covenant is to forsake his promise of obedience to God's com-mands, and most particularly, in this context, to those binding him to a moral sexual life. It also means forsaking that Law which forged the Jews into a single people, set aside from all others.
- . . . *covered over the mark of their circumcision.* As the mark of the Covenant with Abraham, circumcision was a symbol of purification and readiness for Jewish marriage.[34] It

[32] Thus Jonathan Goldstein, who holds that the phrase as used in I Maccabees reflects Num. 25:3, and that in both places sexual connotation is probably intended (Anchor Bible, vol. 41, p. 201).

[33] *An Alexandrian Erotic Fragment*, ed. Bernard C. Grenfell (Oxford: Clarendon Press, 1896), p. 2. The writing of I Maccabees has to be placed between the succession of John Hyrcanus in 135 BC, the last event mentioned in the text, and Pompey's violation of the Temple in 63 BC, which outraged the Jews and would have ruled out the favorable treatment given the Romans in the text. For that same reason, it can be doubted that the translation was made after Pompey's sacrilege.

[34] 'This is my Covenant, which you shall keep, between me and you and your descendants after you,' Yahweh told Abraham. 'Every male among you shall be circumcised . . . So shall my Covenant be in your flesh an everlasting Covenant. Any uncircumcised male who is not circumcised in the flesh of his foreskin shall be cut off from his people; he has broken my Covenant' (Gen. 17:10–14).

As purification, circumcision becomes an extended metaphor: circumcision of heart means humility, and docility to Yahweh. See Lev. 26:41, Deut. 10:16, Jer. 4:4; cf. Rom. 2:29.

Hebrew males born during the four decades of wandering in the desert were not circumcised. The sacred historian, in explanation, says laconically that they 'could not be circumcised on the journey' (Josh. 5:7). But upon crossing the Jordan, the whole nation of the Israelites was circumcised at Yahweh's command (Josh. 5:2–8).

Circumcision is probably the most mysterious and ancient of the rites held sacred by the Hebrews. Its antiquity is attested by the instrument of ritual: a stone knife.

symbolically contradicted the licentious atmosphere of the gymnasium, its homosexuality specifically.[35]

Thus this brief quadripartite passage is packed with meaning, and the act of disguising circumcision (through painful surgery known as *epipasmus*[36]) becomes an act of apostasy. It had to be such if Yahweh's words were to be taken seriously, if the solemn undertakings of the Israelites were to have meaning and effect.

This apostasy, and the inducements to it, outraged a people as determined to keep faith as the Jews of this epoch showed themselves to be.

Another gesture of apostasy, highly explicit and linked to homosexuality to boot, was instigated by a high priest we have seen before: Joshua (or Jesus), alias Jason.[37] On the occasion of the five-yearly games held at Tyre in the king's presence, 'the vile Jason sent envoys as representatives of the Antiochians of Jerusalem, to bring there three hundred silver drachmas for the sacrifice to Heracles.'[38]

Heracles – Hercules to the Romans – was a mythological hero who widely received the sacrifice reserved to the gods. The emissaries themselves knew that such sacrifice 'was not right,' as one of the biblical authors tells us.[39]

The crowning touch: among the Greeks, Heracles was a symbol of homosexual love.[40]

All of this was apparently too much even for the emissaries of the Hellenizers; they themselves 'decided that the money

[35] It has been argued that the Jews did not exercise unclothed in the gymnasium. Josephus (*Antiquities of the Jews*, 12. 5. 1) appears to think otherwise. Indeed it is hard to imagine why anyone would undergo such a painful operation if its results were to be concealed.

Circumcision was an object of mockery in Greek art, as in the representation of Egyptian priests.

[36] This operation is described in bk. 50, ch. 2 of a fourth-century medical collection made for the Emperor Julian by the Greek physician Orabasius. See Aline Rousselle, *Porneia: On Desire and the Body in Antiquity*, tr. Felicia Pheasant (New York and Oxford: Basil Blackwell, 1988), p. 17.

[37] For the name-changing, see Josephus, *Antiquities of the Jews*, 12. 5. 1.

[38] II Macc. 4:19, New American Bible tr.

[39] Ibid.

[40] See Plutarch, *Erotikos*, 761[d] and 761[e].

should not be spent on a sacrifice,' and so suggested that it be used to build triremes.[41] It was a suggestion likely to please the warlike king.

By this time the gymnasium had taken its toll on the formal worship of God in his Temple at Jerusalem, as we touched upon earlier:

> The craze for Hellenism and foreign customs reached such a pitch, through the outrageous wickedness of the ungodly pseudo-high-priest Jason, that the priests no longer cared about the service of the altar. Disdaining the temple and neglecting the sacrifices, they hastened, at the signal for the discus-throwing, to take part in the unlawful exercises of the palestra.[42]

The Temple Desecrated

Moreover the Temple itself became the scene of pagan sacrificial meals and sexual orgies. Here again the author of II Maccabees may be hinting at homosexual acts when, after saying the men 'took their pleasure with prostitutes and had intercourse with women in the sacred precincts,' he adds: 'introducing other indecencies besides.'[43]

The Greek king even erected in the Temple an idol – possibly a statue of Zeus – called by a sardonic pun 'the abomination of desolation' in II Maccabees and Daniel (which latter was probably written during the Maccabean troubles to steel the Jews against the king's syncretic polytheism).[44] The idol was a prime example of syncretism, that attempt to combine and reconcile differing beliefs which was so common in the ancient world as to be considered quite normal. But the Maccabees would have none of it.

[41] II Macc. 4:19 and 20; quotation from the Jerusalem Bible tr.

[42] II Macc. 4:13–14. Where the New American Bible, quoted here, speaks of 'unlawful exercises,' Goldstein uses 'illicit entertainment.' It seems doubtful that the Greek phrase leaves room for sexual activity.

[43] II Macc. 6:4, Jerusalem Bible tr.

[44] I Macc. 1:54; Dan. 9:27 and 11:31.

Josephus (*Antiquities of the Jews*, 12.5.4) tells us the blasphemous object stood atop the altar of holocausts.

The sacrilege of enshrining an idol on the altar of sacrifice was accompanied by sexual orgies that further desecrated the Temple. Says one of the sacred chroniclers: 'This intensified the evil in an intolerable and utterly disgusting way.'[45]

Can it be mere coincidence that when the God who gave life to Israel at Sinai was displaced from his sanctuary, the sanctuary was defiled by the same sexual license of which he was the sworn enemy? by that same sexual license which he had warned would be the death of Israel?

But it was not her death, for she rejected it along with Zeus and his turbulent ménage of lesser gods. Her martyrs – the first known to history, let us recall – died horribly rather than give up even the most arbitrary and, some might think, irrational symbols of fidelity to Yahweh. Her sons, known to us as the Maccabees, fought a seemingly hopeless war against an empire, and won. They credited their astonishing victories not to themselves but to the God who rules history, the God they fought to defend, the God they believed fought on their side. It was the Maccabees who preserved Judaism, belief in the one God and belief in the family, and thus enabled the West to be born. Their achievement has long been recognized by the Church in her liturgy, but her historians have been curiously muted in their regard. Perhaps not too mysteriously, the achievement of the Maccabees has gone unsung by the secularist world in the person of its prestigious historians.

Nor need we, on reflection, be surprised that the role of homosexuality in the Maccabean Revolt has gone unrecognized. The reason, to recall, is that until our own day the West had never been confronted by an open challenge from organized homosexuals.[46] The political potential of this vice went unsuspected. In mid-century, who in the West could have believed it?

Now, however, we have been alerted. Now, when we read the sacred histories of the Maccabees, the evidence of homo-

[45] II Macc. 6:3, New American Bible tr.

[46] Homosexual practices were widely imputed to the Albigenses, but as we shall see there is no extant proof of the charge.

sexuality is clear to us, the overtones of homosexuality are distinct.

Scholars, on the other hand, are constitutionally cautious. The thesis herein advanced, namely that homosexual hedonism was a tool of the Hellenizers and a provocation of the Maccabean Revolt, must meet professional scepticism until every objection, not to say all inertia, is overcome.

But in the path of this thesis there stands a bigger hurdle than inertia or professional scepticism. It is ideology, a shrunken philosophy born of a style of life.

Men have always known that homosexuality can only begin by distorting nature. They now realize that it can only end by distorting society. They are beginning to perceive, dimly perhaps, that it can only continue by distorting history. But those monumental figures of a monumental history, the Maccabees, will not bend. They did not bend before the powers of yesterday, and they will not bend before the powers of today. They will stand by their testimony.

Chapter 4

THE ROMAN EMPIRE: CHASTITY IN DEFENSE OF THE BODY POLITIC

At the very first teaching assembly of the Church, now called the Council of Jerusalem, St James as bishop of the place laid down four simple rules for Gentiles who became Christians.[1] To moderns, all these rules will at first glance appear rather

[1] The Acts of the Apostles recounts in ch. 15 that Paul and Barnabas, while at Antioch, disputed with Jewish converts who held that converts from paganism were bound by the Mosaic law of circumcision. They went to Jerusalem to discuss the problem.

> When they arrived in Jerusalem they were welcomed by the church and by the apostles and elders, and gave an account of all that God had done with them.
>
> But certain members of the Pharisaic party who had become believers objected, insisting that the pagans should be circumcised and instructed to keep the law of Moses. The apostles and elders met to look into the matter, and after the discussion had gone on a long time, Peter stood up and addressed them.
>
> 'My brothers,' he said, 'you know perfectly well that in the early days God made his choice among you: the pagans were to learn the Good News from me and so become believers. . . . God made no distinction between them and us, since he purified their hearts by faith. It would only provoke God's anger now, surely if you imposed on the disciples the very burden that neither we nor our ancestors were strong enough to support?' (Acts 15:4–7, 9–10).

After Paul and Barnabas spoke, James gave his decision: 'I rule then that instead of making things more difficult for pagans who turn to God, we send them a letter telling them merely to abstain from anything polluted by idols, from fornication, from the meat of strangled animals, and from blood' (Acts 15:19–20).

These four prohibitions were repeated in an apostolic letter sent to Christians of pagan birth in Antioch, Syria, and Cilicia, with the assurance: 'Avoid these, and you will do what is right' (Acts 15:23–9).

odd; yet all show themselves, on scrutiny, to be entirely reasonable, and cast a stark light both on the times and on how square the Christian faith stood athwart them.

The first rule requires abstention from meats that had been sacrificed to idols.[2] The Church demands this because she abhors false worship, abhors it to the point of demanding that Christians, like the heroes of Maccabean times, refuse it even if refusal means death. The taint she imputes to animals sacrificed to idols symbolizes this abhorrence.

Two other rules demand abstention from the blood of animals, one explicitly, the other implicitly through prohibition of the meats of strangled animals, because they have not been drained of blood. This was carried over from the Mosaic Law, but offered an important lesson to Christians: blood symbolized life,[3] of which God alone is master; human life comes straight from the hand of God, since the infusion of the soul, spiritual and immortal and therefore bearing his image, is his only ordinary direct intervention in the order of creation.[4] Yet human life, like the human person, was held very cheap in the ancient world.

The remaining demand was that the new Christians who had come from paganism abstain from sexual impurity.[5]

[2] Cf. I Cor. 10:14–33. Here St Paul gives the principle and guidelines for its application in social intercourse.

[3] See Lev. 17:11: 'The life of the flesh is in the blood.'

[4] The note to Acts 15:20 in the Jerusalem Bible says: 'The severity with which the Law forbids it . . . explains the Jews' reluctance to dispense pagans from this prohibition.'

On the other hand Johannes Munck, in the Anchor Bible commentary on *Acts* (Garden City, NY: Doubleday, 1967), p. 140, ties the rules on blood-free meals to the common meals shared by Christians of Jewish and pagan background. The two theses seem compatible.

As for the disregard with which human life was treated in Roman society, the killing of gladiators for the pleasure of spectators was deplored by pagan and Christian alike, and in very similar terms. Seneca the Younger says, 'Man, a being sacred to man, is killed even for diversion and play' (*Epistles*, XCV. 33), while St Cyprian writes, 'Man is killed for the pleasure of man' (*Epistles*, I. 7). We shall see something of the disregard – one might even say contempt – for newborn human life later in this chapter.

[5] In the Greek, *porneia*. This is sometimes rendered 'fornication,' but commonly, perhaps universally, interpreted in the broad sense of sexual impurity. Munck, translates it precisely that way: 'sexual impurity' (*Acts*, p. 140). William

Thus according to the early Church in council, the three sins that set pagan morality apart from the Christian morality were sexual impurity, disregard for life, and false worship.[6] Conversely the three virtues that should set Christians aside from their pagan neighbors were worship of the true God, respect for human life, and chastity. It should emerge from our study that these three virtues are linked ineluctably in history to the social, cultural, and political order we call Western civilization.[7]

The first Christians saw chastity, then, as a distinctive Christian virtue, closely bound up with a reverence for life that was rare among pagans and with a worship of the one true God that was the very antithesis of paganism.

The Pagan Ethos

But chastity was not without its champions even within paganism. Thoughtful men, including some who held the powers and responsibilities of state, deplored the profligacy and dissipation of the times as destructive of society. Among these men was Augustus, styled the 'first citizen' of Rome but in fact the creator and all-powerful master of the Roman Empire, still disguised as the Republic. It was within the

---

F. Arndt and F. Wilbur Gingrich's *A Greek-English Lexicon of the New Testament* [Chicago: University of Chicago Press, 1952], s.v. 'porneia') says this word is used 'of every kind of unlawful sexual intercourse.'

The Jerusalem Bible footnote says: 'This word probably refers to all the irregular marriages listed in Leviticus 18.' Beyond irregular marriages, Leviticus 18 also condemns, and most solemnly, adultery, ritual child murder, sodomy, and bestiality.

Cf. Joseph Fitzmyer, 'The Dead Sea Scrolls and the New Testament after Thirty Years,' *Theology Digest*, 29 (1981), pp. 361–4.

[6] Elizabeth Anscombe, describing the prohibition of fornication as a 'peculiarity of Christian life,' comments: 'the prohibition on fornication must have stood out; it must have meant a very serious change of life to many, as it would today' (*Contraception and Chastity* [London: Catholic Truth Society, n.d.], pp. 3 and 4).

[7] To call it instead 'Western culture' has the advantage of drawing attention to the primary role of worship – cult – in the social, political, and aesthetic orders.

Empire that Christian belief struck its deepest and most far-spreading roots. The capital of the Roman Empire was to become the seat of the Church, and the Empire itself the most important vehicle of the Christian faith the world has yet seen.[8]

At the advent of Christianity, Rome, like all societies of the time, had been at a severe disadvantage vis-à-vis Israel. Israel, both the state and the religion, was of divine origin, and had the prophets. True, the history of Israel as traced in the Old Testament is a saga of infidelity, but again and again these men of inspired courage awakened her to her vocation. She was the creation of Yahweh, they cried, his beloved and his bride. She must return to him in penitence and in renewed fidelity.

Classical Rome, for all her pre-eminence and grandeur and might, had no such divine inspiration. Yet she possessed poets of moral indignation who to this day remind us, if we heed them, of the follies and iniquities that dog us from generation to generation; Juvenal and Martial spring to mind. She had Virgil, whose epic account of Rome's foundation coruscates with the conviction that it was led by divine providence.[9] She also, and perhaps above all, had the great historians, the incomparable Tacitus and, not far behind him, Livy. Even in Sallust, a rather distant third, a man reportedly of deplorable morals, there is a touch of the prophet.[10]

[8] Hilaire Belloc's *Europe and the Faith* (New York: Paulist Press, 1921) expounds the celebrated thesis: 'The Faith is Europe and Europe is the Faith' (p. viii).

[9] P. G. Walsh cites no fewer than seven instances in the *Aeneid*: I. 205, 257, 294, 382, and 777; III. 395; and IV. 224, noting that there are others also (*Livy: His Historical Aims and Methods* [Cambridge: Cambridge University Press, 1963], p. 61).

[10] Because Sallust was preoccupied with the bloody political upheavals of his day – with, that is, the dying spasms of the Republic – his survey of history focuses on the merely personal ambitions that had overridden genuine political needs and had plunged Rome into decades of internecine warfare.

Sallust, says Donald Earl, 'applied his concept of *virtus* both to the broad sweep of Roman history from its beginnings to his own times. . . . From this application he was concerned to demonstrate that both the oligarchs and their enemies who attacked their pretensions and aspired to their position had betrayed the ideals they professed. As a political thinker Sallust was incompetent, as an historian variously delinquent. Yet his basic notion, that the failure of the

Livy on the other hand wrote in a fine prophetic vein from beginning to end.[11] The purpose of his monumental *History of Rome from its Foundation*, he tells us, is not only to explain who were the men and what were the means that made Rome powerful but also to draw attention to 'what was the life and what were the morals.' He would also, he continues in his oft-quoted Preface, 'have the reader trace the process of our moral decline, to watch, first, the sinking of the foundations of morality as the old teaching was allowed to lapse, then the rapidly increasing disintegration, then the final collapse of the entire edifice.'[12]

Finally he speaks of 'the dark dawning of our own day,' a day that finds a reflection in our own 'when we can neither endure our vices nor face the remedies needed to cure them.' With the lapse of the old ethos there had disappeared that virtue by which men are strong and honorable, women chaste and valiant.[13] Those who think nostalgia is no longer what it

---

Roman Republic was connected with a failure in the ideal of *virtus*, was not without merit' (*The Moral and Political Tradition of Rome* [Ithaca, NY: Cornell University Press, 1967], p. 55).

[11] Moreover his style was rich, so rich in Quintillian's eyes, as to cast doubt on its substance (see *Institutio oratoria*, X. i. 32).

[12] Thus Aubrey de Selincourt's translation (New York: Penguin Books, 1972), free but justified in that the Latin metaphor is drawn from a decaying building. De Selincourt's rendering of *haec tempora* as 'the dark dawning of our own day,' cited immediately below in the text, has chiefly beauty and drama to recommend it, but it also harmonizes with the tenor and tone of Livy's work.

[13] Plutarch, writing in Greek, notes: 'the Latin word for virtue . . . is properly equivalent to manly courage' (Coriolanus, in *The Lives of the Noble Grecians and Romans*, tr. John Dryden and Arthur Hugh Clough [New York: Modern Library, n.d.], p. 263).

Earl says: 'The word [*virtus*] . . . is not translatable. "Manliness" is perhaps the nearest we can get. Fundamentally, it describes the peculiar nature and quality of the man, *vir*, as *senectus*, old age, describes the quality peculiar to the *senex*, old man, and *iuventus*, youth, that peculiar to the *iuvenis*, young man' (*The Moral and Political Tradition of Rome*, p. 20).

This scholar makes a claim about the Roman concept of virtue that is worth reporting: 'The service of the state required private virtues, but in their public application. To a purely private cultivation of personal virtue the Roman tradition was always hostile. The tradition prescribed the service of the state as the only fit field of activity. The proper service of the state demanded private goodness, but such goodness without public achievement was of no account' (ibid., p. 23).

used to be can bring forward Livy's lament in evidence: 'Where today will you find in a single person that modesty and fairness, that nobility of mind which in those days belonged to a whole people?'[14] As for chastity itself, his appreciation of it has never been lost on his readers.[15]

Tacitus maintained that to find such chaste manners the Romans now had to look abroad, and he held up the barbarians of Germany for their solid family life and their severity toward marital infidelity.

Among the poets the sensualist Horace, though practically a propagandist for gathering rosebuds while you may, hankered after the virtues of antiquity and preached piety toward the gods.[16] Virgil, like Horace a bachelor but

---

This of course is an extreme claim. But it does point out the importance that Romans saw in the public function of private virtue. I have not encountered any objection to the Roman laws dealing with sexual morality on the ground that that morality had no effect on society and the state.

[14] *History of Rome from its Foundation*, IV. 6. 12.

[15] For example, Walsh notes: 'Livy's lessons on the important role of chastity (*pudicitia*) in the well-ordered state, in the cases of Verginia and Lucretia, had been pondered by his readers as early as 25 B.C.' (*Livy*, p. 13). Walsh here is making a point which is important if we are to understand that Livy wrote of chastity out of conviction, not under pressure from the emperor. He recalls that Augustus had become curator of laws and morals no earlier than 19 BC, and that his legislation discouraging adultery and encouraging stable family life and childbearing came even later.

Livy in fact goes much farther than Augustus in making of marital chastity not merely fidelity to the spouse of the moment, but, more specifically, fidelity to a single spouse. He thus anticipates the Christian standard, unique in practice in the ancient world, of indissoluble marriage.

Here is the passage in which he deals with the patrician matron Verginia's gesture, made celebrated by him: 'she shut off part of her great house, large enough for a shrine of moderate size, set up an altar in it, and then summoned the married plebeian women. After complaining about the insulting behavior of the patrician ladies [who had prevented her from participating in ceremonies at the shrine of Patrician Chastity on the ground that she had married a plebeian], she said, 'I dedicate this altar to Plebeian Chastity, and urge you to ensure that it will be said that it is tended more reverently than that other one, if that is possible, and by women of purer life. Thus, just as the men in our State are rivals in valor, our matrons may compete with one another in chastity.' This altar was then tended with almost the same ritual as the older one, so that no one but a matron of proven chaste conduct, *married to one man alone*, had the right to offer sacrifices' (*History of Rome from its Foundation*, X. 23; emphasis supplied. Translated by Betty Radice [New York: Penguin Books, 1982]).

[16] See, inter alia, *Ode* III. 6.

so sensitive in feeling that he was nicknamed 'the maiden' (*virgo*, a word that alliterated neatly with his name), offered his fellow citizens a poetic picture of ancient morality that can scarcely be excelled for charm and persuasion.[17]

Some of Virgil's didactic poetry was undertaken at the behest of the emperor Augustus, and that is an index of the alarm felt by Roman authorities who took their duties seriously. Those who had the job of thinking about what was called 'the public thing' believed that Rome had grown strong through her virtue (a simple idea, and easy for the Roman to grasp since *virtus* in the language of Rome also meant manly strength), that she had become weak because she was no longer virtuous, and that she would diminish and disappear

[17] Donald Earl sums up the situation:

> For what Augustus's restored Republic meant to contemporaries we have the impressive testimony of the poets Virgil and Horace. At one level Virgil's *Aeneid* expounds the ideal of the new order which had replaced the self-seeking chaos that had gone before. The nobles of the Late Republic by pursuing glory at the expense of the state had destroyed the *respublica*. All that they had meant by glory Virgil showed to be false and disruptive. True glory attended the foundation of a secure society, based not on war but on the rule of law and extending its civilizing influence over the whole world. . . . Aeneas's great quality, emphasized and invoked at every turn of the poem, is *pietas*. It meant nothing else than doing his duty to his gods, his country and his family. . . .
>
> Horace agreed with Virgil that there was no room in the new order for the pursuit of that glory which had ruined the Republic. [Earl might have added that these two and Sallust were agreed on this point.] In the *Carmen Saeculare* he listed the key-notes of the new dispensation: 'Faith and Peace and Honor and ancient Modesty and neglected Virtue dare to return. . . .'
>
> Again and again Horace insisted that it was Augustus alone who prevented the return of chaos. The cynical may dismiss it as propaganda. But Virgil and Horace were not hypocrites – and they were right. . . . The propaganda of Augustus succeeded precisely because, unlike the polemic of the factional strife of the last age of the Republic, it was founded ultimately on real issues (*The Age of Augustus* [London: Elek Books Ltd, 1968], pp. 67 and 68).

On p. 196 Earl again defends the sincerity of Horace, citing the theme frequent in this poet that Augustus had restored order and observing that Horace 'knew from harsh experience how narrow had been the escape from chaos.'

unless she somehow found again that elixir of her pristine vigor.

That of course is what chiefly concerns us in this study, but we would be remiss should we fail to point out a twin concern of Rome's magistrates, one that offers a striking parallel to the mission of Moses. The Rome of history harked back to the Rome of pre-history not only in hopes of restoring the integrity of her citizenry but in hopes of establishing the legitimacy of her authority. This was especially true of the new imperial government, come to power as the victor of civil wars that left much of Italy depopulated, and much of the populace outraged at the ambition that had brought death and destruction on a national scale. Could the fortunes of war confer anything more than power?

Thus it was only natural and of no mean significance that an immense empire, so much of whose economic capital was loot, of whose labor was slavery, of whose land was steeped in the blood of its despoiled tenants, of whose system of income distribution was an unstable equilibrium of taxation, graft, usury, and handouts, of whose political arena had become first a jousting field for personal ambition and then a bloody battlefield, of whose statesmanship was an unsavory admixture of hauteur and hubris, of whose soldiery was a deracinated rabble, of whose familial life, our particular concern, stood awash in a tide of public indecency and private dissolution – it was only natural and of no mean significance that this empire should perpetually hark back to the stern wisdom of her beginnings. Imperial Rome's obsessive scanning of the mists of her distant past, her tireless search for purity of origins, was an attempt to find justification for the authority of her regime and of her empire, as well as an impelling model for the reform of her society.

Rome could scarcely find legitimization for her authority in the props of power: the gold that bribed, the bread and games that drugged, the legions that put nations under the yoke and emperors on the throne. These, rather, were arguments *against* the legitimacy she pretended to and aspired to, and it was to mask their role in maintaining her power, to put on a show of continuity with the Rome of origins, that the Empire preserved republican forms. Throughout the centuries when virtually absolute power was wielded by the emperor and his henchmen, republican forms such as the Senate and the consulate, though a charade, constituted a powerful symbol of continuity, hence of legitimate authority.[18]

From our vantage point we might well conclude that any radical attempt at reform was no less destined to fail than was a search for a divine foundation. The moral resources available to the early Empire, as to the later Republic, were too weak to wrestle with Rome's basic institutions, so crazily askew: especially her slavery-based, usury-ridden economy, and the latifundism that had grown from usury and had uprooted the smallholding class, degrading it into a purposeless, unproductive proletariat. Such distorted and distorting forces in the larger society, paradoxically, both emasculated and defeminized the family, bringing it to what must have seemed, as it did to Livy, a point of no return.

Only a novel and powerful spiritual dynamic could, as it in the event did, lift up the institutions of society, not least the family, and with them erect a transcendentally better order, both public and private: the order found in the village-based society of yeomen and tradesmen that eventually emerged from the villa, and from the slavery that supported the villa. This unique achievement, the abolition, wrought by the Christian ethos, of the universal institution of slavery, was at its briefest to be the labor of half a millennium. We know the

[18] It is no accident that the deepest investigation of the nature of authority and of law itself to be carried out by any Roman is found in this very period of the death of the Republic and the birth of the Empire. Cicero's philosophy of law stands to this day. He sought and, we do well to believe, found a rational justification for political authority and for law. His concept of law stands: 'right reason applied to command and prohibition' (*Laws*, I. xii), expanded in a classic passage in his *Republic*: 'True law is right reason in accord with nature, saturating all, immovable, imperishable, which calls to duty by its commands, and deters from fraud by its prohibitions' (III. xxii). He sought and, we do well to believe, found a rational justification for political authority, even if his justification of the authority of the Roman regime is less than rational; see, e.g., the *Republic*, II. v: 'How then could Romulus have acted with a wisdom more divine?'

fact and can deduce the reason, though the historical record is all but non-existent during the critical centuries from the sixth to the ninth.[19]

[19] For a sweeping and contentious survey of the original servile foundation of Western society, and how the institution of slavery was dissolved in the West, see Hilaire Belloc's *The Servile State* (London and Edinburgh: T. N. Foulis, 1913; reissued in Indianapolis by Liberty Classics, 1977), sect. 2 and 3. Other factors in the decline of servitude are thought to be economic and political, including the creation of free cities by Holy Roman emperors in their struggle against feudal lords, and the decline of the rentability of servitude. But these factors, especially the latter, are more speculative than the religious. The present writer has examined reasons for the disappearance of slavery in an essay, 'Discriminating Multiculturalism,' published in *Christ and Culture in Dialogue*, ed. Angus J. L. Menuge (St Louis: Concordia Academic Press, 1999).

For a survey of more recent literature on this subject, see Pierre Maraval, CSSR, 'L'Eglise du IVème siècle et l'esclavage,' *Studia Moralia*, 8 (1970), pp. 319–46. Father Maraval is nowhere nearly as sure as Belloc that the disappearance of slavery during the unchronicled centuries known as the Dark Ages was the effect of Christian principles at work. Yet he says there is a consensus that Constantine's prohibition of the forced separation of family members held in bondage was a result of Christian influence (p. 334). This is an important concession, and shows the Christian ferment already at work against one of the most inhumane, immoral, and destructive practices of the servile institution.

This practice was to return in the slavery of the United States. Many families were sundered through the sale of father, mother, or children. An echo of this remains in the phrase, 'Sold down the river,' meaning sold to traders in the great slave market in New Orleans, near the mouth of the Mississippi.

It is significant that the recrudescence of slavery within a Christian society was stifled chiefly by the efforts of a man appealing to Christian principles. Abraham Lincoln's statements on the subject of slavery are studded with religious and specifically Christian sentiments, such as:

- '[m]y ancient faith teaches me that "all men are created equal," and that there can be no moral right in connection with one man's making a slave of another.' (speech in Peoria, Ill., 16 Oct. 1854)
- 'But if it [slavery] is a moral and political wrong, as all Christendom considers it to be, how can he [Stephen Douglas] answer to God for this attempt to spread and fortify it?' (speech in Bloomington, Ill., 29 May 1856)
- 'Those principles [that all men are created equal, and that to enslave others is a sacred right of self-government] . . . are as opposite as God and Mammon.' (speech at Springfield, Ill., 16 Oct. 1854)
- 'Pharaoh's country was cursed with plagues, and his hosts were lost in the Red Sea, for striving to retain a captive people who had already served them more than 400 years. May like disasters never befall us.' (speech in Springfield, Ill., 16 July 1852)

Slavery has not been eradicated everywhere. A report of the International Labour Office in Geneva, *World Labour Report 1993* (Geneva, 1993), notes: 'At

The Pagan Reform

What Augustus was able to accomplish was a radical transformation of Rome's political structure. He carried this out step by careful step, always maintaining the forms of the Republic but creating what is now known as the Principate (with himself as *princeps*, the first citizen), or more commonly as the Empire (with himself as commander).[20] If Augustus eventually emptied the republican institutions of all but symbolic – largely palliative and propagandistic – significance, he attempted a genuine restoration of traditional piety, sobriety, and moderation.

Of Augustus's attempts to restore public morals, the most ambitious and most radical was one that concerns us directly in this study: a law against adultery, the *Lex Julia de adulteriis* of 18 BC. There must be significance in the fact that Augustus decided to present this law to the people himself: possibly he felt it to be a matter of such importance that it deserved his personal prestige. Possibly he saw that his prestige was necessary to carry a law previously mooted but judged unworkable.[21]

---

the end of the twentieth century many people assume that slavery has been eradicated. Unfortunately not. Slavery survives even in its ancient forms, and also in more modern forms such as the entrapment of workers into debt bondage and the abduction of men, women and children to work at gunpoint' (p. 1).

The report cites Mauritania and Sudan as countries where traditional slavery survives, and Pakistan, India, Thailand, Haiti, Peru, Brazil and the Dominican Republic as places where forced child labor and debt bondage, described as disguised slavery, still thrive.

It is impossible to calculate or even estimate the total numbers involved, but according to figures published by the International Labour Organization, 20 million men, women, and children were working as bonded laborers in Pakistan alone.

[20] The forms of the Republic were not dropped until the reign of Diocletian at the end of the third century.

[21] One bit of evidence that such an earlier law had been attempted is the poem of Propertius (*Elegies* II, 7) that speaks of the delight of his mistress 'at the abrogation of the law which brought us both long tears at the thought of parting – though Jupiter himself could not separate two lovers against their will.' This poem is dated before 23 BC.

This is held to have been the first time in Roman history that adultery was a civil crime.[22] If so, the severity of the punishment is all the more remarkable. According to the *Institutes* of Justinian, this law 'punishes with the sword not only those who dishonor the marriage-bed of others but also those who indulge their unspeakable lust with males.'[23] Thus adultery and sodomy were subsumed under a common condemnation and a common capital penalty.

Seduction, whether of a virgin or of a 'respectable widow,' incurred confiscation of half of the offender's property, or, where the offender lacked an estate, flogging and relegation, which in Roman law was a mild form of banishment not entailing loss of property or of civil rights. The same legislation outlawed marriage with a convicted adulteress, and penalized failure to dismiss a wife who had committed adultery. Also penalized were renting a house for the commission of adultery and accepting a bribe 'to conceal illicit intercourse.'[24]

Did this severe legislation have the effect intended? It had no more effect than did the severely moralistic literature produced during the Augustan age, we can suppose; yet, we can also suppose, no less. Like literature, the law is a teacher, and a teacher of right and wrong, for better or for worse. In any society with a sense of the common good, citizens tend to give the rationality of a law the benefit of the doubt. Doubt in fact will be rare: a just law will win wide consent for its principle. Even if it is more honored in the breach than in the observance, at least it is honored.

Augustus appears to have done everything a lawmaker could to restore sexual probity in Rome. He complemented the prohibitive legislation on adultery and other sexual misdemeanors with prescriptive laws encouraging marriage, so to speak, by penalizing what too many aristocratic Romans considered single bliss.

[22] Thus Earl, *The Age of Augustus*, p. 67. Frank C. Bourne states: 'Previously adultery had been punished only in family circles' (*A History of the Romans* [Toronto and London: D. C. Heath, 1966], p. 366).

[23] *Institutes*, IV. 18. 4.

[24] *Digest* of Justinian, IV. 4. 37.

Dio Cassius notes:

> He imposed heavier penalties on unmarried men and women, and at the same time offered privileges for marriage and the production of children. And since there were many more men than women among the freeborn, he allowed any who wished, senators apart, to marry freedwomen.[25]

Among the governing classes, married men were given preference for political advancement.[26] Privileges were awarded the parents of three or more children.[27] As an encouragement, women who gave a good example of family life were allowed to receive inheritances in excess of what the sumptuary legislation specified.[28]

The threatened demise of the richer and more highly educated classes through paucity of offspring prompted Augustus to introduce new inducements to procreation through the regulation of inheritance. Under the *Lex Papia Poppaea* of AD 9, a surviving spouse could inherit the entire estate of the deceased spouse provided the prescribed number of children had been born.[29]

But even among the general population there was a dearth of children, a dearth Augustus tried to correct through that same *Lex Papia*. Freeborn women who bore three children, and freedwomen who bore four, were loosed from dependency on guardians.[30] Many more provisions could be cited, all encouraging matrimony and offspring.[31]

[25] *Roman History*, LIV. 16. 1–2.

[26] Augustus 'decreed that the senatorial governors should be appointed annually by lot, except where legal precedence was granted by reason of marriage or number of children' (ibid., LIII. 13. 2–3).

[27] Ibid., LV. 2. 6.

[28] Ibid., LV. 10. The operative legislation was the *Lex Voconia*.

[29] Ulpian, *Rules*, XVI. 1–3.

[30] Gaius, *Institutes*, I. 194, cited in *Rome: The Augustan Age*, eds. K. Chisholm and J. Ferguson (Oxford: Oxford University Press, 1981), p. 184.

[31] R. H. Barrow says: 'at every turn in social and political life, in taxation and privilege, the same questions – married or unmarried? – children or no children? – were asked with resulting rights or disabilities' (*Slavery in the Roman Empire* [London: Methuen & Co. Ltd., 1927], p. 182).

Dio, referring to the consuls who introduced this legislation, M. Papius Mutilus and Q. Poppaeus Secundus, observed: 'It happened that neither had a child or wife, which made the need for legislation obvious.'[32]

That Augustus held out great hopes for such legislation would seem clear enough from the fact that he exiled his own daughter for notorious adultery, and then, ten years later, her daughter also.[33] The exile of Ovid, though its motivation has been obscured by remarks of the poet himself, was a dramatic gesture demonstrating the emperor's refusal to tolerate the public championing of libertinism. He would not let his carefully crafted legislation become a dead letter, done to death by clever or illustrious scofflaws.

To repeat our question: did this legislation succeed? Did the attempt of Augustus to bring back sexual morality, the *pudicitia* of the ancient Romans, have any lasting effect? Did it have a substantial if short-lived effect?

[32] Dio Cassius, *Roman History*, LVI. 10.

[33] Daughter and granddaughter were both called Julia.

Seneca writes: 'The deified Augustus banished his daughter, who was shameless beyond the indictment of shamelessness, and made public the scandals of the imperial house – that she had been accessible to scores of paramours, that in nocturnal revels she had roamed about the city, that the very forum and the rostrum from which her father had proposed a law against adultery had been chosen by the daughter for her debaucheries, that she had daily resorted to the statue of Marsyas and, laying aside the role of adulteress, there sold her favors and sought the right to every indulgence with even an unknown paramour' (*On Benefits*, tr. J. W. Basore, Loeb Classical Library [London: William Heinemann Ltd., 1935], VI. 32. 1).

With an indictment like this, it seems unnecessary to suggest, as so many modern historians have done, that a conspiracy was the real reason for the elder Julia's exile (Pliny, in his *Natural History*, VI. 149, is the only ancient source I know of to give any support for this theory).

Seneca in fact proceeds: 'Carried away by his anger, he divulged all these crimes, which as emperor he ought to have punished and kept secret equally. . . . Afterwards, when with the lapse of time shame took the place of anger, he lamented that he had not veiled in silence matters that he had not known until it was disgraceful to mention them' (ibid., VI. 32. 2).

Tacitus (*Annals*, III. 24) treats the two exiles without a hint of conspiracy, speaking of the emperor's 'calamitous' family life. The great historian's complaint in this matter is uncharacteristically lacking in a sense of stern condemnation: he is upset because Augustus treats everyday adultery as sacrilege and treason. Yet if marriage is a sacred covenant, then adulterous betrayal can reasonably be described in those terms.

It has been doubted on empirical grounds, for history does not record any widespread reform in society. It might be doubted on a priori grounds as well, for as we have observed, the Rome of the early Empire, like the Rome of the late Republic, lacked the moral resources for a deep-rooted reform. As for empirical evidence of the profligacy of the early Empire after Augustus, it is plentiful. That Augustus's law against adultery fell into disuse is shown by the fact of its revival under Domitian in AD 90, a revival that Juvenal made sport of in the Second Satire because of the licentiousness of the lawmaker.[34] We find the great social commentator Seneca the Younger, in his satire on the 'pumpkinification' of the Divine Claudius, deploring the lack of progeny among Romans.[35]

Yet Augustus's determined attempt to bring back chastity deserves more attention, and a more respectful attention, than it is ordinarily given. Historians from Barrow through Dawson to Bourne have credited it with success, however limited.[36]

[34] Domitian was one of the most profligate of Roman emperors. He forced his niece Julia, pregnant with his child, to undergo an abortion. The young woman and, needless to say, her child died from this procedure.

Another emperor who renewed laws on chastity was Caracalla, early in the third century AD. Yet he was a man who murdered his wife. He also murdered his own brother, in the arms of their mother.

R. H. Barrow, citing Tacitus as his authority, recalls that the emperor who succeeded Augustus, Tiberius, thought laws for the reform of society useless: 'Twice in the reign of Tiberius an attempt was made to introduce legislation that should check luxury, and twice Tiberius refused to take any steps, on the ground that sumptuary laws create greater evils than they set out to cure' (*Slavery in the Roman Empire* [London: Methuen & Co., 1928], p. 43).

[35] 'Clotho replied: "Upon my word, I did wish to give him [the emperor Claudius] another hour or two, until he should make Roman citizens of the half-dozen who are still outsiders. (He made up his mind, you know, to see the whole world in the toga: Greeks, Gauls, Spaniards, Britons, and all.) But since it is your pleasure to leave a few foreigners for seed, and since you command me, so be it"' (*Apocolocyntosis Divi Claudii*, III). The implication of course is that once foreigners become Romans, they cease producing children. This is an indictment of Roman decadence.

Seneca had been exiled by Claudius in AD 41 on a charge of adultery with the emperor's niece, Julia Livilla. Penalties against adultery were still in force.

[36] 'To regenerate society by law is an impossible task, and Augustus has often been criticized for attempting the ridiculous. Yet Augustus did not wholly fail,' says R. H. Barrow (*Slavery in the Roman Empire*, p. 179).

Even if it failed outright, it cannot be dismissed on that ground. The achievements of Augustus in statecraft, probably unmatched in secular history, argue that he knew better than just about anyone precisely what should be ventured. He opened his *Res Gestae*, the official account of his stewardship, which he wanted published throughout the Empire, with a factual statement of an astonishing accomplishment: 'At the age of nineteen, on my own initiative and at my own expense, I raised an army, with which I liberated the Republic from the tyranny of a faction that oppressed it, and I restored it to freedom.' His accomplishments in the six decades that followed were no less astonishing.

Hear Philo Judaeus:

> What about the man who pitted himself against the general confusion and chaos as soon as he took charge of public affairs? For islands were struggling for supremacy against the continents, and continents against islands, with Romans of the greatest distinction in public life as their generals and leaders. Again, large parts of the world were battling for the mastery of the empire. Asia against Europe, and Europe against Asia; European and Asian nations from the ends of the earth had risen up and were engaged in grim warfare, fighting with armies and fleets on every land and sea, so that almost the whole human race would have been destroyed in

---

Frank C. Bourne gives Augustus plenty of credit here: 'It would be unjust to label Augustus's legislation on marriage as totally ineffective. It is true that many Romans showed great recalcitrance and invented many interesting subterfuges to escape the law's provisions; but the program was celebrated by contemporary poets as marking the renascence of the family virtues. It was certainly held in high esteem by later writers, and its provisions received elaboration and commentary in the later law' (*A History of the Romans* [Lexington, Mass. and London: D. C. Heath and Co., 1966], p. 366).

Christopher Dawson notes: 'Rome . . . had been founded on the life of the family and the rural community, and the loss of the agrarian foundations of Roman society caused a profound revolution in Roman culture and in the Roman polity. *The national tradition was only saved by an immense effort for social regeneration which was indeed but partially successful*' ('The World Crisis and the English Tradition,' *The English Review*, 56 [1933], repr. in *Dynamics of World History*, ed. J. J. Mulloy [La Salle, Ill.: Sherwood Sugden & Co., 1978], p. 219; emphasis supplied).

internecine conflicts and disappeared completely, had it not been for one man, one *princeps*, Augustus, who deserves the title of 'Averter of evil.'[37]

And Michael Grant:

Augustus was one of the great administrative geniuses of history. The gigantic work of reorganization that he carried out in every field of Roman life and throughout the entire empire not only transformed the decaying republic into a new, monarchic regime with many centuries of life ahead of it but created a durable Roman peace, based on easy communications and flourishing trade. It was this Pax Romana that ensured the survival and eventual transmission of the classical heritage, Greek and Roman alike, and provided the means for the diffusion of Judaism and Christianity.[38]

Clearly such a man does not go to such efforts to create a law, and the ethos that should go with it, if that law and that ethos have no social or political function. The success or failure of the law in achieving its purpose is not the only point: very significant also is the political intelligence of the framer. Some proof of the political and social purposes of chastity is to be found in the resolve of this political genius to restore that virtue within the immense and enduring political structure he was busy raising.[39] Put briefly, the

[37] *Legatio ad Gaium*, 144, given in Chisholm and Ferguson (eds.), *Rome: The Augustan Age*, p. 69.

[38] *The New Encyclopaedia Britannica: Macropaedia* (Chicago: Encyclopaedia Britannica, 1974), s.v. 'Augustus.'

[39] There was of course within the Roman political tradition a strong current of concern at the weakening of family life. Cato the Elder (234–149 BC) 'tried unsuccessfully to tighten sexual morality, blaming the freedom enjoyed by women since the Punic wars for the breakdown of the family, the corruption of civil morality and the decline in the birthrate' (F. Roy Willis, *Western Civilization – An Urban Perspective*, 3rd edn. [Lexington, Mass., and Toronto: D. C. Heath & Co., 1981], vol. 1, p. 148).

The Punic Wars contributed to the breakdown of the family because the small farmers who constituted the chief source of soldiery in those years lost their lands during their absence, partly through inability to keep them in good repair, partly through inability to pay creditors. That is when latifundism and a factory system of farming through slavery began. Former smallholders poured into the cities and formed a client-class proletariat in which the economic

founder of the Roman Empire fostered chastity as if the survival of his tremendous enterprise depended on it.

The emperor's own failures to observe that virtue are no proof that he thought it unimportant.[40] Only a person utterly inexperienced in the dramas of life and the complexities of human nature could reach such a conclusion. Nor are those failures of Augustus a proof of hypocrisy, any more than are

---

functions of the family were radically reduced, hence the cohesion of the family weakened. This was the class to which the Gracchi appealed, and the upheavals of the Gracchean period are generally blamed for weakening the Republic to a point where it could not survive. It was this class that actually decided the fate of the Republic, for the Roman mob would not tolerate the so-called Optimates, or senatorial faction, that had murdered Caesar.

It was this same propertyless class, which had made up the army's legions since the reform of Marius, that decided who was to rule after the death of Caesar, and that decided throughout much of the history of the Empire who was to succeed a dead emperor, or for that matter whether a living emperor was to be allowed to continue living.

A phenomenon that must be grasped in order to understand the decline of the Republic, and to understand the measures that Augustus took to strengthen families both among the populace and the aristocracy, is that as the family declined among the populace, the *role* of the family in Rome's oligarchical structure grew stronger than ever. (An analogous phenomenon could be developing in the United States, where the new elite may one day consist of children who enjoy the rare privilege of being raised in an intact family where the mother remains at home.) S. I. Kovaliov points out (*Storia di Roma*, tr. Renato Angelozzi [Rome: Editori Riuniti, 1955], vol. 1, p. 96) that of the 200 consuls elected in the century beginning 234 BC, 159 were drawn from only 26 families.

In Roman political theory, the family, especially the father, was given a central role. The patrician families that ruled Rome in the earliest centuries of its history took their specifying adjective from the word for father. In those centuries the senate (which takes its name from the word for elder) was composed of the fathers of the ruling families (see Kovaliov, *Storia di Roma*, p. 98, and Willis, *Western Civilization*, p. 165).

Cicero, in his study of political theory, the *Republic*, emphasizes the role of the father in government. He says that Romulus desired his senators 'to be called fathers' (II. viii), and recalls that the first of the Tarquins, Lucius, 'first doubled the number of original fathers [here meaning members of the senate] and called the older ones fathers of the greater families . . . and those added by himself fathers of the lesser families' (II. xx). He boasts 'that no other form of government is comparable . . . with what our ancestors received from their own fathers, and have handed down to us' (I. xlvi).

[40] For a list of the defects, indeed crimes, of Augustus, see Tacitus, *Annals*, 9 and 10.

an alcoholic father's attempts to protect his children from alcoholism.

A formidable obstacle faced by Augustus in his grand strategy to restore the virtue and size of the citizenry was slavery. Marriage and the family were the key to Augustus's strategy, yet slavery had proved itself inimical to both, especially under the factory system of farming now employed in the *latifundia.*[41] Slaves were natural prey to the lust of their masters and mistresses. So strong was the tendency of slaves to intellectual and moral degradation of every kind that many ancients thought slaves lacking by nature in the full humanity that is revealed in virtue, moral virtue especially but also intellectual virtue.[42]

Roman literature exudes an unmistakable aroma of disdain for former slaves who rose to positions of wealth, eminence and power. Even a man such as Horace, only one generation removed from slavery, writes of 'breathless indignation' at the sight of an ex-slave now strutting about as a military tribune: 'hoc, hoc tribuno militum.'[43]

There was widespread criticism of the custom of granting citizenship automatically to freed slaves. Dionysius of Halicarnassus, visiting Rome in the reign of Augustus, writes:

> Many are indignant when they see unworthy men manumitted, and condemn a usage that gives such men the citizenship of a

[41] Both latifundism and widespread slavery had germinated and grown during and after the Punic Wars, especially (see n. 39 above). 'There were very few slaves until the beginning of the overseas wars of conquest – perhaps fewer than 20,000 as late as 300 B.C.,' reports Willis; 'The bulk of the population, even of the city itself, engaged in small-scale agriculture to feed their own families' (*Western Civilization*, vol. I, p. 142).

Ramsay MacMullen estimates that during the early Empire, up to the end of the third century, the slave population 'was enormous, possibly a quarter of the whole' (*Roman Social Relations* [New Haven and London: Yale University Press, 1974], p. 92).

[42] Aristotle raises this in an aporia (*Politics*, I. xiii, 18–28 [1259^b]). For enlightening treatments of the question see the doctoral thesis of Winston Ashley (later Father Benedict Ashley, OP), 'the Theory of Natural Slavery according to Aristotle and St Thomas' (Notre Dame University, 1941), and Charles J. O'Neil, 'Aristotle's Natural Slave Reexamined,' *New Scholasticism*, 27 (1953), pp. 247–79.

[43] *Epodes*, IV. 10 and 20 respectively.

> sovereign state whose destiny is to govern the world. As for me, I doubt whether the practice should be stopped altogether lest greater evil be the result; I would rather that it be checked as far as possible, so that the Republic may no longer be infested by men of such villainous character.[44]

In tackling this problem, which bore directly on the questions of virtue, progeny, and the greater stake that a free citizen holds in the welfare of the state than does the unenfranchised freedman, Augustus was highly systematic.[45] He was the first to modify the custom of vesting freed slaves automatically with Roman citizenship.[46] He restricted the number of slaves to be given freedom under a will.[47] On former slaves he kept a tight rein: citizenship was granted only to those who offered proof of the responsible family life that is the duty of the citizen. Among the biggest class of those who had to prove themselves, the Junian Latins,[48] citizenship could be obtained only by marrying a free person, citizen or not, and producing offspring that survived to the age of a year.

This last requirement hints at an odious custom that had taken root among the Romans. Just how effectively the decline of family life and of sexual discipline had degraded human feelings can be seen not only in the abortion of infants in the womb but the exposure of newborns. The father's decision about the child's fate was absolute; the mother was left with no say, legally, until child exposure was outlawed under the Christian empire.[49]

When Juvenal complained of the corruption of Rome by foreign customs he would have been hard pressed to point

[44] *Roman Antiquities* IV. 24.

[45] Suetonius says: 'He attached great importance to preserving the people pure and untainted by any polluting admixture of foreign or servile blood. He seldom gave Roman citizenship, and narrowly determined the limits of manumission' (*Augustus*, XL).

[46] Through the *Lex Aelia Sentia* of AD 4.

[47] In the *Lex Fufia Caninia*.

[48] So called because created by the *Lex Junia*.

[49] For a list of ancient and modern authorities on this matter, see Aline Rousselle, *Porneia: On Desire and the Body in Antiquity*, tr. Felicia Pheasant (New York and Oxford: Basil Blackwell, 1988), p. 51.

to a more hideous example than child exposure, largely a Greek import and most widely practiced in those parts of the Empire, such as Egypt, which had been under Greek cultural domination.[50]

More than a century after the death of Augustus a Christian apologist expresses his outrage at the exposure of infants. Justin Martyr, in pleading Christian rights and the reasonableness of the Catholic faith before the emperor, responds to charges of immorality among Christians by pointing to that custom. He tells Antoninus Pius:

> But as for us, we have been taught that to expose newborn children is the part of wicked men; and we have been taught this . . . first, because we see that almost all so exposed (not only the girls but the boys also) are brought up to prostitution. And it is said that as the ancients reared herds of oxen, goats, sheep, or grazing horses, so now we see you rear children for this shameful use only.[51]

There exists throughout your empire, St Justin continues, an entire class of persons dedicated to this abominable kind of pedagogy. You take their taxes, but you ought to extirpate them from your realm.[52]

We see then how sexual license, in breeding new classes for its exploitation, perpetuated itself through its victims. In the literature of the times there is a recurrent theme dealing

[50] For Juvenal's rantings against foreign influence, see especially Satire III. Polybius, himself a Greek, traces the 'vicious tendencies' – sexual misbehavior – of Roman youths in the time of Scipio Aemilianus to the war with Perseus of Macedon, when young men were 'speedily infected by Greek laxity in such matters' (*The Histories*, XXXI. 25).

Livy opines: 'it was through the army serving in Asia [under Cneius Manlius Vulso against the Asiatic Gauls] that the beginnings of foreign luxury were introduced into the City. . . . Banquets were made more attractive by the presence of girls who played on the harp and sang and danced, and by other forms of amusement, and the banquets themselves began to be prepared with greater care and expense. The cook whom the ancients regarded and treated as the lowest menial was rising in value, and what had been a servile job came to be looked on as a fine art' (*History of Rome from its Foundation*, XXXIX. 4).

[51] *First Apology*, XXVII.

[52] Ibid.

with the incest that this source of inmates for brothels inevitably produced.

There is more. Children rescued from exposure (in many cases they were flung upon garbage heaps, and in Alexandria the custom was to dispose of them on a particular trash dump) ordinarily found themselves in slavery, not just a social, economic, and political slavery but, as Justin remarks, very often a moral slavery as well. This throws light on the link between institutionalized lust and institutionalized slavery, and conversely between chastity and liberty.

The Church, which stood for chastity and liberty both, was unable to bring liberty to the slaves of the Roman Empire. It must be remembered that the servile institution was universal in the ancient world, indeed in all subsequent worlds save the Christian West. As rich Romans adopted the Catholic religion, the Church even found herself with slaves of her own, bequeathed to her along with the vast properties they worked. It has been argued that she could scarcely have freed them without exposing them to want.[53] In any event it is probable that she could not have maintained her landed properties, the chief source of her discretionary income, indeed virtually the only source of wealth in that epoch, without the employment of the slaves that were attached to them; her immense works of charity, it is argued, depended on income from these estates.[54]

The Christian Ethos

Against the sexual immorality of the age the Church could bring the intellectual armament of her teaching, the wholesome severity of her discipline, the unsettling example of her

[53] P. Maraval, citing St John Chrysostom, argues thus ('L'Eglise du IVème siècle et l'esclavage', p. 344). He continues: 'Certain historians even think that the emancipations effected by the Christians created more beggary, against which the emperors had to take harsh measures' (ibid.).

[54] Ibid., p. 345. He cites a detailed examination of the question by E. J. Jonkers in a more general treatment entitled 'De l'influence du christianisme sur la légalisation relative a l'esclavage dans l'antiquité', *Mnémosune* (1934), pp. 253–9.

faithful adherents, and, finally and perhaps most important for the eventual disappearance of Roman pansexualism, the astonishing countersign of consecrated virginity and celibacy.

Christians, faced with slanderous accusations of mother–son incest and other gross immoralities, could point to the celibacy practiced among them. 'Indeed you will find many among us, both men and women, growing old unmarried, in hope of living in closer communion with God,' writes Athenagoras of Athens to the emperors Marcus Aurelius and his youthful son Commodus.[55] The celibacy of men and

[55] *Supplication for the Christians*, XXIII. Athenagoras continues: 'But if it brings one nearer to God to remain a virgin and in the state of a eunuch, while indulgence in carnal thought and desire leads away from him, when we avoid the thought, much more do we reject the deeds' (ibid.).

In the following chapter he charges the accusers of the Christians with hypocrisy, for they 'accuse us of the very things they know they do.' They are the 'adulterers and pederasts' who range abroad like predators and 'feed upon human flesh, working such violence in contravention of the very laws that you and your ancestors, with due care for all that is fair and right, have enacted' (XXIV).

Then, defending Christians against the charge of cannibalism in the next chapter, he turns his indignation against the disregard for human life so widespread in the ancient world. He cites gladiatorial combat, and the pleasure taken by the crowd at the sight of one man killing another: 'And when we say that those women who use drugs to bring on abortion commit murder, and will have to give an account to God for the abortion, on what principle should we commit murder? For it does not belong to the same person to regard the very fetus in the womb as a created being, and therefore an object of God's care, and when it has passed into life to kill it; and not to expose an infant, because those who expose them are chargeable with child murder, and on the other hand, when it has been reared to destroy it' (XXV).

There is a horrifying parallel in Western society today. The murder of children in the womb has been licensed by the law. In many cases it has been underwritten by public funds, so that the entire public is drawn willy-nilly into material complicity. Yet nothing could threaten the future of a nation more directly than the sanctioned killing of children, whether ritual, as among certain ancient Semites, or for convenience, as in decadent societies of ancient or modern times.

It is taboo in our times to link the killing of children to unchastity, yet it is precisely the disregard of chastity that has led moderns to this desperate and unspeakable custom. Abortion becomes the ultimate defense against the responsibilities of sexual congress. In fact a broader definition of chastity than the one we have adopted for our purposes puts the crime of abortion in another light: if chastity is conceived in terms of the entire reproductive process, from the glint in the father's eye to the cry of the newborn child, then abortion is a crime against chastity.

women both was not only a powerful defense against charges of sexual immorality but a powerful antidote to the defeatism in sexual matters that is bound to arise in a pansexual society.

The sworn enmity of Christian belief to libertinism is seen further in the repeated condemnations of abortion as a sin that stems from sexual license and that, as Clement of Alexandria points out, destroys not only the child but all human feeling.[56] Even wealthy women, far from welcoming orphans into their home, will expose their own newborn children and instead take pet animals, 'preferring irrational creatures to rational.'[57]

In decrying the wickedness of the Roman world, Christian writers of this period put the emphasis on *world*, not on *Roman*. They took seriously Jesus Christ's warnings against the world, and echoed them. The wickedness they denounced was chiefly a worldly wickedness, not a wickedness peculiar to Rome, however accentuated and even institutionalized it may have been within the Empire.[58] Indeed, for most men who lived within the Roman ambit in those times, the Roman Empire and the public thing, the *res publica*, were simply synonymous.[59]

But Christians did more than denounce the evils of the world, more than defend their religion against argument, their co-religionists against slanders. They preached conversion in faith and morals, and in this effort met substantial success. Whatever effect this had on the mores of civil society may not have been evident to secular historians of the time. This, after all, was the planting season. Moreover, its firstfruits had to be internal. And beyond that, Christians remained a minority for centuries.

[56] *The Instructor*, II. 10. The exact date of this work is not known, but it was written before the year AD 202. Clement lived from the mid-second century to the second decade of the next.

[57] Ibid., III. 4.

[58] It is true of course that Roman writers, both Christian and pagan, did point to the virtue of earlier times, and of some barbarian societies. Tacitus and Livy, as we have seen, are cases in point.

[59] The Empire, like the Principate before it, still bore the proud title *Res Publica*.

But not an impoverished minority, despite St Jerome's later remark that the early Christians came 'from paltry common people.'[60] Minucius Felix, writing no later than the first third of the third century, claims that Christians are 'not from the lowest levels of society.'[61] But his real pride is Christian moral integrity, chastity in particular:

> We cling freely to the bond of one marriage. In the desire to procreate we know one wife or none. . . . With chaste discourse and even more chaste in body, many of us enjoy rather than boast of the perpetual virginity of a body undefiled. In fact, so far from us is the desire for incest, that some blush even at the thought of a chaste union.[62]

Christians sought converts not only among the virtuous few but also among the unvirtuous many. In this they were faithful to the example of Jesus Christ, who was reproached for associating with sinners and the stooges of the foreign oppressor, and replied that he had come 'not to call the virtuous, but sinners to repentance.'[63]

This search for the riff-raff of this world, for waifs and strays, provoked the contempt and reproach of pagans, but boded well for the moral regeneration of society. To a pagan who complained of 'this preference for sinners,' Origen replied by distinguishing between great sinners who come to repentance and lesser sinners who take pride in their virtues.[64]

St Paul reminds his converts at Corinth that some of them had been 'idolaters, adulterers, catamites, sodomites, thieves, usurers, drunkards, slanderers and swindlers.'[65] Here St Paul

[60] 'de vili plebicula' (*In Gal.*, III).

[61] *Octavius*, XXXI. 6. (For speculation on the date of this work, and of Minucius Felix himself, see William A. Jurgens, *The Faith of the Early Fathers* [Collegeville, Minn.: Liturgical Press, 1970], p. 109.)

Shortly after the middle of the third century, the Emperor Valerian ordered the death penalty for Roman knights and senators who held to belief in Jesus Christ (see Robert M. Grant, *Augustus to Constantine* [New York: Harper & Row, 1970], p. 171).

[62] *Octavius*, XXXI. 5.

[63] Luke 5:32.

[64] *Against Celsus*, III. 44.

[65] I Cor. 6:9–11.

draws a significant distinction: Christians are not to associate with such persons, *if they are Christians.*[66] That ban does not extend to association with those outside the Church, for to shun pagans who were immersed in such vices would be a practical impossibility. In order to avoid 'all the people in the world who are sexually immoral . . . , you would have to withdraw from the world altogether.'[67]

Without condoning immoral behavior, he writes: 'It is not my business to pass judgment on those outside. . . . But of those who are outside, God is the judge.'[68]

The decision of the Council of Jerusalem cited at the opening of this chapter casts light on this policy. To become a Christian is to leave these sins behind. As for pagans, they are simply expected to lead a life of sin, and sexual sin especially. Now if it is the business of faith in Christ to rescue men from what might be called the institutionalization of sin, that faith should work a radical change on society.

What in fact were these teachings of Jesus Christ on chastity, teachings destined to work such a change? In what ways did they differ from the chastity, the *pudicitia*, so esteemed by the Romans of Our Lord's own time?

Doctrines on chastity that are distinctively Christian might be reduced to two, namely the indissolubility of marriage and the superior dignity of virginity. Even this brief outline reveals differences between Christian chastity and the *pudicitia* of Rome, indeed the marital fidelity of the Hebrews.[69] But here, in order to meet the exigencies of the Christian teaching, we must expand, or rather enrich, the definition of chastity that we gave at the outset of this work, which was the confinement of genital activity to husband and wife. For with the arrival of

[66] I Cor. 5:11.

[67] I Cor. 5:10.

[68] I Cor. 5:12–13.

[69] It was a commonplace among early Catholic apologists to contrast the virginity widespread among Christians with the license that prevailed among Romans, even among those few women formally dedicated to virginity. Minucius Felix charges, not implausibly, that there was virtually no virginity among the vestals (*Octavius*, XXV).

Jesus Christ, the world was given what he himself called 'a new commandment,'[70] and with it a paramount virtue that breathed its soul into every other, from justice to playfulness.

In his farewell discourse to his disciples, Jesus declared: 'I give you a new commandment: love one another, just as I have loved you.'[71] What this meant for marriage was explained by St Paul: 'Husbands should love their wives just as Christ loved the Church and sacrificed himself for her to make her holy.'[72] Fidelity, therefore, did not suffice. It had to be inspired by a self-sacrificing love of the kind Christ had shown in climbing Calvary.

Again it is St Paul, declaring that without love neither eloquence nor prophecy avails, nor does understanding of every mystery, or even faith 'to move mountains,'[73] who offers the explanation:

> Love is always patient and kind; it is never jealous; love is never boastful or conceited; it is never rude or selfish; it does not take offense, and is not resentful. Love takes no pleasure in other people's sins but delights in the truth; it is always ready to excuse, to trust, to hope, and to endure whatever comes.[74]

A marriage imbued with such love seems less of earth than of heaven, and so it is. In it infidelity is unthinkable, while chastity, now expressly a part of the love of God and of neighbor, is lifted into a transcendentally loftier realm.

Christian chastity, as we have seen, also embraced a virginity chosen for that same love of God. Christ taught that such virginity was a higher state than marriage. The most celebrated passage in the Gospels dealing with virginity follows the discussion of divorce, when Our Lord declared: 'Now I say this to you: the man who divorces his wife – I am not speaking

[70] John 13:34.
[71] Ibid.
[72] Eph. 5:25–6.
[73] I Cor. 13:1–3.
[74] I Cor. 13:4–7.

of fornication – and marries another, is guilty of adultery.'[75] The Gospel account continues:

> The disciples said to him, 'If that is how things are between husband and wife, it is not advisable to marry.' But he replied, 'It is not everyone who can accept what I have said, but only those to whom it is granted. There are eunuchs born that way from their mother's womb, there are eunuchs made so by men and there are eunuchs who have made themselves that way for the sake of the kingdom of heaven. Let anyone accept this who can.'[76]

This seems to be a departure from the Jewish ethos making marriage and children a duty to the nation, but the departure is more apparent than real. There are several reasons for this. One is that consecrated virginity, when lived and not merely professed, acts as a wholesome antidote to defeatism in sexual matters, thus helping ensure a chaste and therefore prolific society. Another is that it frees men and women to devote themselves more directly to the common good through works of charity and mercy. A third is that the number of consecrated virgins is unlikely to be sufficient to lower the number of families to a point where the common good is endangered.

The teaching of Jesus Christ on virginity is echoed by St Paul. Speaking of widows and the unmarried, he says:

> it is a good thing for them to stay as they are, like me, but if they cannot control the sexual urges, they should get married, since it is better to be married than to be tortured.[77]

The Christian Reform

The change brought about by Christian teaching on chastity, as we have seen, was quiet and gradual, working as it did like a seed in the ground or a leaven in the mass. Moreover the hostility of the government dictated discretion. For example, a Christian who in a spirit of Christian forgive-

[75] Matt. 19:9.
[76] Matt. 19:10–12.
[77] I Cor. 7:8–9.

ness took a guilty wife back risked public disgrace and even exile or hard labor for connivance in adultery or for procuring.[78]

Early in the fourth century, however, this picture altered. With the arrival on the throne of an emperor who credited Jesus Christ with putting him there, and who not only decreed toleration for the long-proscribed Catholic Church but showed it progressively greater favor, we see virtually immediate changes in the character of society. They were effected by changes in the law, and these Christian-inspired laws of Constantine the Great offered a foretaste of the transformation that the Catholic faith would eventually work upon the West.

Although the emperor did not seek baptism until his last illness, he made known from the outset his sympathies with the newly tolerated religion, indeed his belief in it. Every bit as conspicuous as the Christian symbol on the coins he minted was the Christian inspiration of laws he inscribed in the imperial code.[79]

Of course he was careful not to abolish outright the pagan religions or, *a fortiori*, to abolish those civic forms, based on pagan piety, which had given such strong support to the imperial institutions. The cult of the emperor is perhaps the most important case in point.[80] Whatever fate Constantine may have had in mind for paganism – and as his rule grew

[78] For early Christian teaching on forgiveness of a guilty but repentant spouse, see Hermas, *The Shepherd*, Mandate 4. 1. 4–8. Hermas, who wrote in the middle of the second century, was a brother of Pope St Pius I.

An accessible account of punishments in store for a forgiving husband is given in Rousselle, *Porneia*, p. 103.

[79] Even a historian like Andrew Alfoldi, who clearly misunderstands the accoutrements of the Catholic faith, referring to nails from the Cross as 'talismans,' is constrained to declare: 'But to deny the sincerity and urgency of his religious convictions is to make a very grave mistake' (*The Conversion of Constantine and Pagan Rome*, trs. Harold Mattingly [Oxford: Clarendon Press, 1948], p. 23).

This view of Constantine's conversion has become predominant; see, for example, the *New Encyclopaedia Britannica*, *Micropaedia*, s.v. 'Constantine the Great.'

[80] '[e]ven Christians enjoyed dignities in the "sterilized" cult of the Emperors' (Alfoldi, *The Conversion of Constantine*, p. 106).

more secure he restricted it progressively – he moved from the very beginning to put a Christian stamp on the society he governed.[81]

Among the Constantinian laws of Christian inspiration, the one instituting a weekly day of rest is probably most often cited. This law was the first to impose the calendar of the Church on society at large. Weekly rest was not only salutary for the physical health of the members of society but fostered regular religious worship.[82]

Beyond a regular day of rest, two major civil institutions that were, and in a sense remain, unique to Christian society, namely freedom from the servile institution, and indissoluble marriage, got strong support from Constantine's legislation. The emperor made unilateral divorce more difficult and forbade the keeping of concubines by married men.[83] This latter prohibition not only helped protect women and their status in society, but also struck a blow against that slavery which is concubinage.[84]

[81] For the tenacity of pagan beliefs, or at least of adherence to pagan forms, see Samuel Dill, *Roman Society in the Last Century of the Western Empire*, 2nd edn. (London and New York: Macmillan, 1899), ch. 1.

[82] Constantine decreed a weekly holiday on the 'venerable day of the Sun' in 321. Alfoldi observes: 'The Christian day of rest fell, of course, on the *dies Solis*, the day dedicated to the very popular Sun-god. But the fact does not make the step "neutral." All days of the week were assigned to their special deities, and any other choice might equally well be called an "ambiguous gesture." But there was nothing in Sol or in any other pagan god to justify the Sunday rest, which is based on the authority of the Bible. Christianity had long been holding its regular services on the Sunday. Eusebius, then, is only telling the truth when he says that the Emperor, because of his Christian views, raised Sunday to the rank of a festival. Nor can we doubt that Constantine himself observed the festival with the greatest reverence and caused it to be so observed by his army' (*The Conversion of Constantine*, pp. 48–9).

[83] See Joseph Vogt, *The Decline of Rome*, tr. Janet Sondheimer (London: Weidenfeld & Nicolson, 1967), p. 105. Constantine also abolished certain penalties for the unmarried state (*Codex Theodosianus*, VIII. 16. 1). In so doing he gave precedence, in the Catholic manner, to consecrated virginity over marriage, and perhaps recognized the role that consecrated virginity plays both in enhancing general esteem for chastity and in counteracting sexual defeatism.

[84] For an examination of concubinage in Rome before Christian-inspired legislation was enacted, and of the notion that concubinage constituted a kind of liberation from the laws of the early Empire holding married women in subjection, see Aline Rousselle, *Porneia*, pp. 97–100.

It is no empty coincidence that the first Christian legislation dealing with slavery focused on family life. 'For who,' asks Constantine in justifying his decree ordering that slave families be kept intact, 'could bear the separation of children from parents, sisters from brothers, wives from husbands?'[85] Nor is it sheer coincidence that the Catholic Church was empowered, under Constantinian law, to be an official registrar of the manumission of slaves enacted in the presence of clergy.[86] Thus what seems to have been the first assignment of civil magistracy to the clergy of the Catholic Church, the Church's first civil empowerment, was in mitigation of slavery.[87]

Of course outright abolition of the servile institution, on which the economy of the Empire depended heavily, was unthinkable. But Constantine's legislation loosened the bands of bondage, and aimed at extirpating some of its most cruel and degrading abuses. It began the long series of gradual mitigations that, by the end of the Dark Ages, rendered slavery an anachronism in Christendom and saw, in its place, yeomanry and a serfdom circumscribed by rules now long traditional guaranteeing the intrinsic rights and accrued prerogatives of the serfs.

A third characteristic of Christian society, respect for human life, was incorporated into the Constantinian laws with the abolition of gladiatorial combat. Constantine outlawed the very existence of gladiators, and hence the custom of relegating convicts to gladiatorial status and pitting them against one another in the arena.[88] Other laws, such as the guarantee of sunlight, fresh air, and physical safety to those awaiting trial, and the guarantee that debt-ridden farmers

[85] *Codex Theodosianus*, II. 25.

[86] See *Codex Theodosianus*, IV. 7. 1, and *Codex Justinianus*, I. 13. 2. This became law in AD 321.

[87] Eventually episcopal courts of arbitration, empowered by the emperor to decide disputes of all kinds, were found across the Roman Empire; see *Codex Theodosianus*, I. 27. 1. Thus bishops were positioned to fall heir to full civil authority when the centralized administration of the Western Empire grew weak and finally collapsed.

[88] Edict of 1 Oct. 325 (*Codex Theodosianus*, XV. 9. 12).

could keep their farming tools and draft animals, were evidence of the emperor's Christian mercy.[89]

Thus already, in what can be called the opening years of the Christian empire, we see imperial law enshrining the characteristic Christian respect for human life and dignity, for human freedom, and for the indissolubility of marriage.

That the Church's teachings had a measure of success in leading society to a respect for the source of human life and for human life itself is widely accepted as historical fact, but her claim to success against slavery is ignored. Yet to bring liberty to a world where slavery held sway was a monumental work, uniquely Christian and otherwise unknown to history.[90] Only when the Christian leaven had worked its way through society could it begin to push aside the universal institution of slavery and start raising the slave to the status of the serf, bound indeed to the land of his lord and also to certain services, but with established rights and prerogatives that expanded with the passage of the centuries. Eventually the serfs either left the land or became freeholders. In England this was the work of half a millennium; in other parts of Europe such as Germany a mitigated feudalism remained in force even at the time of the French Revolution, though in France the peasants had by then been free so many centuries that no one, not even historians, knew when serfdom had been abolished.[91]

[89] For the protection of the livelihood of farmers, and other humanitarian provisions such as that prohibiting tax officials to drag mothers from their children, see Vogt, *The Decline of Rome*, p. 105. The Constantinian law on the treatment of persons in custody of the court is found in the *Codex Theodosianus*, IX. 3. 1.

[90] Winston Ashley says about the replacement of classical slavery by serfdom: 'Roman slavery declined with Roman civilization but its very roots were removed by the revolutionary introduction of Christianity. It was abolished slowly but for a revolutionary reason' ('The Theory of Natural Slavery according to Aristotle and St Thomas', p. 20). He thus adopts the thesis most widely known in the English-speaking world through the writings of Hilaire Belloc.

[91] Alexis de Tocqueville, *The Old Regime and the French Revolution*, tr. Stuart Gilbert (Garden City, NY: Doubleday & Co., 1955), p. 23. De Tocqueville proceeds to say that more recently, historians had learned that serfdom had ceased to exist in Normandy 'as early as the thirteenth century.'

If the world was delivered from slavery through an appreciation of human dignity, if, that is, an abiding awareness of human worth proved to be the historical foundation of universal freedom, then freedom becomes, along with virtue, a living symbol of our worth.[92] This impinges on chastity itself. Because human sexuality is an integral part of the human person, because it is the source of human life, its dignity, like human freedom, stems from human dignity itself. Now the perfection of human sexuality is chastity. By perfecting human sexuality, chastity enhances human dignity. But in perfecting our sexuality it also enhances our freedom, because it makes us master of our sexual instincts rather than their servant, or even slave. It frees us from what Sophocles, according to Plato, called 'a sort of frenzied and savage master.'[93]

Aristotle went further and linked promiscuity not to metaphorical slavery but to actual slavery. Slaves should not have their own family, he counselled, but rather should share wives and children in common. That way, he claimed, 'they will be bound to one another by weaker ties, as a subject class should be, and they will remain obedient and not rebel.'[94]

Be that as it may, it is mere history that the deliverance of society from slavery meant the deliverance of women, and men as well, from the sexual exploitation and degradation that accompanied the servile condition. The Christian society that comes into view with the dawn of the Middle Ages gave human sexuality the respect due it, fully on the level of principle if less so in the lives of Christians. This new ethos stood in stark contrast to the pansexualism of classical antiquity.

But early in the Middle Ages another worldview, vigorous and self-confident, arises to challenge the Christian concept

[92] Logically it should be the symbol of a Christian society too, as it was historically. But the Enlightenment wiped that symbolism out of the collective consciousness, and it continues to be excluded by the amnesic secularism that is the bequest of the Enlightenment.

[93] *Republic*, I (329c).

[94] *Politics*, II. 4 (1262b). Here he is speaking of 'husbandmen,' but he later specifies, 'the husbandmen should be slaves' (VII. 9 [1330a]).

not just of sexuality but of the body, hence of human nature. Its roots reached back to the Christian community of the Roman Empire, where it had flourished as an excess of reaction to the dissolute sexual mores of the pagan world. Yet its opposition to the Christian ethos was if anything even more radical than its opposition to pagan pansexualism. Its adherents struggled with the Catholics for dominance. It was called, variously, Catharism and Albigensianism.

Not least, this formidable heresy was an assault, at once subtle and confrontational, on chastity. It attacked chastity head on through hatred of the human body; but the assault was also indirect, through a hatred of all material things and, in a sense that we shall examine in the next and final chapter, their Creator himself.

Chapter 5

THE MIDDLE AGES: CHASTITY IN DEFENSE OF THE BODY

The dark gods of antiquity never died. As Christian belief arose they found their way into it, and there, hiding themselves in a miasma of gnosticism and consolidating themselves into a rival god, they survived the old paganism.[1]

[1] Gnosticism does not lend itself to any single definition. The word itself comes from the Greek *gnosis*, or knowledge, and if understood as *knowledge of divine mysteries* can encompass orthodoxy as well as heresy. That literal meaning turns out to be historical as well, so that Clement of Alexandria can repeatedly refer to orthodox Catholics as gnostics. See, for example, *Stromata*, V. 1: 'We, then, are those who are believers in what is not believed, and who are Gnostics as to what is unknown and disbelieved by all, but believed and known by a few.'

For that reason and others, not least the endemic elitism and esotericism of gnostic movements, anyone venturing into a study of gnosticism finds himself in a maze. Academic literature on gnosticism demonstrates that this remains so despite the discovery in late 1945 of a sealed hoard of more than fifty Coptic texts, more than forty of them new to scholarship, near the ruins of the monastery of Chenoboskion in Egypt, which have given greater clarity and authenticity to our understanding of gnosticism. Whereas most of our knowledge of Christian gnosticism had come from the hostile writings of the Church Fathers, we now possess, in what is called the Nag Hammadi Library, abundant writings by gnostics themselves.

One of the clarifications afforded by these writings is to clear St Irenaeus of the suspicion that he had distorted gnosticism in his polemical writings. See 'Twenty Years After' by Robert McL. Wilson, in *Proceedings of the Colloque International sur les Textes de Nag Hammadi, Quebec, 22–5 Aug. 1978* (Quebec: Les Presses de l'Université Laval, 1981), pp. 59–67, esp. pp. 60 and 61; for reservations about the writings of Irenaeus and other Fathers, see Frederik Wisse, 'The Nag Hammadi Library and the Heresiologists,' *Vigiliae Christianae*, 25 (1971), pp. 205–23.

This rival god became a powerful subversive force within early Christianity, especially where he was conceived as the very author of evil in the world, and most dangerously where evil was identified with matter. The gnostic dualism of two gods, one ruling over a realm of spirit and light, the other over matter and darkness, generated a dualism of body and soul. Theological dualism became anthropological dualism,

---

Some of the confusion that remains might be blamed on the a prioris of modernity, which have prompted what the Oxford researcher M. J. Edwards calls 'efforts of such scholars as Elaine Pagels to use these [Nag Hammadi] writings as evidence for a pervasive spirit of protest, anticipating projects for intellectual freedom or the emancipation of women' ('New Discoveries and Gnosticism: Some Precautions,' *Orientalia Christiana Periodica*, 55 [1989], p. 266). Dr Edwards is referring specifically to Dr Pagels's widely promoted *The Gnostic Gospels* (New York: Random House, 1979), which popularized Walter Bauer's theory of almost half a century earlier that orthodoxy was merely the position that happened to prevail, among the many competing positions of early Christian times. (A team-translation of Bauer's somewhat neglected book, *Rechtgläubigkeit und Ketzerei im ältesten Christentum* [Tübingen: Mohr-Siebeck, 1934], was published in 1971 as *Orthodoxy and Heresy in Earliest Christianity* [Philadelphia: Fortress Press]. This translation, a British edition the following year, and an expanded German edition of 1964 provoked a torrent of reviews, virtually all critical of Bauer's thesis and methods.)

Presuppositions of modernity may also explain the widespread but unsupported assumption that gnostic writings have been suppressed; here Dr Edwards again singles out Elaine Pagels ('New Discoveries and Gnosticism,' p. 258).

But prejudices and special pleading apart, and despite the Nag Hammadi Library and other gnostic writings discovered over the past two centuries (see Wisse, 'The Nag Hammadi Library', pp. 205 and 206), an aura of vagueness still envelops gnosticism. Ugo Bianchi observes: '*the* gnostic system . . . evidently does not exist' ('A propos de quelque discussions récentes sur la terminologie, la définition et la méthode de l'étude du gnosticisme,' in *Proceedings of the International Colloquium on Gnosticism, Stockholm, August 20–5, 1973* [Leiden: E. J. Brill, 1977], p. 18).

On the other hand, Edwards holds that a comprehensive examination of neoplatonist literature, of the Church Fathers, and of gnostic documents themselves reveals a 'well-defined' sect ('Neglected Texts in the Study of Gnosticism', *Journal of Theological Studies*, n.s. 41 [1990], pp. 26–50). If this thesis survives scholarly scrutiny, it will be a breakthrough in the study of gnosticism.

For an attempt to draw a comparison between, on the one hand, 'the different gnostic ideologies of the second and third centuries constituting the great heresy' that confronted the Church, and on the other hand the 'vaster' gnosticism revealed by discoveries since World War II, see Jacques-E. Menard, 'La Gnose et les textes de Nag Hammadi,' in *Proceedings of the 1978 Colloque Internationale sur les Textes de Nag Hammadi*, pp. 3–17.

digging a chasm between the spiritual and the corporal, between body and soul, and setting man at odds with himself irreconcilably.

Because the human body belonged to the kingdom of evil, it itself became evil. Once the body was evil, it followed that marriage and procreation were evil.

What this implies for chastity is clear enough upon reflection. Dualism means the death of that virtue, for in making the body evil it makes the works of the body evil. Procreation above all becomes evil since it is the prolongation of bodily evil. It is the imprisonment of a soul in an evil body. If chastity can be called a virtue in the dualistic scheme of things, it is mere abstention. Psychologically then, chastity is horror of genital activity.

What this means for the family is manifest, and sinister, and in the long run disastrous: the family is evil.

Now if the basic cell of the body politic is evil, that larger society must choose between two evils, one physical and one moral: either to sustain itself through the radically corrupt institution of the family, or to disappear from the earth.

This cruel and unrealistic dilemma, after arising early in Christianity as part of gnosticism and then declining with it, presented itself insistently again as the Middle Ages were reaching their height, toward the end of the twelfth century and the beginning of the thirteenth. It was very energetically promulgated by a dualistic heresy known most correctly as Catharism, the religion of the pure, and most commonly as Albigensianism, although how it acquired this latter name can only be guessed.

For fully a century the Catholic Church fought for the moral survival of society, and very possibly for its physical survival as well. Yet from the Enlightenment on, historians have not seen the Church's struggle in a good light. She has found herself accused of alarmism and even of base motives. Presumably the Church violated too many taboos of the Age of Reason: she founded the Inquisition to seek out the carriers of the heretical virus, she waged a war over religion, and – most unforgivable of all, one might be tempted to think –

she displayed all the resolve and rigor of an institution confident of her divine foundation.

It is important to remember that although the dualism that split both God and man in two reached its most dangerous pitch in the High Middle Ages, when the times drew their character from Catholicity, such dualism got a strong start in the earliest centuries of our era, when Christians were a persecuted minority. Not for nothing does the Nicene Creed begin: 'I believe in *one* God.'

Of the early sects calling themselves Christian but giving shelter to a second god, and raising him into virtual equality with the God of the Fathers, foremost was one taking its name from Marcion, a rich shipowner of Asia Minor. So powerful was the appeal of Marcion's dualistic teaching, so plausible a solution did it offer to the mystery of evil, that a veritable counterchurch grew out of it. This Marcionite church spread to the ends of the Empire and beyond, remaining strong in the East until the fifth century at least, and surviving in one form or another in the West until the Middle Ages.

Polycarp, who was instructed by the Apostles, had a face-to-face encounter with Marcion. In the denunciation that this martyr levelled at the heresiarch we can discern how basic is the dualistic heresy: he was, Polycarp told him, 'the firstborn of Satan.'[2]

The dualism of two gods, one of them responsible for evil in the world, took diverse forms in the early centuries of Christianity. Common to most of them was a hatred of the flesh and of procreation.[3] Other heresies might display a tendency to such hatred – Priscillianism is a case in point – but dualism, most sharply where the second god or demiurge

[2] Irenaeus, *Adversus Haereses*, III. iii. 4. Marcion died about 160. As the letters of St Paul show, he was far from the first heretic.

[3] An exception is the system of Bardaisan. He 'did not regard generation and birth with abhorrence as a further enmeshing of the Divine substance in matter. . . . Conception and birth, therefore, is the process by which something is produced which has the chance of escaping from this mixed world and rejoining the pure region of Light' (F. C. Burkitt, *The Religion of the Manichees*, Donellan Lectures for 1924, Trinity College, Dublin [Cambridge: Cambridge University Press, 1925], p. 77).

or disposing angel was outright evil, despised the flesh out of principle because it was part of the kingdom of evil.[4]

That is our chief interest here: the principled hatred of things material, and the seemingly inevitable consequences, intellectual and practical, of that hatred.

Marcion taught that there are two gods, but it is not clear whether one of them was outright evil. For him the God of the New Testament was distinct from the God of the Old Testament. Marcion construed the latter to be the *source* of evil in so far as he had created matter, principle of evil, or perhaps had just organized pre-existing matter.[5] On the other hand the pure God of the New Testament, who begot Jesus Christ and was manifested in him, was the source of mercy and love. Even if the God responsible for the material universe was not himself evil, he had bungled the job and made a further mess of things through his pettifogging legalism and vindictiveness.

Because matter was evil, the human body this God produced was evil. Human procreation was wrong. Marriage was nothing less than rape and fornication.[6] Little wonder that Marcion rejected the infancy narrative of St Luke's Gospel! Jesus was not born of woman, but came to earth full-grown.

Another dualistic heresiarch was Mani, whose influence outlasted Marcion's. Born in Babylonia in the third century, Mani called himself 'an apostle of Jesus Christ,' but posited a cosmogony wildly divergent from the Judaeo-Christian

[4] Priscillianism was an ascetic, mystical movement, with strong docetic and Sabellian components, that began in the late fourth century and was still considered dangerous enough in the sixth century to merit official condemnation. Whether its founder, Priscillian, was heretical has not been demonstrated, but the movement eventually showed itself hostile to marriage, meat, and wine.

[5] There is confusion, stemming from contradictory reports of the Church Fathers, over the nature of Marcion's second deity, the God of the Old Testament: whether he is evil or simply too juridical, and whether he is the creator of matter or just its organizer. See R. Joseph Hoffmann, *Marcion: On the Restitution of Christianity* (Chico, Calif.: Scholars Press, 1984), p. 190; also E. C. Blackman, *Marcion and his Influence* (London: SPCK, 1948), p. 66.

[6] '*Phthora kai porneia*,' cited by E. Amman, *Dictionnaire de théologie catholique* (Paris: Letouzey et Ané, 1951), s.v. 'Marcion,' col. 2024.

doctrine of creation.[7] His is a religion of two uncreated principles, one of light and one of darkness, whose kingdoms find themselves intermingled after a titanic struggle. He left a highly organized church with two categories of members, the perfect and the hearers.[8] The latter were permitted to marry but were enjoined to avoid procreation – something of special interest to moderns – while the former had to abstain from marriage and all genital activity, from meat and wine, from work, and from the destruction of plants and animals.

We have touched on the implications for chastity of any principled rejection of the body. If the body is evil, then human reproduction is evil, and marital chastity as known to Christians and to the paganism of classical antiquity is left without a role. There can be no such virtue unless understood as total abstinence or, perhaps, perfect contraception.

The Manichaean aversion to offspring, with its dismissal of chastity and its reliance on contraception, is strikingly like modern anti-natalist ideology. Modern 'population control,' especially the conjoined propaganda that babies

[7] Burkitt opines 'that St Ephraim is right when he regards the main principle of the cosmogony of Mani as derived from Bardaisan' (*The Religion of the Manichees*, p. 77). But he holds that Mani took his moral and social teachings from another source: 'Ephraim's *Refutations* go far to show that here Mani's master was Marcion' (p. 80).

Burkitt points out (p. 14) that Ephraim had the advantage of being able to read Mani's writings in the language original to most of them, Syriac, and that he died in 373, only a century after Mani himself.

[8] Two such categories of adherents was a characteristic of dualist sects. Among the Cathars, the special subject of this chapter, they were known as the Perfects and the Believers. Jonathan Sumption writes: 'after Marcion, all dualists had two fundamental points in common. The first was a belief in the creation of matter by the Devil, or Demiurge, and thus in the desirability of total continence and extreme asceticism. The second, arising out of this, was a church organization which divided its members into practitioners and believers, the two separated by an imposing ceremony of initiation. Hence the distinction between *gnosis*, the knowledge of the initiated practitioner, and *pistis*, the faith of the ordinary believer' (*The Albigensian Crusade* [London and Boston: Faber & Faber, 1978], pp. 33–4).

Sumption is not right in all respects. Some Cathar sects thought matter pre-existing, merely cast in its current form by an evil agent. Nor, as we have seen, did Bardaisan think matter evil, or demand total continence.

are a plague on the earth and that chaste behavior is not a realistic option, has had a powerful impact on modern society, modern politics, and even the modern economy. We shall see other similarities between the older dualisms and modern ideologies, and their effect on modern society, when we study the medieval Manichees known as Cathars.

Rebirth of a Second God

Although the doctrine of Mani, and some forms of Manichaean ecclesiastical organization, extended from the Atlantic across the Eurasian land mass to Chinese Turkestan,[9] it is not possible in the present state of research to trace any direct development of Manichaeism into medieval dualisms. What we do know is that by the opening of the High Middle Ages dualism was in the air. To become infected by it was probably easy enough wherever orthodoxy had lost its vigor.

During the seventh century an anti-hierarchical movement among Armenian Christians had adopted a dualist doctrine and become known by the name *Paulician*, possibly from a son named Paul of the legendary Manichaean woman Kallinike.[10] The Paulicians were rigorously dualistic, positing two gods and abhorring material creation. These heretics grew into a formidable military force in Thrace, where groups of them from various parts of the Byzantine Empire had been deported in the eighth century. From their headquarters in Philippopolis (modern Plovdiv, in Bulgaria) they ravaged the territories of their neighbors in the ninth and tenth centuries. The terror they inspired left on dualism the mark of Cain, and could account for much of the odium that fell upon

[9] Some notion of how wide the doctrines of Mani had spread can be deduced from the fact that Manichee documents discovered early in the twentieth century in Chinese Turkestan were written in Middle Persian (Soghdian) and Proto-Turkish, while other documents found there and bearing on Manichaean doctrine are in Chinese. See Burkitt, *The Religion of the Manichees*, pp. 15 and 16.

[10] This movement, which played a political and military role in the Byzantine Empire, finds treatment in standard sources such as the *Dictionnaire de théologie catholique* and the *New Catholic Encyclopedia.*

dualistic heretics during the Middle Ages. However, it appears to have left little impression on those historians who dismiss the Church's alarm at the rise of dualism in the medieval West. The precedent of subversion within the Byzantine world only two centuries earlier seems to have raised no questions among them.

Yet it is virtually impossible to exhaust all the ways in which dualism, and specifically the dualism known as Catharism, threatened society. The Catharist rejection of oaths is sometimes cited, since the order of society in medieval times depended heavily on the oath; for instance, the refusal of secular Franciscans to take feudal oaths speeded the decline of feudalism and the serfdom that was attached to it. Yet nothing, realistically speaking, could pose a more direct or dangerous threat to civil society than the Catharist condemnation of the family and of procreation. It struck at the heart.

Henry Charles Lea, who has probably devoted more time than any other writer in English to searching out and delving into original documentation on the Cathars, and who was no friend of their foes, pronounces severe judgment on their religion:

> however much we may deprecate the means used for its suppression, and commiserate those who suffered for conscience' sake, we cannot but admit that the cause of orthodoxy was in this case the cause of progress and civilization. Had Catharism become dominant, or even had it been allowed to exist on equal terms, its influence could not have failed to prove disastrous.[11]

Hilaire Belloc called Catharism 'an attack not only on the religion that made our civilization, but on that civilization itself.'[12] We shall see that its principal point of attack was against chastity; indeed a term for sodomy, ensconced both

[11] *A History of the Inquisition of the Middle Ages* (New York: Harper & Bros., 1887), vol. 1, p. 106.

[12] *The Great Heresies* (n.p.: Sheed & Ward, 1938; repr. edn., Manassas, Va.: Trinity Communications, 1987), p. 97.

in vulgar speech and in the vocabulary of the law, is taken from a name widely applied to the Cathars, 'Bougres.'[13]

Despite the Cathar teaching that marriage and procreation were evil, ordinary believers lived as they thought themselves able to live, or found themselves willing to live: they married and had children. Rather than do this evil, some might think it better to spill their seed *in vas indebitum*, as their opponents would put it; hence the vulgar yet, in the Common Law, correct term *buggary* for the behavior imputed to these disciples of Bulgarian dualists.

Certainly the imputation was plausible enough in view of their dogmatic hatred of normal sexual intercourse. Given this teaching, and the strength of the sexual drive, the practice was probably far from unknown among them. None the less the Cathar *perfecti* were so widely esteemed for austerity of life that only the few Catholics of equal asceticism could win equal esteem and thus combat the heresy effectively.

The Cathar threat to the West was deadly not only because its dogmas attacked the family, which is at once the basic unit of the body politic and the principle of regeneration of that larger society when it falters or fails. Nor was it deadly only because Cathar doctrine constituted a rival to the institution that had carried the cultural and ethical elements of Western civilization into the Middle Ages, indeed stood as the very embodiment of that civilization, and as its sole defender of consequence. The deadliness of the Cathar threat stemmed also from the great wealth and high culture that flourished in the land where Catharism most flourished, plus the commercially and militarily strategic situation of that land, in what now makes up southern France.

Hilaire Belloc writes:

> For the country over which the Albigensians had power was the wealthiest and best organized of the West. It had the highest culture, commanded the trade of the Western Mediterranean

[13] Term of the times, from medieval Latin, for Bulgarian, testifying to the belief, probably justified, that Catharism found its way to the West from Bulgaria.

> with the great port of Narbonne, it barred the way of all northern efforts southward, and its example would have been inevitably followed.[14]

Thus the defeat of the Cathars was not just an episode in the history of the Middle Ages. It ranks with the containment of the West's military enemies, the rise of communes and of the monarchy, the revival of commerce and of letters, and the recovery of Aristotle as a turning point of the times and of history.

Just where the Cathar dualists got their doctrine, no one really knows. A direct line from the Paulicians to the Cathars is sometimes traced, though it has little more than superficial plausibility, and the lack of a plausible alternative, to recommend it. The line would run through a Bulgarian priest of the tenth century named Bogomil, who is said to have drawn his dualistic doctrines from the Paulicians and from other gnostics.[15] But whatever the source of the Bogomil doctrines, the Bogomiles are the likeliest source of the dualistic doctrines that made themselves felt in Europe in the eleventh century. Perhaps, as is sometimes suggested, soldiers of the First Crusade were infected in the Balkans or in Constantinople, itself a Bogomil center by then.[16]

[14] *The Great Heresies*, pp. 110–11.

[15] Thus the *Dictionnaire de théologie catholique*, s.v. 'Bogomiles,' referring to Euchites, also known as Messalians. (Both names come from a word meaning 'prayer,' the former from the Greek, the latter from the Syriac.) These gnostics arose in Mesopotamia, just when is not known, and were found in Syria and Asia Minor by the second half of the fourth century. Before all mention of them as a contemporary phenomenon had ceased in works of the early twelfth century, they had spread throughout the East. They bore less the characteristics of an organized sect than those of bands of vagabonds. It is not thought that they posited two gods, but they did offer placatory rites to Satan. See *Dictionnaire de théologie catholique*, s.v. 'Euchites.'

[16] Cf. *Handbook of Church History*, vol. 4, ed. H. Jedin and J. Dolan (Freiburg: Herder, 1970), p. 99. Here merchants are mentioned as well as Crusaders.

Christine Thouzellier attributes the contagion to the Second Crusade; see *Catharisme et Valdéisme en Languedoc à la fin du XIIe et au début du XIIIe Siècle*, 2nd edn. (Louvain: Editions Nauwelaerts, 1969), p. 12. However, this would not explain earlier phenomena such as, it seems, the Liège trial cited below in the text; nor would it explain another case referred to later in the text, the presence near Cologne in 1143, several years before the Second Crusade, of heretics

No doubt it would be highly ironic if the Crusaders, embarked on a self-sacrificing enterprise to regain the Holy Places for Christendom, became carriers of the virus that threatened Christian civilization, or rather civilization *tout court.* We can only speculate how such a thing could happen.

One element of a solution, probably, is the fact that not all who marched on the Crusades bore arms. When Pope Urban II uttered his rallying cry for a Crusade at the Council of Clermont in 1095, a 'popular element' rallied to it along with the nobles, knights, and men-at-arms.[17] Many would prove themselves less pilgrims than adventurers. Moreover as privation, disease, and decimation overtook the forces bound for the Holy Land, disillusion followed close behind. The most idealistic especially, as always, were prey to bitterness and cynicism at the occasional degeneration of the enterprise into plunder, at self-serving among the leaders, at the growing custom of redeeming the Crusader's vow through the purchase of fighting men. By the thirteenth century there were open and widespread challenges to the very principle of the Crusades.[18]

In the previous century, however, and within less than half a century from the papal summons to the first Crusade, 'a regular hierarchy of hearers, believers, priests, and prelates was discovered' among heretics put on trial in Liège.[19]

---

answering the description of Cathars; see Eberwin of Steinfeld's appeal to St Bernard (Walter Wakefield and Austin Evans, *Heresies of the High Middle Ages* [New York and London: Columbia University Press, 1969], pp. 126–32).

[17] 'it was not only warrior knights who responded: a popular element, apparently unexpected and probably not desired, also came forward' (*Encyclopaedia Britannica, Macropaedia* (Chicago: Encyclopaedia Britannica, 1974), s.v. 'Crusades'). 'Contrary to the intentions of Urban II, unarmed pilgrims joined the first and the following Crusades. These noncombatants, who lived on alms, were a burden to the army and suffered severely from the privations to which they, first of all, were exposed. They were a turbulent element within the crusading body' (*New Catholic Encyclopedia* [New York: McGraw-Hill, 1967–], s.v. 'Crusades').

[18] See *Handbook of Church History*, vol. 4, p. 286. For the opinions of Roger Bacon, Blessed John Duns Scotus, and Marsilius of Padua, see p. 391.

[19] *Handbook of Church History*, vol. 4, p. 100, where it is suggested that the defendants may have been 'the first representatives of this new but soon increasingly threatening movement.'

Heretics answering the description of Cathars cropped up near Cologne shortly thereafter.[20] By the seventh decade of that same twelfth century heresy made itself known in England and Italy; it took firm root in the north of the Italian peninsula, specifically Lombardy and Tuscany, and sent its tendrils southward.[21] But it made its deepest inroads in that country which extended, roughly, from the marches of Gascony eastward to the Rhône, and where *yes* was heard as *oc.* Because of this linguistic peculiarity the country eventually became known as Languedoc, and is known by that name to this day.

The name, which was not used until well into the period we are dealing with, was imposed by conquerors, whose own language used *oïl*, that is, in modern form, *oui*, for *yes.* This form derived from the Latin *ille*, the other from *hoc.* Because the region was not known as Languedoc until after its conquest by the North, in the middle of the thirteenth century, the name, strictly speaking, is anachronistic when used, as it is in this work and indeed almost universally, to describe the region before that time.

But to refer to this region as southern France is worse than an anachronism; it is seriously misleading. The political struggle that emerged from the doctrinal struggle was fought by men of the North – France, roughly speaking, but also Germany and Burgundy – against men of the South. The point is not merely technical: it is pivotal to an understanding of the military struggle against heresy in the Middle Ages, though it is of course irrelevant to the theological foundations of the struggle. The region later known as Languedoc was not a part of France, which in those days was more properly confined

[20] P. Timko calls Eberwin's letter to St Bernard about these heretics 'a milestone in the history of popular heresy, because it provides the first unambiguous evidence of the infiltration into Western Europe of the Bogomil missionaries who brought dualism from the East' ('What is the Church? The Ecclesiology of Moneta of Cremona's *Adversus Catharos et Valdenses*,' doctoral diss., Catholic University of America, 1989, p. 37).

[21] For an account of the spread of Catharism in central Italy, see Mariano d'Alatri, OFMCap, 'L'Inquisizione francescana nell'Italia centrale nel secolo XIII,' *Collectanea Franciscana*, 22 (1952), pp. 225–50, and 23 (1953), pp. 51–165. The final 33 pages consist of documentation.

to what was then called Francia and is today known as the Ile-de-France. True, some of the Languedocian nobles were vassals of the king of France, but some were vassals of the king of Aragon.

Far from considering themselves Frenchmen, the men of Languedoc deemed Frenchmen aliens: these men of the North, these Franks, were of different allegiances and different blood and different language. In language, and to a certain extent in culture too, the men of Languedoc were closer to the Aragonese and Piedmontese than to the northerners. Hence the Albigensian Crusade took on the color of conquest. It became a political struggle of Languedocians against intruders from the north, especially 'Frenchmen' (more properly *Franks*). This helps explain how some whose Catholicity could not be doubted took sides against the Crusaders.

Near the chief city of Languedoc, Toulouse, in a town called St-Felix-de-Caraman, the Cathars are said to have held a decisive council by 1167, and to have set up at that meeting their own ecclesiastical organization throughout Languedoc and Lombardy.[22] There may be doubt about the historicity of the council, but there is none about how widespread was the heresy. Nor are there doubts about how thoroughly organized it was even if, lacking a central doctrinal and disciplinary authority and an established canon of authoritative books, it inevitably fragmented into dissenting groups. It is said that at that council of St-Felix-de-Caraman the Cathar hierarch Nicetus, having come from Constantinople, united the Cathars of Languedoc in belief in absolute dualism.[23]

However, the distinction between absolute and mitigated dualism is vague and variable. Definitions not immediately applied to the case at hand are misleading because there are many different kinds of theological dualism.[24] The absolute

[22] See Thouzellier, *Catharisme et Valdéisme eu Languedoc*, pp. 13 and 14 for an account of this council and for doubts about its date and historicity.

[23] Thus, e.g., Thouzellier, ibid., p. 13.

[24] The definition in *Handbook of Church History*, vol. 4, pp. 99–100, is one example, and another is found in Timko, 'What is the Church?', p. 64.

and mitigated forms frequently distinguished those who held to the *creation* of matter by an evil principle, the devil, from those who held that the devil merely *divided* the elements, created by the one God. However, other Cathars spoke of the principle of evil as a god. Another form of dualism held that matter was not created but pre-existed, and that an evil force shaped it into its present form; this was attributed to Marcion.[25]

[25] The shadowy figure Bonacursus, a twelfth-century Italian convert to Catholicity from Catharism, writes of differences among the Cathars: 'Some of them say that God created the elements, while others say no, rather the devil. However the opinion of all is that the devil divided them.' (Cited by Thouzellier, *Catharisme et Valdéisme eu Languedoc*, p. 107. Mlle Thouzellier takes the lines from the text of Bonacursus' *Manifestatio haeresis catharorum quam fecit Bonacursus* as given by Raoul Manselli, 'Per la storia dell'eresia nel secolo XII,' in *Bullettino dell'Istituto storico italiano per il medio evo e Archivio Muratoriano*, 67 [1965]).

Ranerius Sacconi, who after his conversion from Catharism became a Dominican friar and an inquisitor, wrote in his *Summa de Catharis* (1250) of the 'general beliefs of the Cathars,' saying that they believe 'the devil made this world and everything in it' (Wakefield and Evans, *Heresies of the High Middle Ages*, p. 330). In the same *Summa*, Sacconi analyzes the divergent doctrines found among the sixteen Cathar churches he lists, while asking the reader not to blame him for calling them churches 'since this is how they refer to themselves.' He lists three in Languedoc: the Toulousan, that of Carcassonne, and the Albigensian. (This last held none of the pre-eminence ascribed to it by authors seeking to find in it an explanation for the name applied to Cathars throughout Languedoc: Albigensian. One who falls into this facile error is G. G. Coulton in his *Inquisition and Liberty* [London and Toronto: William Heinemann Ltd., 1938], p. 70. The reason for calling the Cathars Albigenses is not known.)

Sacconi says that the doctrine of the Cathar heresiarch John de Lugio holds 'that there are from eternity two principles, or gods, or lords, namely, one of good and the other of evil' (*Summa*, 19, given in Wakefield and Evans, *Heresies of the High Middle Ages*, p. 339).

The Book of Two Principles, widely but not universally attributed to John de Lugio, maintains: 'there is, in addition to the faithful Creator . . . , another god and lord who is a creator and maker' (part IV, cited in ibid., p. 561).

Moneta of Cremona, a Dominican inquisitor, wrote in a *summa* against the Cathars about the year 1241:

> Some of them assert that there are two principles, without beginning or end. One they say is the Father of Christ and of all the Just, the God of Light; the other they believe to be him of whom Christ said in John 14:30, 'The prince of this world cometh.' Him they believe to be the god . . . of darkness.
>
> These persons believe that the latter created these four elements which we can see. . . .

In the presence of these varieties of theological dualism, the distinction between absolute or radical dualism on the one hand and mitigated dualism on the other is not helpful without further specification.

It is outside our purpose to examine and categorize all the variations of Cathar doctrine. They do not affect our study of chastity since common to all Cathars was a belief that matter was evil, hence that procreation was a prolongation of the evil of material existence, and chaste wedlock a hoax. That belief alone would have sufficed to move the Catholic Church to marshall its outstanding men, from the monk Bernard of Clairvaux to the soldier Simon de Montfort, and thousands of others, soldiers and scholars and preachers and inquisitors, not a few of them saints, for the struggle against Catharism. Yet there was a deeper reason for the Church's alarm, a dogmatic reason for her decisive and indeed drastic action; nor does our own focus on the socially destructive dynamic of Catharism exempt us from examining this fundamental theological teaching. It is the source and principle of the Cathar teaching on – or rather against – chastity, hence of the social dynamic that sprang from that teaching.

The very first article of the Nicene Creed professes belief in one God, the Father Almighty, creator of heaven and earth,

---

They also believe him to be the God of whom Moses spoke in the first chapter of Genesis: 'In the beginning God created heaven and earth' [clearly this is the Marcionite God of the Old Testament] . . . Those who assert there is one Creator . . . suppose that there is a prince of the world whom the Scriptures call the devil and Satan, who, after the creation of primal matter by God, divided that matter into four elements' (translation in Wakefield and Evans, *Heresies of the High Middle Ages*, pp. 308 and 312, from *Monetae Cremonensis adversus Catharos et Valdenses libri quinque* i, ed. Thomas A. Ricchini [Rome, 1743]).

Bernard Gui, a Dominican inquisitor whose account of Cathar doctrine utilizes the confession he got in 1310 from the Cathar pastor Peter Authier, wrote that the Manichaeans 'declare and confess that there are two gods and two lords, to wit, a beneficent God and an evil one.' But he continues: 'Thus they postulate two creators, namely, God and the devil' (*The Conduct of the Inquisition*, V. i. 1, Wakefield and Evans, *Heresies of the High Middle Ages*, p. 379, translated by them from an edition published in 'Les Classiques de l'histoire de France au moyen âge,' VIII, IX [Paris, 1926–7]).

and of all things visible and invisible. To deny God's existence, then, might seem the basic heresy, but it is not. Atheism is rather the basic *unbelief*; it is not heresy since what it denies is the whole supernatural order, not some part of the Catholic Faith.[26] The basic *heresy*, denying the opening proposition of the Creed, is theological dualism. God is not one, but two. Nor is he almighty. He may be our Father, but only of our spiritual selves, not of our bodies. He created heaven but not earth. Earthbound things, including the flesh and all that goes with it such as nourishment and procreation, were brought into being or at least shaped by another god or demiurge or principle, who might or might not be evil. The one God and Lord of all creation is a Catholic illusion.

Theological dualism, dogged by irresoluble inconsistencies stemming from its cavalier disregard for metaphysics, found itself, as we know, wavering between one or another attempt to reconcile them. Despite the many such variants found among the Cathars, even touching basic theological dualism itself, also called *ditheism*, the doctrine that interests us especially remained a constant, a theme of unity among them. It was a profound hatred of matter as the visible element of evil, a hatred that turned against the human body and all other material creation as well.

The Cathar Mystery

What was the attraction of this heresy? Of a heresy that posited two gods, or at least a principle rivalling God in creation or

[26] The classic definition of heresy is St Thomas's: 'a species of unbelief pertaining to those who profess the faith of Christ but corrupt its dogmas' (II-II. 11. 1).

Belloc, after giving a definition of heresy that can apply to secular matters, namely 'the dislocation of some complete and self-supporting scheme by the introduction of a novel denial of some essential part therein' (*The Great Heresies*, p. 10), comments astutely: 'The denial of a scheme wholesale is not heresy, and has not the creative power of heresy. It is of the essence of heresy that it leaves standing a great part of the structure it attacks. On this account it can appeal to believers and continues to affect their lives through deflecting them from their original characters. Wherefore, it is said of heresies that "they survive by the truths they retain"' (p. 12).

in the disposition of material things? Of a heresy that was at one, however great its divisions, in holding the body and its delights not just in contempt but in abhorrence? That made of marriage a moral pigsty, literally no better than prostitution?

The real Cathar mystery is not what the Cathars taught but how they could believe it.

There are several ways of approaching this question, none of them wholly satisfactory in the present state of our knowledge. We simply do not know enough about Cathar psychology to say with certainty why they believed what they did, nor do we know enough about particular problems of theirs that may have led them to seek a solution in Catharism. We do know that the impoverishment of knights and certain nobles was such that they entrusted their daughters to convents of Cathar women for shelter and education, but the socio-economic explanation attempted by Marxists has not proved convincing, to say no more.[27]

We are forced back onto hypothesis. Because we know the nature of the heresy, and because we know human nature, we can deduce with some confidence what attractions it probably held. The two principal approaches are

[27] See, e.g., Gottfried Koch, *Frauenfrage und Ketzertum im Mittelalter*, Forschungen zur mittelalterlichen Geschichte, vol. 9 (Berlin: Akademie-Verlag, 1962).

This book, by a Marxist historian, is subjected to a sympathetic but eventually destructive critique by E. Delarouelle in 'Problèmes socio-économiques à Toulouse vers 1200,' in *Cahiers de Fanjeaux*, vol. 1 (Toulouse: Edouard Privat, 1966). A work produced by N. Todorov and others for the former Marxist regime of Bulgaria, *Bulgaria: Historical and Geographical Outline* (Sofia: Foreign Languages Press, 1965), assumes without any attempt at proof that the Bogomiles of medieval Bulgaria were social revolutionaries and freedom fighters:

> The teaching of the Bogomils gave vivid expression to the people's indignation and resentment; it was social in its essence, but religious in form....
>
> It was from their ranks that the fearless fighters for social justice, equality and freedom emerged. They fought arms in hand and shook the foundations of the Bulgarian state' (pp. 37–8).

Curiously, the same book reports that the Bogomile preachers 'preached against wars and the bloodshed they caused' (p. 38).

theological: one moral and the other intellectual, yet focused, both of them, on the problem of evil, probably the most vexing problem in theology, certainly the most anguishing problem in human life.

By positing two gods, or two principles of creation, or two masters of the universe, Catharism offered a solution to the theoretical question of how evil entered the world, a question that may seem all but intractable within a theology of the one God. More important for Cathar proselytizing than that intellectual approach was the moral approach. By making material creation the work of the evil principle or god, or by making material creation subject to an evil master, Catharism offered a solution, however gimcrack, to the existential question of evil in the lives of men.

It is true enough that only men in desperate situations will grasp at desperate solutions, and the Cathar solution was nothing if not desperate: the body is evil; all material creation is evil; hence the creator of material things is evil, and God is not one but two.[28] True also, the men of Languedoc were no more desperate, so far as we know, than the rest of men. But we all find ourselves on the edge of the abyss. What might without undue pessimism be called the drama of the human condition, the only too ordinary drama of deep discontents, of sin, and finally of death, can quite adequately explain the historical fact that a religion damning so much of what makes life worth living, including the human body itself, very nearly swept away a highly cultured society.[29]

[28] According to Tertullian (*Adversus Marcionem*, I. 2) Marcion deduced the evil of the principle of material creation from the evil of material creation itself.

[29] Belloc calls Albigensianism 'the peril which had proved so nearly mortal to Europe' (*The Great Heresies*, p. 111). Speaking of Muret, the astounding yet all-but-ignored battle of 1213 in which Simon de Montfort and his Catholic knights routed an Albigensian force one hundred times their number, Belloc makes the claim: 'Had Muret been lost, instead of being miraculously won, ... almost certainly the new heresy would have triumphed. With it our culture of the West would have sunk, hamstrung, to the ground' (p. 110).

The genius of Alexander Pope poses the dilemma that faces almost any man:

> Placed on this isthmus of a middle state,
> A being darkly wise and rudely great:
> With too much knowledge for the Sceptic side,
> With too much weakness for the Stoic's pride,
> He hangs between, in doubt to act or rest;
> In doubt to deem himself a God or Beast;
> In doubt his mind or body to prefer;
> Born but to die, and reas'ning to err.[30]

Here, in the near-despair that comes upon men through the awareness of their fallibility and mortality, the poet finds the chink through which the absurdities of Catharism could seep into the mind of Languedoc. Men knew they were going to die. They knew they must suffer and knew they would sin. They dared not reason too deep about these tragic mysteries. An easy if desperate answer was proferred them, and they seized it, desperately perhaps, and no doubt too easily. Yet so precious did it become to them that many of them died rather than yield it.

For the terrors of death, Catharism offered solace. No one need fear hell, for there is no such place.[31] If a man died in sin, he could do penance in another existence, imprisoned indeed in an even baser body than this human carcass but able to work himself back into the human state eventually, and have another crack at heaven. Moreover, he could prepare himself for death prudently through the *consolament*, the sacred initiation into the life of the Perfect which guaranteed salvation, and was indeed the only road to salvation; it became in practice the extreme unction, so to speak, of Catharism.[32] And if he recovered physically and then fell morally, there was the hope that before death he might receive the *consolament* again.

[30] *Essay on Man*, Epistle II, 3–10.

[31] See, e.g., *Brevis summula contra errores notatos hereticorum*, section on the Albanenses, in Wakefield and Evans, *Heresies of the High Middle Ages*, p. 355.

[32] The term usually employed, *consolamentum*, is a Latinized form of the Provençal (that is, Languedocian) *consolament*.

Since the *consolament* was administered both to usher a healthy person into the austere life of the Perfect, and also to ready an infirm person for death, two kinds of *consolament* have been distinguished.[33] However, no difference in the ritual has been discovered, so the intention of the recipient was probably decisive. An ordinary Cathar who received the *consolament* in danger of death but who returned to health also returned, ordinarily, to his former way of life. That would mean living a normal married life despite the Cathar condemnation of marriage, and despite the Cathar condemnation of procreation.

To speak plainly, there are many repulsive teachings of Catharism, such as the clinically pathological rejection of material things, including the beauties of sensible creation; such also as the *endura* or ritual suicide.[34] But none of these

[33] René Nelli, in advancing this distinction, cites Alain of Lille, the Cistercian *doctor universalis* and adversary of Catharism in Languedoc, and Jean Duvernoy, who published copiously about the Cathars in the 1950s and 60s. He admits however that no distinction in the rites has been discovered. See his *La Philosophie du Catharisme* (Paris: Payot, 1978), p. 194.

Nelli also wrestles with the problem of the *aparalhament*, or Cathar confession of faults. Without further specification he ascribes to J. Duvernoy (presumably in a work listed in Nelli's bibliography, 'La Liturgie et l'église cathares,' *Cahiers d'études cathares*, Spring 1965, Autumn 1967) the view that it was a monthly confession of the Perfect before the bishop or an elder. See Nelli's *Les Cathares* (Paris: Grasset, 1972), pp. 236, 234.

[34] *Endura* is a Languedocian word meaning privation or fast. Nelli, who unfailingly puts a benevolent construction on Cathar customs, describes it thus:

> A sort of mystic suicide in no way blameworthy: to leave this life for love . . . has always been the desire of truly spiritual members of all religions.
>
> In the 13th century it came about that the Cathars, hating the world and having only a few days to live, allowed themselves to die of hunger, after having received the *consolamentum*, because they were no longer able to say the *Pater* before eating and drinking, and because they feared falling back into sin and losing the benefit of the relative and provisory sanctification that they had received from God and the circumstances, without much 'meriting' it.
>
> The *endura* consisted ordinarily in letting oneself die of inanition, or of cold (more rarely). It was never encouraged by the Perfects or, *a fortiori*, imposed by them. It was never moreover widespread except at the end of the 13th century and especially in the county of Foix,

teachings is more distortive of human feeling, more destructive of the common good, than the Cathar teaching on sexuality, the teaching that all genital activity is evil, the procreation of children evil, so that marriage is no better than prostitution. What, we find ourselves asking again, as indeed at every turn, could possibly be the attraction of a doctrine like that?

Here the hypothetical character of our explanation is most manifest, yet the hypothesis itself is most compelling. Although the historic origin of this Cathar doctrine has not been documented, we find a clue in a hatred of genital activity carried to the extreme, grotesque, and – one might find – revolting point of calling offspring evil. Catharism must in part originate from the self-contempt men feel at their subjection to sexual passion, at their submission to the tyranny of lust, at the unhappiness they create through indulging this appetite where reason demands that they abstain, conceiving children where those innocent and defenseless young persons cannot be properly nurtured and educated.

Far less speculative are the practical effects of such doctrines, and it is significant how little is made by modern scholars, especially those writing in English, of the perversions of thought and behavior that must perforce stem from the dogmatic root of this heresy. Jonathan Sumption, for example, does not even suggest that Cathar principles were corrosive of personal morality, the family, and the broader society. Rather, he makes antagonism toward Cathar doctrine and practice subjective, and a peculiarity of the people who lived in certain places at certain times. 'In a society which regarded religion as the foundation of secular life,' he observes in explaining the 'persecution' of Cathars by secular princes, lynch mobs, and finally the Inquisition, 'their attitude is not surprising. A mediaeval community was defined as much by

---

under the influence of the pastor Pierre Authier, in times when the Inquisition strove to render life impossible for believers. (*Les Cathares*, pp. 238–9)

its religion as by its political allegiance or geographical cohesion.'[35]

Joseph Strayer offers another case in point. Asserting a lack of sufficient historical evidence, he dismisses the charge that Catharism led to lax living. And to the charge, 'more logical but almost as lacking in proof,' that Catharism would have extinguished the human race by its denunciation of sexual intercourse, he responds that few Believers (Cathars who did not live according to the fulness of teaching) became Perfects (those who did) during the child-producing years.[36] But he gives no sign of considering the schizoid psychology inherent in the Cathar ethos: the split between belief and behavior, the perhaps more destructive dichotomy between hatred of the body and love of offspring.

Albert Camus, ordinarily a perceptive writer, falls into outright absurdity when dealing with this historical question. He writes in *The Rebel*:

> Hellenism, in association with Christianity, then produces the admirable efflorescence of the Albigensian heresy on the one hand, and on the other Saint Francis. But with the Inquisition and the destruction of the Albigensian heresy, the Church again parts company with the world and with beauty.[37]

We shall examine, in the context of poetry, the contrast between the Catholic, and particularly Franciscan, apprecia-tion of the beauty of all creation and the Cathar hatred of the visible world, work of Satan.

Camus prefaces his remarks with the claim:

> For the Christian, as for the Marxist, nature must be subdued. The Greeks are of the opinion that it is better to

[35] *The Albigensian Crusade*, p. 40.

[36] *The Albigensian Crusade* (New York: Dial Press, 1971), pp. 31 and 32. Adducing no evidence, Professor Strayer asserts: 'The real problem for the Catholic Church was not that Catharism was leading to immorality or race suicide, but that it was interesting a very large part of the population of Occitania and gaining the support of a sizeable minority' (p. 32; *Occitania* is a term coined in modern times as a substitute for *Languedoc*; it was designed to avoid the opprobrious overtones of a name imposed by conquerors).

[37] Tr. Anthony Brower (New York: Vintage Books, 1956), p. 190.

obey it. The love of the ancients for the cosmos was completely unknown to the first Christians.

If this last charge is not too extravagant to merit rebuttal, rebuttal can be found in a constant of Christian literature: praise of the Creator through the glory of his creatures. 'None of the glorious creatures of God should remain silent,' says an early hymn of Oxyrhynchos in Egypt. 'The waters of the rustling stream should give praise to our Father and Son and Holy Ghost.'[38]

Just what Camus means by saying Christians think nature must be subdued is not clear. He is literally correct in that Christians follow the Genesis injunction to subdue nature, but he seems to take it to mean that Christians believe nature must be crushed. Of course a venerable principle of Christian thought holds that grace does not destroy nature but perfects it.[39]

Perhaps the most elaborate modern rebuttal of the Catholic opposition to Cathar teaching comes from Bernard Hamilton. He writes:

> Within a generation of the arrival of the first Cathars the people of Languedoc and Lombardy had found that the heretics were not a threat to their society at all. Catholic polemicists were quick to point out the logical consequences of Catharism on a social level: the Cathars were pacifists and their presence would weaken the power of rulers to wage just wars; the Cathars refused to take oaths, and this would undermine the whole fabric of tenurial and legal structures; while the Cathars' abhorrence of sex would, if generally adopted, depopulate whole regions. These fears were found, in practice, to be groundless, because although many people admired the holy lives led by the Cathar elect and believed the explanation which they gave about the nature of evil, few were prepared to emulate them and embrace the austere life of the perfect. Moreover, the Cathars themselves were rigorously selective in the admission of postulants to full membership of their

[38] Johannes Quasten, *Patrology*, vol. 1 (Westminster, Md.: Newman Press, 1950), pp. 159–60.

[39] See I. 1. 8, ad 2.

> church. Yet in Cathar belief only those who had been consoled were members of the church and were bound by its rules. An unconsoled Cathar believer might behave as he chose: he might marry and beget children, own property, take part in war, swear oaths, eat meat, and even take part in Catholic worship.[40]

This passage ignores the canker planted within the Cathar society itself, hence in society at large were it to become Cathar, by defeatism in the order of morality, by the resulting consecrated tolerance of sinful lives among the vast majority of that society's members, the Believers, and by the schizoid psyche that the members of such a society must carry around with them. Understood broadly, the right of the ordinary man to 'behave as he chose,' in Hamilton's phrase, is a formula for a social order that is no order at all, and hence something worse than barbarism. It is a formula for the rule of brute strength and lust. It is a formula for the destruction of the family, which is the best and only secure haven for the weakest and most in need of help, for the youngest and most in need of protection and training, for the oldest and most in need of support, and which is the regenerating principle of the larger society should it weaken and fail.

We might note further that our author does not even mention the corrosive implications of Cathar doctrine for the family.

The passage is thoroughly modern in its received notions: scepticism about the consequences of convictions, indiffer-

[40] *The Medieval Inquisition* (New York: Holmes & Meier Publishers, Inc., 1981), p. 26. Lea, writing almost a century earlier, took quite another tack: '[Catharism's] asceticism with regard to commerce between the sexes, if strictly enforced, could only have led to the extinction of the race, and as this involves a contradiction of nature, it would have probably resulted in lawless concubinage and the destruction of the institution of the family, rather than in the disappearance of the human race and the return of exiled souls to their Creator, which was the *summum bonum* of the true Catharan. Its condemnation of the visible universe and of matter in general as the work of Satan rendered sinful all striving after material improvement, and the conscientious belief in such a creed could only lead man back, in time, to his original condition of savagism' (*A History of the Inquisition*, vol. 1, p. 106).

ence to convictions themselves. How else but through such indifference, such scepticism, can we explain the force attributed to the thesis that one generation of experience with a novel doctrine, held by a minority and cloaked in secrecy, suffices to demonstrate its eventual effect on society, or in this case lack of effect?

The writer himself, quite probably, is a victim of a doctrine first held in the seventeenth century by a minority of one, namely René Descartes, an epistemological error adopted within a generation by philosophers and theologians alike with no evident deleterious effects on society or belief, attacked only here and there and against all plausibility by prophetic spirits only too likely to be regarded as cranks, such as Blaise Pascal, or by antiquarian, not to say antediluvian, pedants such as Aristotelians and Thomists, then after several generations suffered in its consequences by philosophers who, like Kant, attempted to find a way out of the scepticism it had engendered in them. Where those children of this seemingly harmless error failed to clarify the understanding left clouded by its original sin, others, most illustriously of the school of Edmund Husserl, tried again; whether they have failed remains perhaps to be seen, but half a century and more after the death of Husserl, who himself fell back into the idealism he had set off to combat, philosophical realists still feel pressed to defend their position, while the received wisdom in academe still holds bewilderment to be the basic intellectual virtue, and the font of the supreme moral virtue, tolerance.

It is significant that none of the dismissals of the Catholic condemnation of Catharism deals with the virtue of chastity. A typically modern mindset shows little concern for the effect of Catharism on chastity, or the effect of anything on chastity. Such an ethos, aspiring as it usually does to a universal toleration consistent with its scepticism and moral indifference (though neither moral indifference nor complete scepticism, nor universal toleration for that matter, is humanly possible), can scarcely base an argument on the good of chastity. Because we live in an age of license, most men tend to be indifferent or even sympathetic toward the judgment that Catharism pronounces on chastity.

The Cathar verdict on chastity is *guilty*, the sentence it passes on it is death. While that can scarcely be over-emphasized, it is not a judgment that has much interested men of an age that has gone to the length of anointing the licentious as victims of bigotry, without realizing or without caring what destruction the abandonment of chastity wreaks on the familial society, on the body politic, and on the members of both.

We find that the chief defense of society against the ravages of dualism is twofold: faith in the one God, and chaste behavior.

We cannot sensibly speculate on the particular adventures that would have befallen Western society had it followed Cathar principles to any degree, but if *actio sequitur esse* and if convictions have consequences, then that society would sooner or later have reached the end of the road, however many twists and turns it took before arriving there. Plausible protests from academe notwithstanding, a society that depends as heavily on the oath as medieval society did, or as the medical profession did until its precipitous decline from Nazi days onward, a society that depends as utterly on progeny and its quality as any society must, cannot survive too many generations of reasoned hostility toward marriage and oathtaking, both of them sacred in any healthy society.

In the oath, a man puts the integrity of his person at the service of the moral survival of society, no matter how onerous the sacrifice. In the act of wedding, bride and bridegroom make an oath of mutual allegiance, pledging themselves to the service of one another no matter how onerous the sacrifice. Through that quasi-oath, through the child and the education they give him, husband and wife put themselves at the service not only of the physical survival of society but of its moral survival also, again no matter how onerous the sacrifice.

Despite the scepticism of modern commentators toward the manifest destructiveness of the Cathar heresy, or because of that scepticism, it can scarcely be repeated too often that at stake in this struggle was civilization itself, the dynamic of the West, quality of life as measured by quality of conscience, by temper of mind, above all by the objects of love and the objects of abhorrence.

Would men look on the visible world as good or evil? Could they with good conscience enjoy daily life and the pleasures it brings? Could husbands love their wives in the flesh as well as in the spirit? Could mothers look on the bodies of their babies with heartfelt delight, and teach those children to thank their heavenly Father for the wonders of creation? Was motherhood itself evil? Was fatherhood a species of irresponsibility, if not villainy? What would poets praise? Where would their contempt fall?

Heresy, Orthodoxy, and Poetry

Of Cathar poetry we know little, and there is even good reason to doubt that what little has been identified as Cathar poetry is actually such. René Nelli estimates that there were about twenty troubadours 'that one can hold with some probability to be Cathars or favorable to Catharism.'[41] That would be five percent of the 400 troubadour poets known to us through extant texts.[42] Since Nelli cites only one by name, Guilhem of Durfort, presumably he considers Guilhem among the more clearly Cathar of the twenty, for he would not adduce weak evidence to prove or even illustrate his case. Yet he refers to Guilhem's Catharism as 'a hypothesis,' and calls this hypothesis only 'probable enough.'[43]

Nelli admits that even the 'very light Cathar tonality' he gives Guilhem's sole known poem in his translation is also hypothetical.[44] To impart this Cathar coloring to the poem he feels obliged, for example, to give a Cathar religious meaning to a phrase previously understood and translated as having sexual intercourse with a woman.[45] Given the

[41] *Le Phénomène cathare* (Toulouse: Editions Privat, 1964), p. 150.
[42] See A. V. Roche in the *New Catholic Encyclopedia*, s.v. 'Troubadour.'
[43] *Le Phénomène cathare*, p. 154.
[44] Ibid., pp. 154–5.
[45] Ibid., pp. 160–1.

lubricious tenor of the poem, Nelli's construction is on the face of it forced and implausible.

That does not mean that Guilhem of Durfort was not a Cathar. Nelli gives some historical indications, or rather hints, that he was.[46] If so, that would offer some historical support for the speculative theory of a link between Catharism and the amoral love poetry of Languedocian troubadours, which exalted adulterous adventures. But he was one of only 400 known troubadours, a single swallow with no other sign of summer.

Hence we can ask whether there was even such a thing as Cathar poetry. We can ask what this has to say about Cathar doctrine. So far as I know the questions have not been raised, but the answers to them should cast light on the Albigenses.

One question that has been asked is whether there was a strong streak of Catharism in the troubadour movement. This has been a subject of considerable speculation, and understandably. C. S. Lewis and Denis de Rougemont have engaged in it.[47] The troubadours lived in Cathar days and Cathar places, and a harmony can be posited between what Cathars taught and troubadours sang. Some alliance between the two, some dependence between them, would seem entirely possible. Where troubadours exalted adulterous love (and not all did), the Cathars encouraged it by their tolerance and by the sexual defeatism which can be placed at the source of that tolerance, if not of Catharism itself. The Cathars encouraged it by making marriage no better than fornication, hence making fornication no worse than marriage. Again, the high position that the troubadours accorded to women was in accord with Cathar practice.[48]

[46] Ibid., pp. 153–4.

[47] Lewis in *The Allegory of Love* (London: Oxford University Press, 1938) and de Rougemont in *Love in the Western World*, tr. Montgomery Belgion (New York: Pantheon, 1956). Both can be described, and the latter dismissed, as less works of scholarship than of scholarly intuition.

[48] 'The lady ... may be addressed with the masculine *midons* (my lord); and the relation, in many of its formal aspects, between lover and lady is a highly conventional sexual version of the feudal relation between lord and vassal'

Yet Jonathan Sumption observes that a recurring theme among troubadours was 'the idealization of chastity.' He notes:

> It is far from clear that they had any connection with the spread of the Albigensian heresy. Those *troubadours* (and they were few) who expressed any opinion on the Albigensians were almost invariably hostile, and their hostility must be taken to represent the hostility of most of their patrons.[49]

A vivid example of the kind of troubadour that Sumption writes about is Folquet of Marseilles. After living as a married man, he entered a Cistercian monastery and became abbot. Then, as bishop of Toulouse, he stood as one of the most formidable adversaries of the Cathar heresy, working closely with St Dominic and Simon de Montfort. Dante places this forceful character in Paradise.[50] Stanislaw Stronski observes that he is the only troubadour whom Dante puts there.[51] And Dante makes it clear how much he esteemed Folquet's poetry.[52]

(R. H. Green, in *New Catholic Encyclopedia*, s.v. 'Courtly Love'). Canon Delaruelle remarks in 'Problèmes Socio-economiques à Toulouse vers 1200': 'one would really say from these poems that everything is decided in the name of the woman: it is for her that one goes on the Crusade or that one begins a war' (p. 123).

[49] *The Albigensian Crusade*, p. 30.

[50] *Il Paradiso*, IX. 67–108.

[51] *Le Troubadour Folquet de Marseille* (Cracow: 1910; repr. Geneva: Slatkine Reprints, 1968), p. 145*.

[52] See *De vulgari eloquentia*, II. vi. 5–6). Folquet's first love song begins thus:

> Ben an mort mi e lor
> mei huel galiador
> per que's tanh qu'ab els plor,
> pos ylh so an merit,
> dont hanfach fallimen,
> e qui n'aut pueia bas deissen;
> per, en sa merce m'aten,
> car ieu no cre que merces aus faillir
> lai on Dieus volc totz autres bes assir.

> (My deceiving eyes have truly caused my death as well as theirs; it is just, then, that I make them weep, because they deserve it, having made their choice of such a woman that in so doing they fell into a fault; and who climbs high, falls deep; however I put my hope in her pity, for I do not believe that pity can be lacking where God willed to put all other qualities.)

(Text from Stronski, *Le Troubadour Folquet de Marseille*, p. 11. I have given an English version of his French translation, which is found on p. 119.)

Now if we have no Cathar poetry, we possess powerful anti-Cathar poetry. It comes from the pen of a Catholic mystic, one of the great figures of his age, or any age, St Francis of Assisi. Standing athwart the Albigensian dogmas of two divine principles, one responsible for the good kingdom of the spirit, the other for the evil kingdom of matter and the flesh, Francis invokes all creatures in praise of the one God. His 'Canticle of the Creatures' is a paean to the goodness of creation, evoking not only its beauty but, before all else, 'the praise, the glory, and honor' it gives the one Creator. Thus the canticle begins:

> Altissimu, onnipotente, bon Signore,
> tue so le laude, la gloria, e l'honore
> et onne benedictione.
> Ad te solo, Altissimo, se konfano
> e nullu homo ene dignu te mentovare.
>
> (Most high, all-powerful, good Lord,
> yours are the praise, the glory, and the honor
> and all blessing.
> To you alone, Most High, do they belong
> and no man is worthy to call you to mind.)[53]

Then comes the great strophe that has given this poem its popular name, the Canticle of the Sun:

> Laudato sie, mi Signore cun tutte le tue creature
> Spetialmente messor lo frate Sole
> [per] lo quale iorna et allumini noi per loi.
> Et ellu e bellu e radiante cun grande splendore,
> De te, Altissimo, porta significatione.
>
> (Praised be you, my Lord through all your creatures
> Especially my lord brother Sun
> through whom comes day and you light us by him.
> And how handsome he is and radiant with great
> splendor,
> Your likeness, Most High, he carries.)

[53] The Umbrian text is taken from *Il Cantico di Frate Sole* by Luigi Foscolo Benedetto (Florence: G. C. Sansoni, 1941), pp. 25–40. I have followed his editing down to the use of *cun tutte* instead of the customary *cum tucte*. In translating I have also followed Benedetto's understanding of the prepositions *per* and *cun*.

The poet then invokes God's praise 'by sister Moon and the Stars, ... by brother Wind and by Air' in fair and stormy weather, 'through which you give sustenance to all your creatures.'

Praise goes to God from 'sister Water, who is so useful and humble and precious and chaste.'

Fire too, because a creature of God, praises him and becomes a brother to Francis: 'And he is beautiful and playful and robust and strong.'

The poet then sings of the bounty and beauty of 'our Sister, mother Earth,' for through her go praise to God and sustenance to men as she brings forth 'divers fruits with colored flowers.'

Francis has confronted the Cathars with the goodness of creation, and the praise that creatures give their Author. He then turns to men, their sufferings and their sorrows, their pardon and their love. Through all these go praise to the Lord.

Even death becomes a sister to Francis, an occasion of praising God:

> Laudato si', mi Signore, per sora nostra Morte
> corporale
> dalla quale nullu homo vivente po skappare.
>
> (Praised be you, my Lord, by our sister bodily Death
> whom no man living can escape.)

When we consider the tumults of the age of St Francis, when we consider in particular the Franciscan struggle against dualism, it is hard to understand how historians can fail to see that this earliest surviving poem of the Italian *volgare* was a weapon in the battle for Europe's soul. True, in Languedoc itself the outstanding adversary of heresy was St Dominic, along with the Order of Preachers, which he founded, and this undoubtedly helps explain why modern historians overlook the highly effective opposition of Francis and his Friars Minor to the hatred of material things.

The apostrophes that Francis addressed to the sun and the moon and the elements, as we have seen, taught love for the whole of creation, and through it for the one Creator. So did his celebrated but little understood intimacy with animals, from the ravaging wolf to the chirping grasshopper; this too was a forceful blow against Catharism. The heretical antagonists of the Franciscans in the *Little Flowers of St Francis* are our dualist acquaintances, and it is significant that when, in a charming account in the book, the heretics of Rimini refuse to listen to the Franciscan preacher Anthony of Padua, he summons the fishes to lift up their heads and hear him, and to honor their Creator by bowing their heads in reverence, and to show the astonished heretics that material creation not only is good but understands how good it is, and gives glory to its Maker.[54]

No less integral to St Francis's struggle against the Cathars (although he is not known to have even pronounced their name, and never disputed with them[55]) was his struggle against his own body. Here he showed that good as all creation is, man has been weakened and rendered unruly by original sin, and therefore must be disciplined severely. Not for him the sanctioned choice between a widespread abandonment to the

[54] *Little Flowers of St Francis*, I. xxxix.

[55] Thus Omer Englebert, *St Francis of Assisi* (2nd English edn., revd. and augmented by Ignatius Brady, OFM, and Raphael Brown, trs. Eve Marie Cooper [Chicago: Franciscan Herald Press, 1965; repr. edn. Ann Arbor, Mich.: Servant Books, 1979]), p. 66. Raoul Manselli, in outlining the diverse origins of the Dominican and Franciscan orders, offers an explanation of the silence of St Francis on the Cathars: 'The second group [Franciscans] sprang from an impetus of charity, from the desire to repeat on earth the experience of Christ in poverty, in suffering, and in mortification. St Francis did not assign to them any task of disputing with heretics beyond the sincere and fervent preaching of penance' (*L'eresia del male* [Naples: A. Morano, 1963], p. 261).

For Catharism in Francis's own region of Italy, see Ilarino da Milano, OFMCap., 'Il dualismo cataro in Umbria al tempo di San Francesco,' *Atti IV Convegno di Studi Umbria* (1966), pp. 175–216. The Italian Capuchin, a widely-published theologian of his day, essays an explanation of the absence of any direct mention of St Francis's opposition to Catharism in the early Franciscan sources (pp. 211–16). His answer is that St Francis, who was constitutionally averse to controversy and ill-prepared for it theologically, worked against Cathar pessimism through the joy and austerity of his life, and through devotional means such as the Canticle of the Creatures. He echoes Manselli's remark that the Canticle sounded in the ears of the Cathars 'as a long series of horrid blasphemies.'

flesh on the one hand, and on the other an asceticism of the few, these few living tolerantly and complacently side by side with the abandonment of the many. What St Francis taught by his life was an asceticism to which all men were in some degree bound if they were to govern the instincts of fallen human nature and live by the laws of their true nature and of the one Lawgiver.

The Christmas crib that St Francis made popular in the Italy of his day, and in Christian custom to our own day, was an effective weapon against the dualistic abhorrence of the body and of procreation. It aroused love of the infant Jesus in his full humanity, body and soul. St Francis held Mary in reverence precisely because of his reverence for the sacred humanity of Christ, which was her gift to her son. Catholics must love her, he used to say, 'because she made the Lord of Glory our brother.'

But the Church sought not only to win over the Cathars by persuasion, by devotions and poetry and the preaching of missioners such as St Dominic and his friars and, earlier, St Bernard and his fellow Cistercian monks. She sought also to uproot Cathar belief through a new institution, the Inquisition, so named because it searched out heretics instead of waiting for them to make themselves known or to be denounced. She finally turned to arms.

The heretics and their protectors met military defeat, but this did not root out the heresy.[56] It lingered in Languedoc for a century, cropping up also in various parts of Western Europe, and sank from sight only in the fourteenth century.[57]

Has it vanished altogether? Some modern authors, such as Belloc, have spied it in Puritanism. One American legislator who was in the thick of the struggle over Prohibition was so struck by similarities between the Albigenses and the advocates

[56] Nor did it spell political defeat for all the protectors of heresy. The most notorious of them, Raymond VI, Count of Toulouse, found himself restored to all his possessions at the time of his death. See René Nelli, *La Vie quotidienne des Cathares du Languedoc* (Paris: Librairie Hachette, 1969), p. 286.

[57] The execution of the zealous Perfect, Peter Authier, in 1311 is taken as marking the effective end of Catharism in Languedoc.

of Prohibition that he wrote a book on the Albigensian struggle.[58] Prohibition and some other relics of Puritanism are in bad odor today, while the radical otherworldliness of Catharism has nothing to do with modern unbelief.

That leaves us with a curious puzzle. Why do contemporary historians treat Catharism, which tried to cram reality into an outlandish religious mold, which held manifestly anti-social notions, as a progressive movement? Why does sympathy with Catharism abound among works of research and *haute vulgarisation*, not to mention fiction, making it a religion of high morality and romance? With some effort we might imagine this deriving from a dogmatic condemnation of drink

[58] Hoffman Nickerson, *The Inquisition* (Boston and New York: Houghton Mifflin, 1923). As its title suggests, the book ended up as a study of the Inquisition. Nickerson treats of the Manichaean roots of Prohibitionism in ch. 7, 'Epilogue on Prohibition.' Hilaire Belloc contributes a typically feisty preface; Mrs Nickerson was Belloc's secretary.

Belloc's own analysis is worth noting:

> The false doctrine of which the Albigensians were a main example has always been latent among men in various forms, not only in the civilization of Christendom but wherever and whenever men have had to consider the fundamental problems of life, that is, in every time and place. But it happened to take a particularly concentrated form at this moment of history. . . . By what its effects were when it was thus at its highest point of vitality we can estimate what evils similar doctrines do whenever they appear.
>
> For this permanent trouble of the human mind has swollen into three great waves during the Christian period, of which three the Albigensian episode was only the central one. The first great wave was the Manichean tendency of the early Christian centuries. The third was the Puritan movement in Europe accompanying the Reformation, and the sequel of that disease, Jansenism. The first strong movement of the sort was exhausted before the end of the eighth century. The second was destroyed when the definite Albigensian movement was rooted out in the thirteenth century. The third, the Puritan wave, is only now declining, after having worked every kind of evil (*The Great Heresies*, pp. 97–8).

Half a century after Belloc observed the progressive decline of Puritanism, it appears to be a spent force in the United States, except perhaps among the exclusively Bible-based Christians of the South. These Christians have emerged as leaders of the struggle against rampant libertinism in the United States. Not all of them however are puritanically inclined, and that appears to be true even among those who are struggling within their denominations for fidelity to Christian doctrine as those denominations have understood it.

– but of meat? And who would put marriage on a par with prostitution? As for the attempt to induce others to take their own lives, who would find that noble?

Maybe – just maybe – we catch a scent here. For an age that has smashed through virtually every taboo, the barrier now to be swept aside obstructs 'assisted suicide' or 'the right to die.' Compound that with other modern nostrums, such as the absolute condemnation of capital punishment, the notion that to bear children is anti-social, and scepticism of the just war concept.[59] Add, say, the acceptance of high interest as a fact of life.[60] Throw in, finally, a flirtation with nihilism.[61] What emerges is a pattern of parallels between Catharism and modernity that may explain why modern scholars demonstrate a vague if vociferous sympathy for that implausible and indeed sinister creed.

That cannot be the whole answer. It omits what must enter into the judgment that modern scholars pass on things medieval, because our historians are children of our time and sharers in its judgments. They can scarcely escape an inherited, residual suspicion of anything Catholic. A serious definition of modernity is the escape from Catholic dominance over culture and morality. Many moderns take it for granted that without that escape, modern progress could never have been achieved.

Such a temper of mind seems to offer the core explanation for the curiosities we find in modern scholarly treatment of

[59] Cf. the codified list of heretical tenets of three sects of Italian Cathars, dating from the thirteenth century, reproduced in Wakefield and Evans, *Heresies of the High Middle Ages*, pp. 359–61.

[60] Ibid.

[61] Cathars made much of equating evil with both the visible world and with nothingness, hence reducing matter to nothing. See Thouzellier, *Catharisme et Valdéism en Languedoc*, pp. 403–4, and Nelli, *Les Cathares*, 252–5.

Nelli defends the Cathar thesis, and in another work (*La Philosophie du catharisme*, pp. 187–8) disputes the Catholic position defended by Mlle Thouzellier in 'Les Cathares languedociens et le nihil (Jean I,3),' published in *Annales: Economies, sociétes, civilisations*, Jan.–Feb. 1969, p. 3.

Camus does not seem aware of the position of the Cathars on *nihil*, but does link nihilism with suicide: 'absolute nihilism ... accepts suicide as legitimate' (*The Rebel*, p. 6).

the Albigenses. How else can we explain the curious inability of scholars to spy a connection between the Albigensian heresy and the much-admired devotion of St Francis to the glories of material creation and to the child Jesus warmed by the breath of beasts? Another is the failure of historians to see the Cathar struggle in the light of the undeniable greatness of the chief men engaged in it: not only St Francis and St Dominic but the pope who recognized their worth and encouraged them, Innocent III, and Bernard of Clairvaux, *the* man of the twelfth century, who among his other feats saved the Jews of the Rhineland from slaughter, single-handed and at risk of his own life; to this day the number of Jews named Bernard bears testimony to Jewish gratitude for this feat of courage. Bernard and Innocent, Dominic and Francis, all stand among the giants of history.

The endemic bias, to be frank about it, of historians in treating the Cathars is not lost upon René Nelli, who in his many works on the Cathars shows every sympathy for them and their doctrines, and little sympathy for Catholic doctrine, discipline, or institutions. Yet he has still less sympathy for the undiscriminating admirers of the Cathars, and accuses them of bigotry and ignorance. This scholar writes:

> At the beginning of the nineteenth century, the *Philosophes* lost no occasion to stigmatize Simon de Montfort in the name of Tolerance, and the Albigensian Crusade in the name of Humanity. But it is clear that in so doing they obeyed their anti-religious feeling, their hatred of 'Fanaticism,' rather than a concern to rehabilitate the work of the Pure, of whose history and doctrines they were, moreover, ignorant.[62]

Our own age, as heir of the Enlightenment, has been no less cavalier. For example, the Modern Library edition of Dante's *Divine Comedy* brands the Albigensian Crusades 'infamous.'[63]

[62] *Le Catharisme* (Toulouse: Editions Privat/Presses Universitaires de France, 1953), p. 210.

[63] New York: Random House, 1930; p. 460, n. 14 to canto IX of the *Paradiso*.

Admittedly it is not easy for men of cultures once predominantly Protestant, now predominantly secularist, to accept that the ethos of the Catholics who fought the Cathars inspires the deepest convictions and aspirations of the West; that the Catholic ethos, as distinct from the Cathar ethos, shaped our civilization from poetry to politics until the arrival of Machiavelli. This traditional Christian view of good and evil, of death and regeneration, all within the creation of the one God, is spelled out by the greatest poet of our language:

> The earth that's nature's mother is her tomb;
> What is her burying grave that is her womb,
> And from her womb children of divers kind
> We sucking on her natural bosom find,
> Many for many virtues excellent,
> None but for some and yet all different....
> For nought so vile that on the earth doth live
> But to the earth some special good doth give,
> Nor aught so good but strain'd from that fair use
> Revolts from true birth, stumbling on abuse:
> Virtue itself turns vice, being misapplied;
> And vice sometimes by action dignified.[64]

[64] *Romeo and Juliet*, II. iii. 9–14, 17–22. Thomas Carlyle recognized that the traditional Catholic ethos was to be found in Shakespeare, calling him 'the noblest product' of the Catholicism of the Middle Ages' ('The Hero as Poet,' lecture delivered in 1840, published in Thomas Carlyle on *Heroes, Hero-Worship, and the Heroic in History* [Lincoln, Neb., and London: University of Nebraska Press, 1966] p. 102). However, that Shakespeare was a Roman Catholic remains a minority view, advanced mostly by Catholics. This is so despite strong evidence that his father, John Shakespeare, held to the Catholic faith at considerable sacrifice until his death. It is so despite persuasive evidence – if only cumulative and converging – that the poet himself was a Catholic.

A thorough investigation of the question is carried out by Heinrich Mutschmann and Karl Wentersdorf in a book of almost 450 pages systematically studying many aspects of Shakespeare's life, times, and works. These authors conclude: 'Shakespeare belonged to the [Catholic] party which compromised without, however, undergoing an interior change: he avoided attending Anglican church services as far as possible, and retained his Catholic outlook, consorting chiefly with Catholics.... Above all, he gave expression to his love of the old faith in his works. In these incomparable poetic creations, his Catholic outlook repeatedly manifests itself' (*Shakespeare and Catholicism* [New York: Sheed & Ward, 1952], p. 384).

Although religion plays a major part in the works of Shakespeare, and though scholars such as Mutschmann and Wentersdorf have shown with high probability

Shakespeare has his character, significantly a Franciscan priest, turn to the herbs he is gathering:

---

that he was a Catholic, the question of his religion is scarcely touched in modern criticism. For example, the 15th edition of the *New Encyclopaedia Britannica*, in a twenty-page article on Shakespeare in its *Macropaedia*, makes no mention of religion as an element in Shakespeare's plays or in the England of his day. It cites as the only evidence of Shakespeare's religion a statement by Richard Davies, archdeacon of Lichfield, that he 'died a papist,' and questions its trustworthiness (p. 266).

How is one to explain this epidemic neglect of a matter central to the understanding of our major poet and his works? There seems to be no single overarching reason. In some cases it is a failure, or refusal, to understand the role that religion can play in the creative imagination of an artist. In others, it is a failure to link history with literary criticism.

Hugh Ross Williamson blames the latter for two errors of that titan among students of Shakespeare, the inspired amateur Sir Edmund Chambers (*The Day Shakespeare Died* [London: Michael Joseph, 1962], pp. 39–40 and 53). Even among cultured Englishmen the history of the English Reformation was colored and obscured by the self-serving version that the English Crown, largely through control of the printing trade, imposed on literature for almost two centuries.

From the viewpoint of national statistics, the odds that Shakespeare was Catholic stand at one in two, if we accept the demographic estimates of Brian Magee in *The English Recusants* (London: Burns Oates & Washbourne, 1938). Dr Magee produces evidence tending to show that a good half of the English nation remained Catholic when Shakespeare entered manhood, that is until the Crown was able to exploit the Spanish attempt at invasion to paint Catholics as unpatriotic. William Raleigh Trimble, in *The Catholic Laity in Elizabethan England* (Cambridge, Mass.: Belknap Press of Harvard University Press, 1964), concludes that the number was considerably smaller. Because Dr Trimble limits his study to the reign of Elizabeth, he does not consider evidence adduced by Magee that during the Civil War, more than a third of the officers in the royal army were Catholics. But Trimble appears to ignore Magee's work entirely. A critical comparison of the two studies may offer fertile ground for postgraduate work.

Scholarly treatment of evidence for Shakespeare's Catholicity can verge on the bizarre. There is, for example, an 838-page survey of the 'quest for knowledge of Shakespeare the man,' as the author describes it, which delves not only into the results of sober scholarship but into what the author calls the 'antics' of forgers and the 'deviations' of Oxfordians, Baconians, and devotees of other claimants upon the authorship of Shakespeare's works. To 'the amateurs, the eccentrics, the cranks with theories . . . , the heretics,' this survey devotes fully 100 pages, plus seventy or more to forgers. But to a century and more of investigation into Shakespeare's religion it allots a dismissive three pages (S. Schoenbaum, *Shakespeare's Lives* [New York: Oxford University Press, 1970], pp. 122–4, plus a paragraph beginning on p. 459). This is scarcely more than the two pages devoted to defending the scholar Sir Sidney Lee against sneers for concealing his given names, Solomon Lazarus (pp. 506–7). Professor Schoenbaum's conclusion is deeper than his survey: 'Thus does each man convert Shakespeare to his own belief or infidelity' (p. 460).

Within the infant rind of this small flower
Poison hath residence and medicine power:
For this, being smelt, with that part cheers each part;
Being tasted, slays all senses with the heart.[65]

The poet applies this lesson of dumb nature to human nature:

Two such opposed kings encamp them still
In man as well as herbs, grace and rude will;
And where the worser is predominant,
Full soon the canker death eats up that plant.[66]

This is the Catholic, not the Cathar, understanding of man and of the drama he lives: a struggle between God's grace and his own wilfulness, the wellspring of moral evil. Outside of that, in material creation, there is no moral evil, only a variety of powers to be used well or ill, or suffered well or ill. Among them is the power to bring new human life into being, and it is to consecrate its use that the young Romeo approaches the priest, whose Franciscan habit may symbolize detachment from earthly things but also recalls, because of the first man to wear it, their goodness.

To the friar's attempts to find out why he had come, Romeo responds that he seeks 'holy marriage.' Romeo and Juliet, the darlings of Shakespeare's imagination and ours, were husband and wife, their marriage blessed by a priest who stood for the rule of the one God and for the goodness of his creation.

At this writing the most detailed recent enquiry into Shakespeare's religion appears to be Ian Wilson's *Shakespeare: The Evidence* (London: Headline Book Publishing Ltd., 1993).

[65] *Romeo and Juliet*, II. iii. 23–6.

[66] Ibid., II. iii. 27–30.

REFLECTIONS

A work aspiring to the status of philosophy will ordinarily, as it closes, draw conclusions. But our conclusions have already been drawn, in the Introduction and in Part I, the properly philosophical sections of this work. The historical illustrations comprising Part II are just that: illustrations, drawn from history, of philosophical principles already established. They are examples of principles in action. They are images needed, so to speak, to accompany our concepts.

To bring imagination to the support of principle and thus forge conviction is a function of art, not of philosophy. As for history, while it may be as Burke held it to be, a preceptor of prudence rather than of principles, it is certainly an illustrator of how principles thrust themselves home. If, on Aristotle's ground that history deals in accidents, we were to hold with him that it cannot be a science, we could still study it with a view to testing our principles and, if they proved true, making convictions of them. That is why the historian should be an artist. But only atheists, it seems to me, are bound to hold that history cannot in principle be a science. The believer contends that Providence rules history, his writ being large of course, whatever scribbling may be assigned to men.

Whether a science of history is a *practical* human possibility is quite another question. God's Providence, along with his forgiveness, is the deepest mystery of Faith. In my view it is humanly unfathomable; amid the tempests and doldrums of human experience we can at best discern its drift. Still, to do that is vital to the moral and perhaps physical survival of mankind.

To focus this necessary reflection on the recent history of chastity, and catch its drift, is easy. One might say *only too easy*. There is no need to labor the painfully obvious, the destruction of families and with them of cultural and economic vigor, the moral destruction of children, indeed their physical destruction in a frenzy of fleshly lust turned to bloodlust. Not only commonly but very aptly is this upheaval termed the sexual revolution. It was quite akin to the revolution in statecraft worked by Machiavelli. Admittedly, before the sexual revolution men misbehaved in sexual matters, as before the Machiavellian revolution they misbehaved in matters of state. But in both they did so with a guilty conscience, in so far as they had a conscience (to borrow Maritain's wry phrase).

The change in philosophy is exemplified by a sudden switch in the meaning of hypocrisy between the mid-sixties and the mid-seventies. Until that unhappy period, hypocrisy had been the tribute that vice paid to virtue; it now became the epithet that vice hurled at virtue. The implication was that nobody lived chastely, and that those who criticized the new ethos were themselves its secret practitioners. The latter charge may in many cases have been true, but that need not imply hypocrisy, merely an understanding of the importance of chaste behavior even by men unwilling or unable to live it.

Many books have been written touching on this unhappy history. Many of them, especially those of a feminist cast and some pretending to expound Catholic moral theology, have actually contributed to the tragedy. Some on the other hand are excellent, and here one of the earliest might be singled out: George Gilder's *Sexual Suicide*.[1] A still more important book remains to be written, one that would offer a masterplan for the restoration of chastity.

Undoubtedly a far-sighted statesman can, given the right powers and propitious circumstances, accomplish much

[1] New York: Quadrangle, 1973.

toward that restoration. Augustus showed the way. But something more than law is needed; not even charismatic leadership suffices. In this field corporate reform, wholesale repentance, national conversion, is demanded, and only truly prophetic powers can turn the trick. There is but one exception, and we scarcely dare think of that: cataclysm, the supreme reality-therapy. Yet by course of nature this seems destined to come, barring prophetic intervention.

Both from the floor of the US Senate and in widely-published articles, Daniel Patrick Moynihan has warned that the illegitimacy rate in the United States threatens national stability. He has spoken in apocalyptic terms, in seismic metaphors, calling the present proportion of out-of-wedlock births unprecedented in history.

So, in the eyes of veteran social scientist Peter Drucker, is the *dearth of children.* 'For at least two hundred years, all institutions of the modern world and especially all businesses have assumed a steadily growing population,' he writes in *Management Challenges for the 21st Century.* 'For the next twenty or thirty years demographics will dominate the policies of all developed countries. And they wiil inevitably be politics of great turbulence.'[2]

But the weakness of our power to foresee the future has been demonstrated by the collapse of communism in Eastern Europe, to universal astonishment. Perhaps the same will happen to the empire of sex. Perhaps the emptiness of sexual pleasure when indiscriminate and voided of purpose will disgust an entire society. Perhaps there will be a corporate discernment, born of unhappy experience, that if we are not spiritual even in the flesh we will not even be fleshly in the flesh. The disorder and debasement wreaked in certain communities by the failure of the family has aroused alarm; perhaps the broader society will make the obvious diagnosis, apply the obvious prognosis to itself, and prescribe the necessary medicine. Or will it turn its alarm and disgust against the sexual faculty, and revert to puritanism?

[2] New York: HarperBusiness, 1999, pp. 45–6.

If it does, the West will have a new struggle on its hands, against a foe scarcely less dangerous than the license that now threatens to dissolve it.

BIBLIOGRAPHY

Philosophical Foundations

AQUINAS, THOMAS. *Summa Theologiae, Summa Contra Gentiles, Sententia Libri Ethicorum, In Aristotelis Libros Physicorum,* Leonine edition, Rome: Commissio Leonina, and Paris: J. Vrin, 1884–1976.

——. *Super IV Sententiarum, Questiones Disputatae de Virtutibus, Super Mattheum, Super Epistolas Pauli Apostoli, Catena Aurea, Sententia Libri Metaphysicae, Super Librum Boethii de Trinitate.* Frette edition, Paris: Vives, 1889.

ARISTOTLE. *The Works of Aristotle.* Translated into English under the editorship of W. D. Ross. Oxford: Clarendon Press/ Oxford University Press: 1928–52. 12 volumes.

BURKE, EDMUND. *Edmund Burke: Selected Writings and Speeches.* Edited by Peter J. Stanlis. Chicago: Regnery Gateway, 1963.

DE KONINCK, CHARLES. *In Defence of Saint Thomas – A Reply to Father Eschmann's Attack on the Primacy of the Common Good.* Quebec: Editions de l'Universite Laval: 1945. (Extrait du *Laval Théologique et Philosophique,* Vol. 1, No. 2, 1945.)

A durable treatment of Thomistic teaching on the common good. Because it takes the form of a point-by-point response to criticisms of the author's work, it lacks organization.

GILSON, ETIENNE. *The Spirit of Medieval Philosophy.* Translated by A. H. C. Downs. New York: Philosophical Library, 1952.

Gilson, Etienne. *Thomist Realism and the Critique of Knowledge.* Translated by Mark A. Wauck. San Francisco: Ignatius, 1986.

Lecler, Joseph. *The Two Sovereignties.* New York: Philosophical Library, 1952.

Maritain, Jacques. *On the Church of Christ.* Notre Dame, Indiana: University of Notre Dame Press, 1973.

——. *The Social and Political Philosophy of Jacques Maritain.* Edited by Joseph Evans and Leo Ward. New York: Charles Scribners' Sons, 1955.

Renard, Henri. *The Philosophy of Being.* 2nd edition. Milwaukee: Bruce Publishing Company, 1943.

Strauss, Leo and Cropsey, Joseph (eds). *History of Political Philosophy*, 2nd edition. Chicago and London: Oxford University Press, 1958.

Tocqueville, Alexis de. *The Old Regime and the French Revolution.* Translated by Stuart Gilbert. Garden City, New York: Doubleday Anchor Books, 1955.

On the Old Testament, and on the Jewish Family

Albright, W. F. *Archaeology and the Religion of Israel.* 3rd edition. Baltimore: Johns Hopkins Press, 1956.

——. *The Archaeology of Palestine.* Harmondsworth, Middlesex: Penguin Books, 1949.

——. *From the Stone Age to Christianity.* Baltimore: Johns Hopkins Press, 1946.

——. *History, Archaeology, and Christian Humanism.* New York: McGraw-Hill, 1964.

——. *Yahweh and the Gods of Canaan.* London: Athlone Press, 1968.

Alt, Albrecht. *Essays on Old Testament History and Religion.* Translated by R. A. Wilson. Oxford: Basil Blackwell, 1966.

Includes the highly influential essay 'The God of the Fathers,' which has come under continual criticism since its publication in German in 1929.

BICKERMAN, ELIAS. *The God of the Maccabees.* Leiden: E. J. Brill, 1979.

BROADT, LAWRENCE, CSP. *Reading the Old Testament: An Introduction.* New York/Mahwah, New Jersey: Paulist Press, 1984.

Father Boadt's survey achieves great clarity through its schematic organization and strong distinctions.

BRIGHT, JOHN. *A History of Israel.* 3rd edition. Philadelphia: Westminster Press, 1981.

Widely regarded as the definitive work in English.

CHILDS, BREVARD S. *Exodus: A Commentary.* London: SCM Press, 1974.

Outstanding as a summary of scholarship at the time of its publication. Its own analyses may be contested.

CROSS, FRANK MOORE. *Canaanite Myth and Hebrew Ethic.* Cambridge, Massachusetts: Harvard University Press, 1973.

Offers a critical summary of theories on early Israelite worship.

DRESNER, SAMUEL H. 'The Return of Paganism?' Published in *Midstream,* June/July 1988, pp. 32–8.

ELAZAR, DANIEL. *Covenant and Polity in Biblical Israel.* New Brunswick and London: Transaction, 1995.

Offers a valuable account of speculation by Jewish thinkers concerning the political function of the Sinaitic Covenant. The author takes no firm position on this question, but is convinced of the superiority of modern political theory and does not, for example, hesitate to criticize the Patriarch Joseph for consolidating the authority of Pharaoh 'as the totalitarian ruler of Egypt.'

GOLDSTEIN, JONATHAN. *The Anchor Bible Commentary: I Maccabees.* Garden City: Doubleday & Co., 1976.

GOLDSTEIN, JONATHAN. *The Anchor Bible Commentary: II Maccabees.* Garden City: Doubleday & Co., 1983.

GOODMAN, PHILIP and HANNA. *The Jewish Marriage Anthology.* Philadelphia: The Jewish Publication Society, 1985.

HARRELSON, WALTER. *The Ten Commandments and Human Rights.* Philadelphia: Fortress Press, 1980.

HYMAN, PAULA E. and COHEN, STEVEN M. (eds). *The Jewish Family: Myths and Reality.* New York/London: Holmes & Meir, 1986.

KAISER, WALTER C., JR. *Toward Old Testament Ethics.* Grand Rapids: Academic Books, 1983.

LÉON-DUFOUR, XAVIER (ed.). *Dictionary of Biblical Theology.* Translated by P. Joseph Cahill, SJ and E. M. Stewart. New York: The Seabury Press, 1973.

LÉVY, LOUIS-GERMAIN. *La Famille dans L'Antiquité Israélite.* Paris: Alcan, 1905.

LINZER, NORMAN. *The Jewish Family.* New York: Human Sciences Press, 1984.

MCCARTHY, DENNIS J., SJ. *Old Testament Covenant – A Survey of Current Opinions.* Richmond, Virginia: John Knox Press, 1972.

Father McCarthy's study offers concise appraisals of theories on the Covenant, and an exceptionally big bibliography.

MCELENEY, NEIL J., CSP. *The Law Given Through Moses.* New York: Paulist Press, 1960.

MCKENZIE, JOHN L., SJ. *Dictionary of the Bible.* Milwaukee: The Bruce Publishing Company, 1965.

MENDELSOHN, ISAAC. 'The Family in the Ancient Near East.' Published in *The Biblical Archaeologist Reader* vol. 3, pp. 144–60. Garden City, New York: Anchor Books, 1970.

MENDENHALL, GEORGE E. *The Tenth Generation: The Origins of the Biblical Tradition.* Baltimore and London: The Johns Hopkins University Press, 1973.

Despite Dr Mendenhall's groundbreaking work in the Covenant as a suzerainty treaty, his distinction between civil law and the Covenant cannot, in the light of the present work, be endorsed.

MENDENHALL, GEORGE E. 'Covenant Forms in Israelite Tradition.' Published in *The Biblical Archaeologist Reader* vol. 3, pp. 25–53. Garden City, New York: Anchor Books, 1970.

MOMIGLIANO, ARNOLDO. *Alien Wisdom.* Cambridge: Cambridge University Press, 1975.

MOSCATI, SABATINO. *The World of the Phoenicians.* Translated by Alastair Hamilton. New York: Frederick A. Praeger, 1968.

NOTH, MARTIN. *The History of Israel.* 2nd edition. New York: Harper & Row, 1960.

Noth discusses at length the similarity of the tribal organization of Israel at the time of the judges to the sacred confederation of the Greeks at a later date. Such a confederation, known among the Greeks as an amphictyony, was thought by Noth to explain the unity achieved by Israel despite the turbulent early history of the tribes. This explanation is no longer accepted as sufficient, but the parallels are illuminating.

OSTERLEY, W. O. E. *A History of Israel.* Oxford: Clarendon Press, 1948.

OGILTREE, THOMAS W. *The Use of the Bible in Christian Ethics.* Philadelphia: Fortress Press, 1983.

Some notion of the premises of this work can be gained from the authors listed under 'Classical treatments of ethical theory.' They include not only Immanuel Kant and John Stuart Mill but Max Scheler, H. Richard Niebuhr, and even John Rawls. The only author from classical antiquity represented is Aristotle. No medieval theologian is cited.

PRITCHARD, JAMES B. *Recovering Sarepta, a Phoenician City.* Princeton, New Jersey: Princeton University Press, 1978.

Recounts the first archeological confirmation of child sacrifice in the Phoenician homeland. This crucial discovery has not yet found its place in the secondary literature.

RAD, GERHARD VON. *Deuteronomy*. Translated by Dorothea Barton. Philadelphia: The Westminster Press, 1966.

SMITH, MARK S. *The Early History of God*. New York: Harper, 1990.

STAMM, J. J. *The Ten Commandments in Recent Research*. Translated by M. E. Andrew. Naperville, Illinois: Alec R. Allenson, Inc., 1967.

TESTA, EMMANUELE. *La Morale dell'Antico Testamento*. Brescia: Morcelliana, 1981.

Methodical and wide-ranging.

VAUX, ROLAND DE, OP. *Ancient Israel – Its Life and Institutions*. Translated by John McHugh. New York: McGraw-Hill, 1961.

This is a compendious work living up to its comprehensive title. It is drawn chiefly from Holy Writ and hence is exegetical, though it liberally employs the findings of archaeology. It is especially informative in its treatment of the family.

On the Society of Classical and Christian Antiquity

ABBOTT, ELIZABETH. *A History of Celibacy*. Toronto: Harper Collins, 1999.

The author warns that she uses 'the words celibacy and chastity almost interchangeably.' This confusion and others bring this work to the brink of editorial chaos. Throughout, the work is informed by a hermeneutic of scorn.

BARROW, R. H. *Slavery in the Roman Empire*. London: Metheun & Co., 1928.

BELLOC, HILAIRE. *Europe and the Faith*. New York: The Paulist Press, 1920.

This contentious and largely undocumented work has remained classic, partly because of its sweeping view of history, partly because of its arresting thesis, 'There is no more a Catholic "aspect" of European history than there is a man's "aspect" of himself.'

BOURNE, FRANK C. *A History of the Romans*. Toronto and London: D. C. Heath, 1966.

CANTARELLA, EVA. *Pandora's Daughters: The Role and Status of Women in Greek and Roman Antiquity*. Translated by Maureen B. Fant. Baltimore and London: The Johns Hopkins University Press, 1987.

This work draws upon and draws attention to a wealth of sources, though it lacks a bibliography. Its interpretations are guided by the thesis that the status of women in classical antiquity was higher than in Christian antiquity. That thesis is supported only by selective citation. It is called into question not only by the title of the book in its English and French translations (*Filles de Pandore*) but also the original title, *L'ambiguo malanno*, 'The Ambiguous Evil,' a term taken from Euripedes' tragedy *Hyppolytus* and referring to woman. The author herself chose the title in English and in French because of the more explicit claim of Hesiod that from Pandora comes 'the accursed tribe of women, a terrible scourge ensconsed among mortal men.'

(The thesis of this book should be examined in the light of a far more serious historical work of a feminist cast, Aline Rousselle's *Porneia*, listed below.)

CHESTERTON, G. K. *The Everlasting Man*. New York: Dodd, Mead, 1925.

CHISHOLM, K. and FERGUSON, J. (eds). *Rome: The Augustan Age*. Oxford: Oxford University Press, 1981.

Key texts in translation.

EARL, DONALD. *The Age of Augustus*. London: Elek Books, 1968.

——. *The Moral and Political Tradition of Rome*. Ithaca, New York: Cornell University Press, 1967.

FOLEY, HELENE P. (ed.). *Reflections of Women in Antiquity*. New York, London and Paris: Gordon & Breach Science Publishers, 1981.

Although marred by incomprehensible gobbledegook and unsupported claims, this collection of essays by American scholars contains much valuable material.

GRENFELL, BERNARD P. *An Alexandrian Erotic Fragment.* Oxford: Clarendon Press, 1896.

MARAVAL, PIERRE, CSSR. 'L'Eglise du IV Siècle et l'Esclavage.' Published in *Studia Moralia* 8 (1970), pp. 319–46.

MCMULLEN, RAMSEY. *Roman Social Relations.* New Haven and London: Yale University Pres, 1974.

PAGELS, ELAINE. *Adam, Eve, and the Serpent.* New York: Random House, 1988.

An investigation into 'how Christians have interpreted the creation accounts of Genesis,' with special focus on St Augustine. Gratuitously speculative.

RHEINHOLD, MEYER. *Diaspora.* Sarasota: Samuel Stevens & Company, 1983.

ROUSSELLE, ALINE. *Porneia: On Desire and the Body in Antiquity.* Translated by Felicia Pheasant. New York and Oxford: Basil Blackwell, 1988.

Neither the thesis nor the seriousness of this work is conveyed by its sensational title. Its principal achievement is to document radical changes in the role of women in the Christian centuries of the Roman Empire.

The author, Assistant Professor of History at the University of Perpignan, does not conceal a feminist bias, which the reader may be inclined to share after perusing this book.

TOYNBEE, ARNOLD. *A Study of History.* 2nd edition. London: Oxford University Press, 1935.

WALSH, P. G. *Livy: His Historical Aims and Methods.* Cambridge: Cambridge University Press, 1963.

WILLIS, F. ROY. *Western Civilization – An Urban Perspective.* Lexington, Mass., and Toronto: D. C. Heath & Co., 1981.

On Dualism and the Cathars

ANONYMOUS. *Istoria de la Guerra dels Albigeses (History of the Albigensian War).* Translated into French; the translator also is anonymous. Carcassonne: CALO, 1971.

The author, a Catholic unsympathetic to the political aims of the crusaders, wrote perhaps a century after the events.

BELLOC, HILAIRE. *The Great Heresies.* Manassas, Virginia: Trinity Communications, 1987 (First published, 1938).

One chapter deals with the Albigenses. This synthetic work draws on the research and reflection of a lifetime; it is not documented.

——. *The Servile State.* Indianapolis: Liberty Classics, 1977. First published in 1913. London and Edinburgh: T. N. Foulis.

BENEDETTO, LUIGI FOSCOLO. *Il Cantico di Frate Sole.* Firenze: G. C. Sansoni, 1941.

BLACKMAN, E. C. *Marcion and His Influence.* London: SPCK, 1948.

BONAVENTURE. *The Life of St. Francis of Assisi.* Anonymous translation from the *Legenda Sancti Francisci.* London: Burns, Oates & Washbourne, n.d.

Cahiers de Fanjeaux. Tolouse: Edouard Privat, 1966– (published yearly).

Proceedings of annual conferences, the first of which was held in 1965, in the Languedocian town of Fanjeaux, center of St Dominic's labors in the region until the foundation of the Order of Preachers. Each conference focusses on a particular theme.

COULTON, G. G. *Inquisition and Liberty.* London: William Heinemann Ltd, 1938.

An exercise in bitterness that too often, as if out of principle, mistakes the branch for the root. Guilty of elemental errors of fact. This work fails to bear out the author's reputation for scholarship, though it fully justifies his reputation for bias.

ENGLEBERT, OMER. *St. Francis of Assisi.* Translated by Eve Marie Cooper. 2nd English edition Chicago: Franciscan Herald Press, 1965; reprint edition, Ann Arbor, Michigan: Servant Books, n.d.

EUSEBIUS OF CAESAREA. *History of the Church.* Translated by G. A. Williamson. Minneapolis: Augsburg Publishing House, 1975.

The only known work dealing with the history of the Church from earliest times. The sections on the gnostic and dualistic heresies are important to an understanding of Catharism.

FALLANI, GIOVANNI (ed.). *Dante Alighieri: La Divina Commedia.* Three volumes. 2nd edition. Messina & Firenze: Casa Editrice G. D'Anna, 1970.

GRIFFE, ELIE. *Les Débuts de l'Aventure Cathare en Languedoc (1140–1190).* Paris: Letouzey et Ané, 1969.

——. *Le Languedoc Cathare de 1190 a 1210.* Paris: Letouzey et Ané, 1971.

——. *Le Languedoc Cathare au Temps de la Croisade (1209–1229).* Paris: Letouzey et Ané, 1973.

——. *Le Languedoc Cathare e l'Inquisition (1229–1239).* Paris: Letouzey et Ané, 1980.

The author began these studies when invited to give a paper at the third session of the Colloques de Fanjeaux.

GUILLAUME DE PUYLAURENS. *Chronicle.* Translated into French by [François?] Guizot. Carcassonne: CALO, 1970.

The chaplain of Raymond VII, Count of Toulouse, begins his account with the preaching of Bernard of Clairvaux in the mid-twelfth century, and ends more than a century later with the submission of the Count of Foix to the French crown.

GUIRAUD, JEAN. *Histoire de l'Inquisition au Moyen Age.* Two volumes. Paris: Editions August Picard, 1935.

——. Translated by E. C. Messenger. *The Mediaeval Inquisition.* London: Burns, Oates & Washbourne Ltd, 1927.

A much more compact treatment, actually extending over a longer period than the highly detailed two-volume work, which concludes in the thirteenth century while this one reaches into the fourteenth.

HAMILTON, BERNARD. *The Medieval Inquisition.* New York: Holmes & Meier, 1981.

Unsympathetic to the institution it deals with.

HOFFMAN, R. JOSEPH. *Marcion: on the Restitution of Christianity.* Chico, California: Scholars Press, 1984.

ILARINO DA MILANO, OFMCap. 'Il dualismo cataro in Umbria al tempo di San Francesco.' *Atti IV Convegno di Studi Umbri* (1966), pp. 175–216.

JEDIN, H. and DOLAN, J. (eds). *Handbook of Church History* vol. 4: From the High Middle Ages to the Eve of the Reformation. Translated by Anselm Biggs. Freiburg: Herder, 1970.

LACORDAIRE, H. D. *Life of Saint Dominic.* Translated by Mrs Edward Hazeland. London: Burns & Oates, 1883. (Original French version published about 1840.)

Father Lacordaire's judgments on political aspects of the Albigensian Crusade, such as the effects of the battle of Muret, the success or failure of Count Raymond VI of Toulouse, and the motives of the King of Aragon, are not those of later historians.

LEA, HENRY CHARLES. *A History of the Inquisition in the Middle Ages.* New York: Harper & Brothers, 1887.

——. *The Inquisition of the Middle Ages.* An abridgement of Lea's *A History of the Inquisition of the Middle Ages* by Margaret Nicholson. New York: The Macmillan Company, 1961.

LECLERC, ELOI. *The Canticle of Creatures: Symbols of Union.* Translated by Matthew O'Connell. Chicago: Franciscan Herald Press, 1977.

LOOS, MILAN. *Dualist Heresy in the Middle Ages.* Translated by Iris Lewitova. The Hague: Martinus Nijhoff N.V., 1974.

Valuable especially for its treatment of heresy in the Balkans.

LUCHAIRE, ACHILLE. *Innocent III: La Croisade des Albigeois.* 2nd edition. Paris: Librairie Hachette et Compagnie, 1906.

MAISONNEUVE, HENRI. *Etudes sur les Origines de l'Inquisition.* Paris: Librarie Philosophique J. Brin, 1942.

A schematized historical treatment demonstrating special expertise in juridical questions but treating theological and political aspects as well.

MANSELLI, RAOUL. *L'eresia del male.* Naples: Morano, 1963.

Especially valuable for its treatment of Catharism in Italy.

MARIANO D'ALATRI, OFMCap. 'L'Inquisizione Francescana nell'Italia Centrale nel Secolo XIII.' *Collectanea Franciscana* vol. 22 (1952), pp. 225–50, and 23 (1950), pp. 51–131.

Documents the role of Franciscans in the Inquisition and, incidentally, the little-appreciated extension of Cathar teaching into central Italy.

MOORE, R. I. *The Birth of Popular Heresy.* New York: St Martin's Press, 1975.

Translations, chiefly by Moore, of key texts in the history of heresy in the High Middle Ages. Useful bibliography. The editor's judgment of modern scholarship in medieval heresy is significant: 'All serious modern work in this field has been based on the fundamental texts published by Father Antoine Dondaine [OP] and his magisterial expositions of them.'

NELLI, RENÉ. *La Philosophie du Catharisme.* Paris: Payot, 1978.

Like all the works of this author dealing with Catharism, this must be treated with caution.

——. *La Vie Quotidienne des Cathares du Languedoc au XIIIe Siècle.* Paris: Hachette, 1969.

——. *Les Cathares, ou l'Eternel Combat.* Paris: Culture, Art, Loisirs, 1972.

—— (ed.). *Le Catharisme.* Paris: Presses Universitaires de France.

Essays by Nelli and Charles P. Bru, Canon Louis de Lacger, Déodat Roche, and Luciano Sommariva.

——. *Le Phénomène Cathare: Perspective Philosophiques.* Paris: Editions Privat et Presses Universitaires de France, 1964.

NICKERSON, HOFFMAN. *The Inquisition.* Boston and New York: Houghton Mifflin, 1923.

PETERS, EDWARD (ed.). *Heresy and Authority in Medieval Europe: Documents in Translation.* Philadelphia: University of Pennsylvania Press, 1980.

Despite the title, this collection also offers a few texts from what ordinarily falls under the heading of antiquity; texts of Tertullian and St Augustine are cases in point.

RUNCIMAN, STEVEN. *The Medieval Manichee.* Cambridge: University Press, 1955.

Despite its title, an account of dualism from its appearance in the early Church. Errors creeps into its pages through confusion of Christian doctrine with the doctrine of some Christians ('To the orthodox Christian, Matter is bad, as a result of the Fall, but can be made good through Christ's sacraments'), and, probably, the unqualified acceptance of Philip the Fair's charges against the Templars.

RUSSELL, J. B. *Dissent and Reform in the Early Middle Ages.* Berkeley and Los Angeles: University of California Press, 1965.

An admirable effort at synthesis, marred by unsupported claims.

STRAYER, JOSEPH R. *The Albigensian Crusades.* New York: The Dial Press, 1971.

STRONSKI, STANISLAW. *Le Troubadour Folquet de Marseille.* Cracow, 1910; reprint edn, Geneva: Slatkine Reprints, 1968.

A critical edition of the poetry of the troubadour who became a Cistercian monk and abbot, and eventually bishop of Toulouse and a collaborator of St Dominic and Simon de Montfort in the struggle against Catharism.

SUMPTION, JONATHAN. *The Albigensian Crusade.* London and Boston: Faber & Faber, 1978.

THOUZELLIER, CHRISTINE. *Catharisme et Valdéisme en Languedoc à la fin du XIIe et au début du XIIIe Siècle.* Louvain: Editions Nauwelaerts, 1969.

A systematic assembly of documents dealing with Cathars, Waldenses, and the struggles that surrounded them, together with a historical matrix of these documents and a running analysis, chiefly theological and canonic.

VACANDARD, E. *The Inquisition.* Translated by B. L. Conway. New York: Longmans, Green & Co., 1915.

A work of apologetics that maintains high standards of scholarship and fairness. These qualities, plus its historical acumen, have earned it the status of a classic.

VICAIRE, MARIE-HUMBERT, OP. *Dominique et ses Prêcheurs.* Paris: Editions du Cerf, 1977.

For the moment, the definitive work on St Dominic. However, it lacks a treatment of the saint's use of devotion to combat heresy.

WAKEFIELD, W. L. and EVANS, A. P. *Heresies of the High Middle Ages.* New York and London: Columbia University Press, 1969.

Professor Wakefield claims that this is the first substantial collection of sources for the study of medieval heresies in English translation since S. R. Maitland's published collection of 1832.

WARNER, H. J. *The Albigensian Heresy.* New York: Russell & Russell, 1967. A reprint of Volume I (1922) and Volume II (1928).

Demonstrates naive bias against the institution that overcame Catharism, the Catholic Church.

INDEX OF NAMES